WITCHBLADE
DEMON REBORN

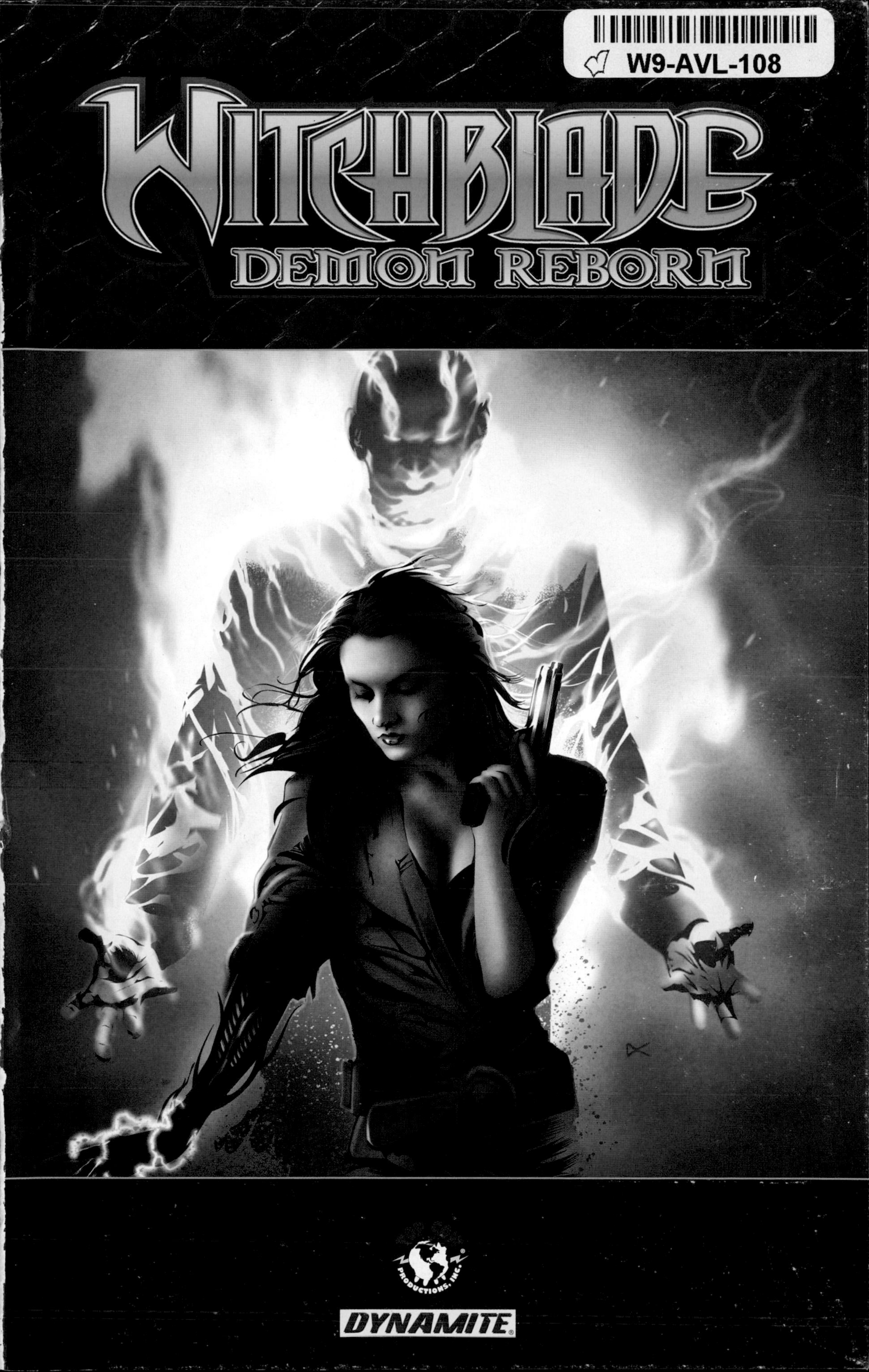

DYNAMITE

MARC SILVESTRI • CEO
MATT HAWKINS • PRESIDENT AND COO
FILIP SABLIK • PUBLISHER
BRYAN ROUNDTREE • ASSISTANT TO PUBLISHER
ELENA SALCEDO • SALES ASSISTANT
JESSI REID • INTERN

DYNAMITE®

NICK BARRUCCI • CEO / PUBLISHER
JUAN COLLADO • PRESIDENT / COO
JOSEPH RYBANDT • SENIOR EDITOR
JOSH JOHNSON • ART DIRECTOR
RICH YOUNG • DIRECTOR BUSINESS DEVELOPMENT
JASON ULLMEYER • SENIOR GRAPHIC DESIGNER
JOSH GREEN • TRAFFIC COORDINATOR
CHRIS CANIANO • PRODUCTION ASSISTANT

ISBN-10: 1-60690-398-5   ISBN-13: 978-1-60690-398-8   First Printing   10 9 8 7 6 5 4 3 2 1

WITCHBLADE: DEMON

originally published in Witchblade: Demon #1 (2003) by Top Cow and Dynamic Forces

written by
MARK MILLAR

illustrated by
JAE LEE

colored by
JUNE CHUNG

lettered by
ROBIN SPEHAR/
DREAMER DESIGN

original design & production
JOSH JOHNSON, RICH WENZKE & JEFF ELLER

WITCHBLADE: DEMON REBORN

originally published in Witchblade: Demon Reborn #1-4 (2012)
by Top Cow and Dynamite Entertainment

written by
ANDE PARKS

illustrated by
JOSE LUIS

colored by
VINICIUS ANDRADE

lettered by
TROY PETERI

collection cover by
DENNIS CALERO

collection design by
JASON ULLMEYER

WITCHBLADE
DEMON

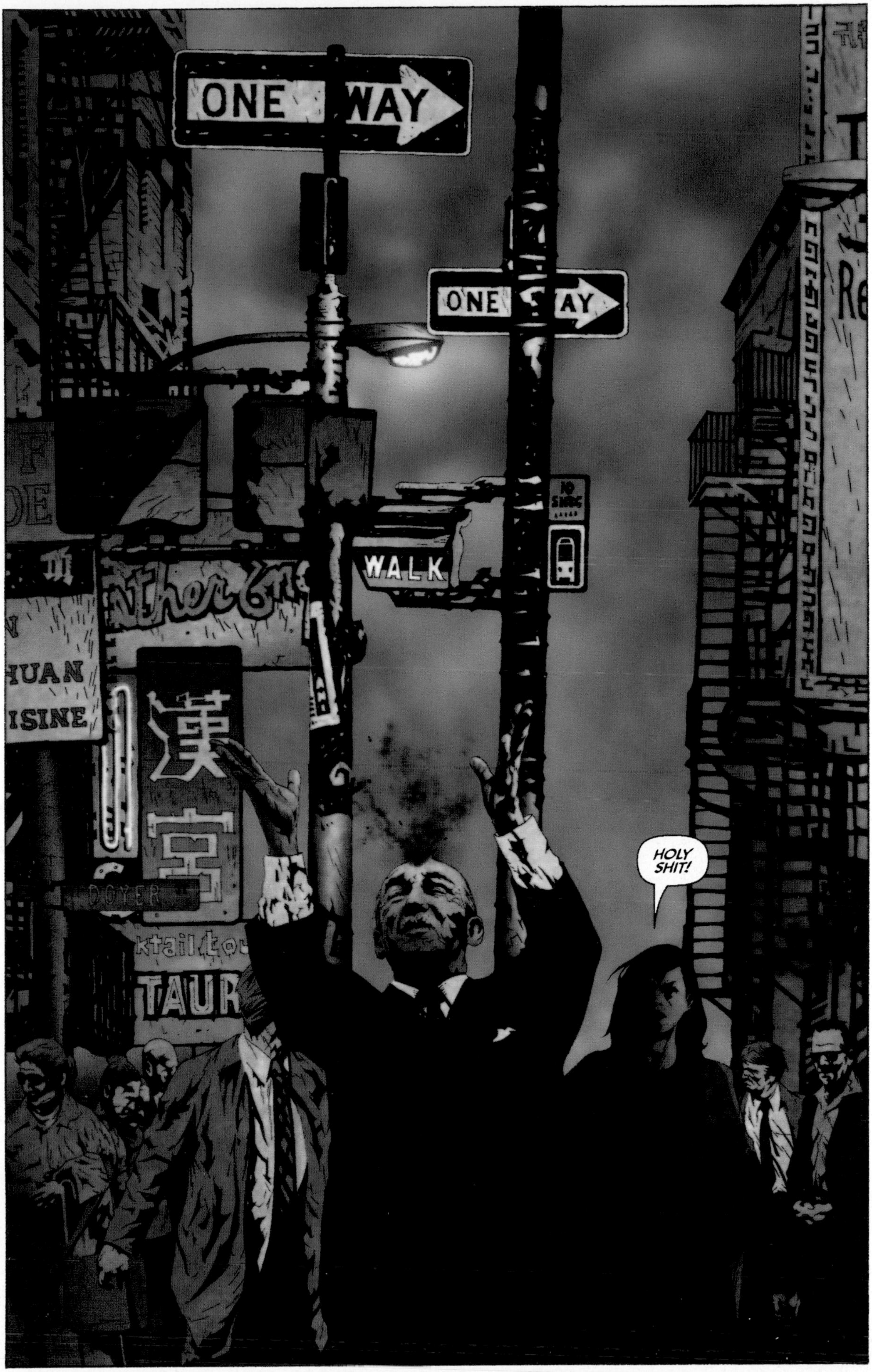
ONE WAY
ONE WAY
WALK
漢宮
DOYER
HOLY SHIT!

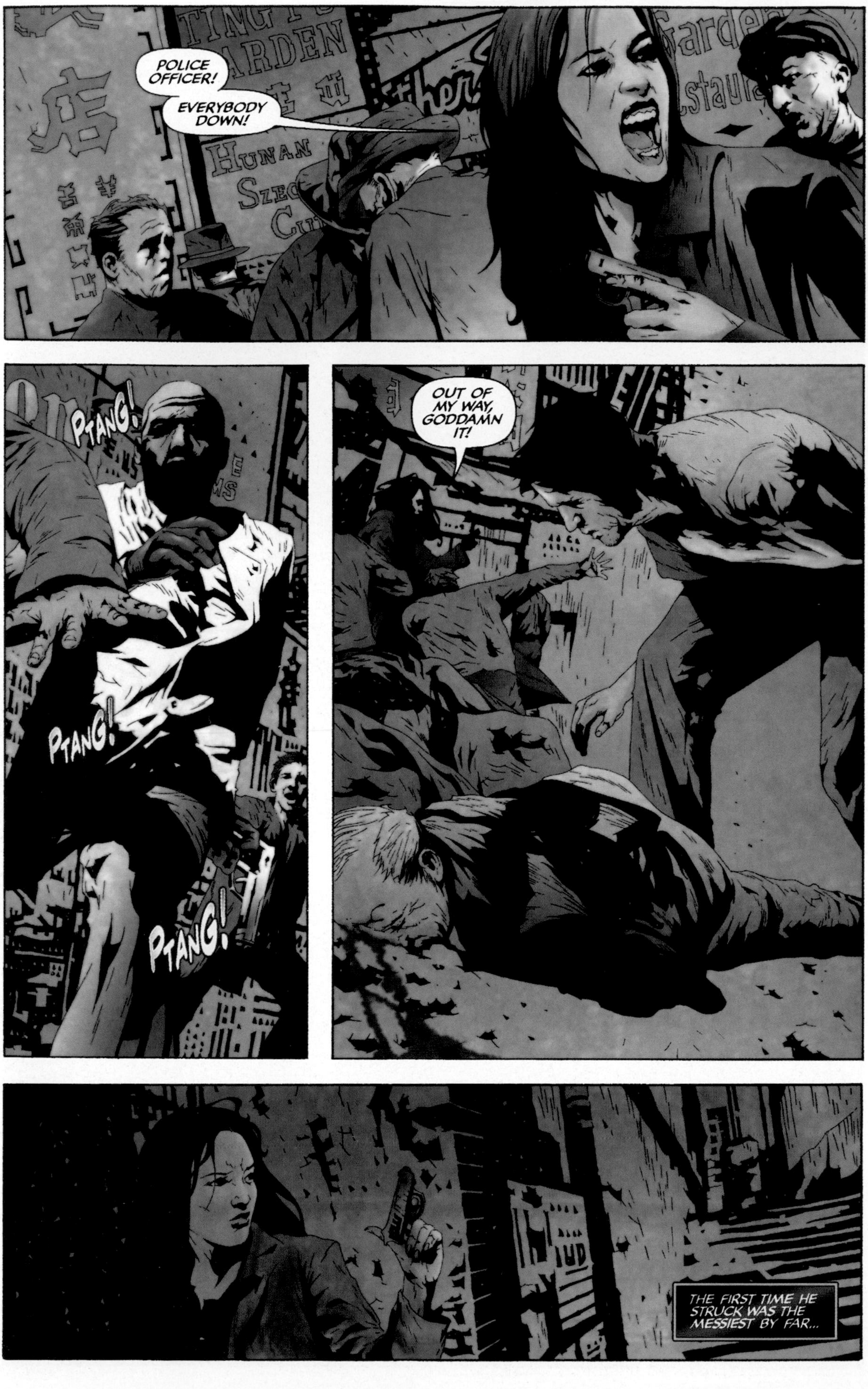
POLICE OFFICER!
EVERYBODY DOWN!
PTANG!
PTANG!
PTANG!
OUT OF MY WAY, GODDAMN IT!
THE FIRST TIME HE STRUCK WAS THE MESSIEST BY FAR...

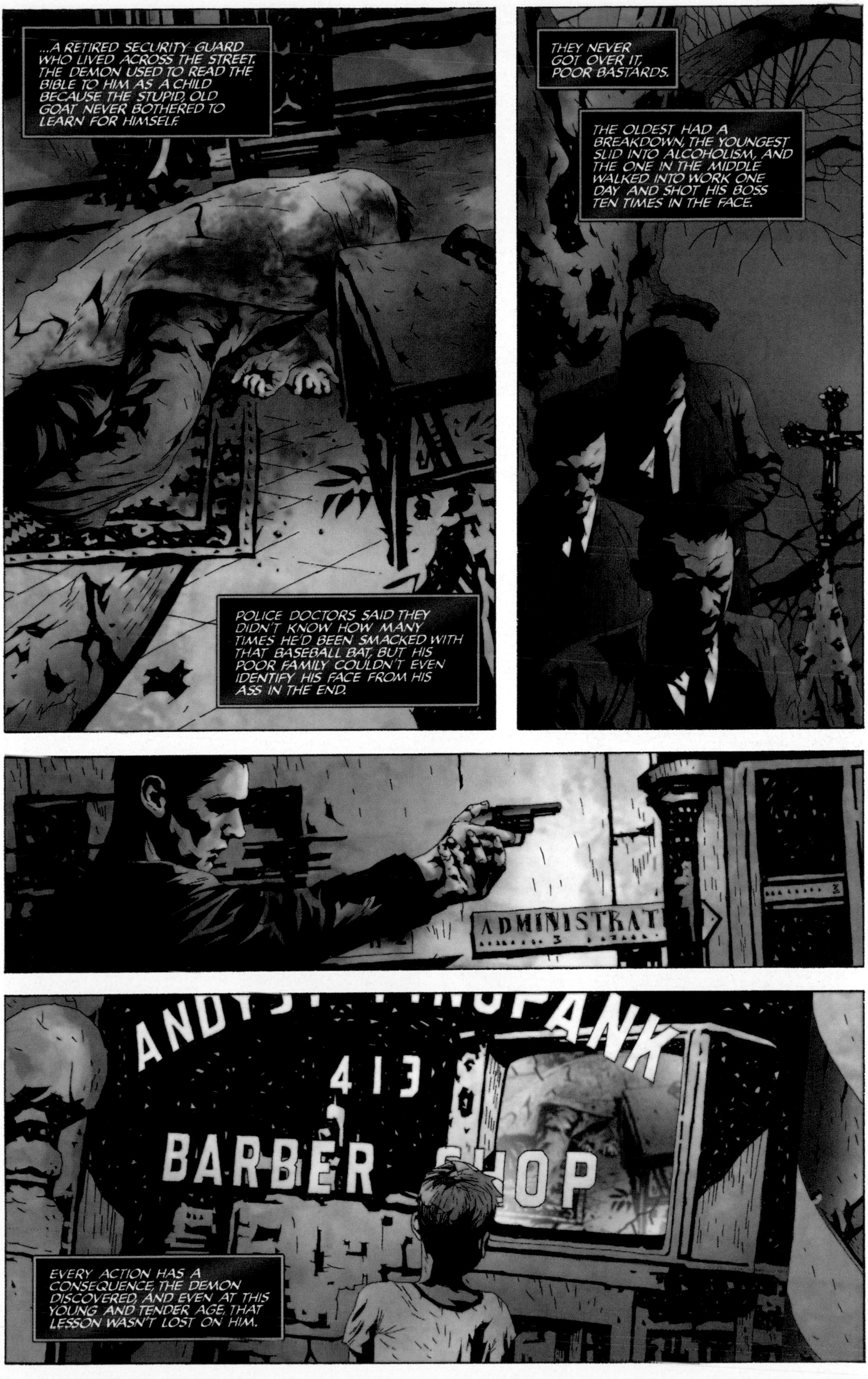
...A RETIRED SECURITY GUARD WHO LIVED ACROSS THE STREET. THE DEMON USED TO READ THE BIBLE TO HIM AS A CHILD BECAUSE THE STUPID, OLD GOAT NEVER BOTHERED TO LEARN FOR HIMSELF.
POLICE DOCTORS SAID THEY DIDN'T KNOW HOW MANY TIMES HE'D BEEN SMACKED WITH THAT BASEBALL BAT, BUT HIS POOR FAMILY COULDN'T EVEN IDENTIFY HIS FACE FROM HIS ASS IN THE END.
THEY NEVER GOT OVER IT, POOR BASTARDS.
THE OLDEST HAD A BREAKDOWN, THE YOUNGEST SLID INTO ALCOHOLISM, AND THE ONE IN THE MIDDLE WALKED INTO WORK ONE DAY AND SHOT HIS BOSS TEN TIMES IN THE FACE.
ADMINISTRAT
413
BARBER
EVERY ACTION HAS A CONSEQUENCE, THE DEMON DISCOVERED, AND EVEN AT THIS YOUNG AND TENDER AGE, THAT LESSON WASN'T LOST ON HIM.

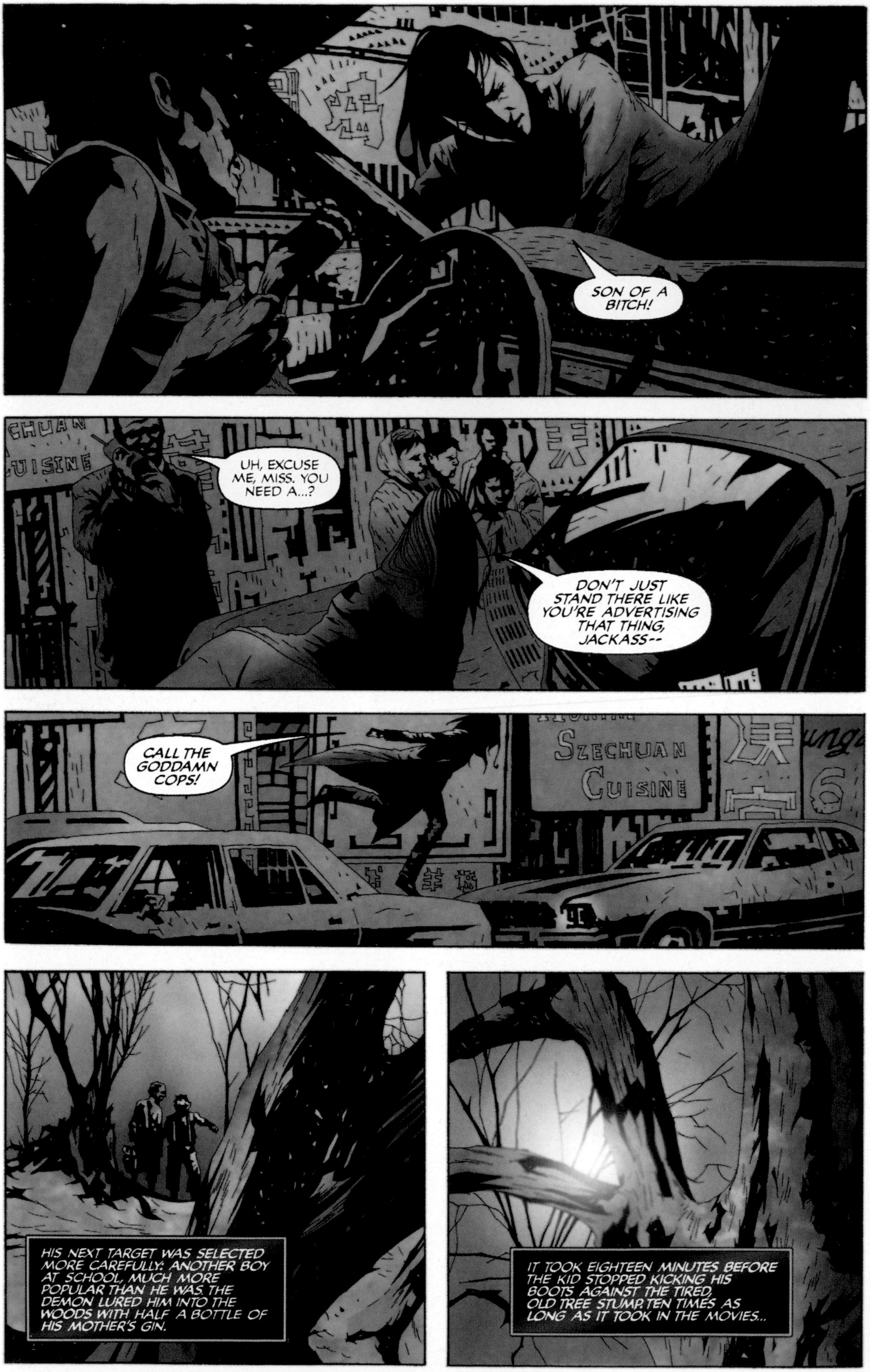
SON OF A BITCH!
UH, EXCUSE ME, MISS. YOU NEED A...?
DON'T JUST STAND THERE LIKE YOU'RE ADVERTISING THAT THING, JACKASS--
CALL THE GODDAMN COPS!
SZECHUAN CUISINE
HIS NEXT TARGET WAS SELECTED MORE CAREFULLY: ANOTHER BOY AT SCHOOL, MUCH MORE POPULAR THAN HE WAS. THE DEMON LURED HIM INTO THE WOODS WITH HALF A BOTTLE OF HIS MOTHER'S GIN.
IT TOOK EIGHTEEN MINUTES BEFORE THE KID STOPPED KICKING HIS BOOTS AGAINST THE TIRED, OLD TREE STUMP, TEN TIMES AS LONG AS IT TOOK IN THE MOVIES...

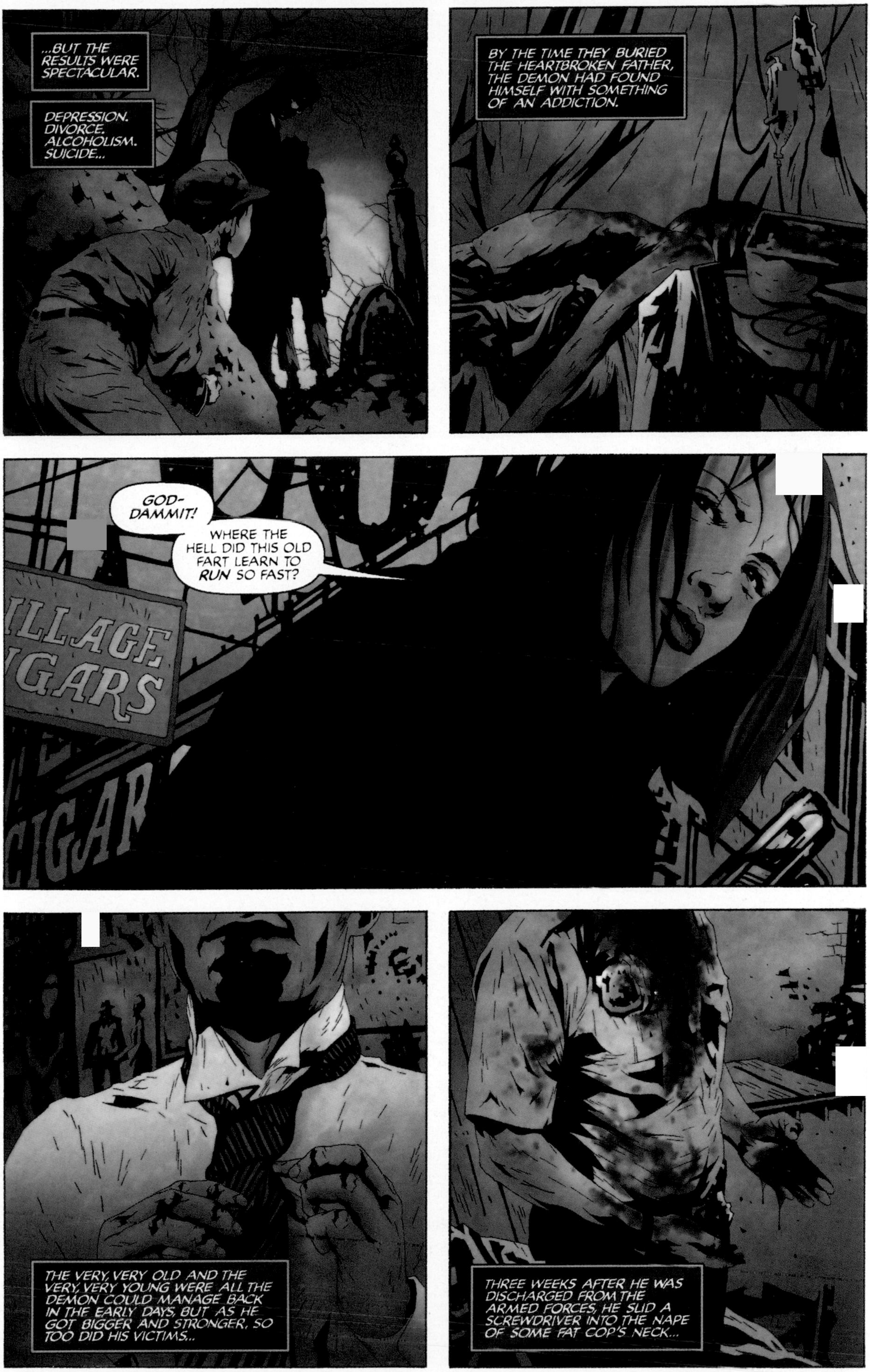
...BUT THE RESULTS WERE SPECTACULAR.
DEPRESSION. DIVORCE. ALCOHOLISM. SUICIDE...
BY THE TIME THEY BURIED THE HEARTBROKEN FATHER, THE DEMON HAD FOUND HIMSELF WITH SOMETHING OF AN ADDICTION.
GOD-DAMMIT!
WHERE THE HELL DID THIS OLD FART LEARN TO RUN SO FAST?
ILLAGE IGARS
CIGAR
THE VERY, VERY OLD AND THE VERY, VERY YOUNG WERE ALL THE DEMON COULD MANAGE BACK IN THE EARLY DAYS, BUT AS HE GOT BIGGER AND STRONGER, SO TOO DID HIS VICTIMS...
THREE WEEKS AFTER HE WAS DISCHARGED FROM THE ARMED FORCES, HE SLID A SCREWDRIVER INTO THE NAPE OF SOME FAT COP'S NECK...

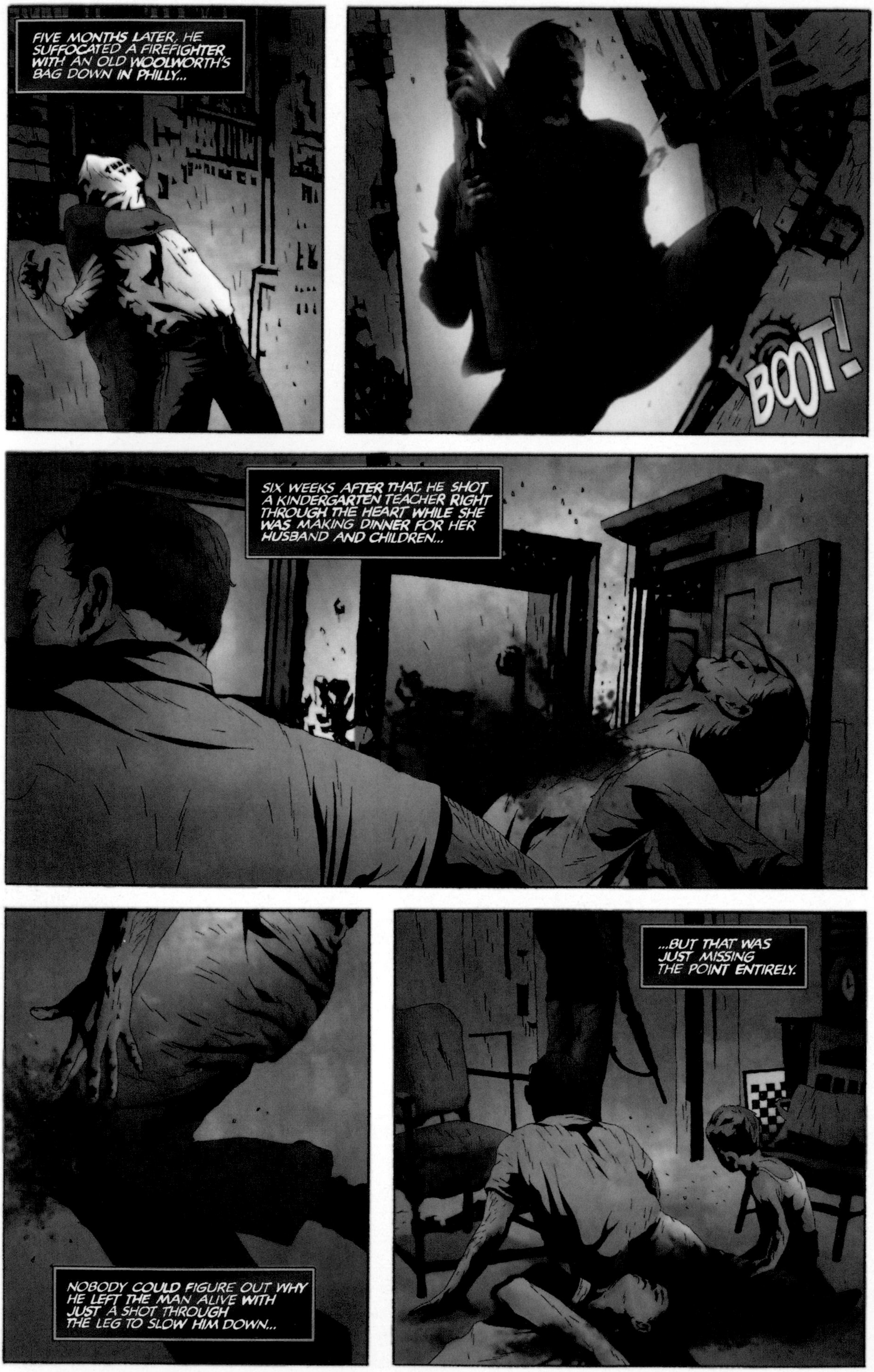
FIVE MONTHS LATER, HE SUFFOCATED A FIREFIGHTER WITH AN OLD WOOLWORTH'S BAG DOWN IN PHILLY...
BOOT!
SIX WEEKS AFTER THAT, HE SHOT A KINDERGARTEN TEACHER RIGHT THROUGH THE HEART WHILE SHE WAS MAKING DINNER FOR HER HUSBAND AND CHILDREN...
NOBODY COULD FIGURE OUT WHY HE LEFT THE MAN ALIVE WITH JUST A SHOT THROUGH THE LEG TO SLOW HIM DOWN...
...BUT THAT WAS JUST MISSING THE POINT ENTIRELY.

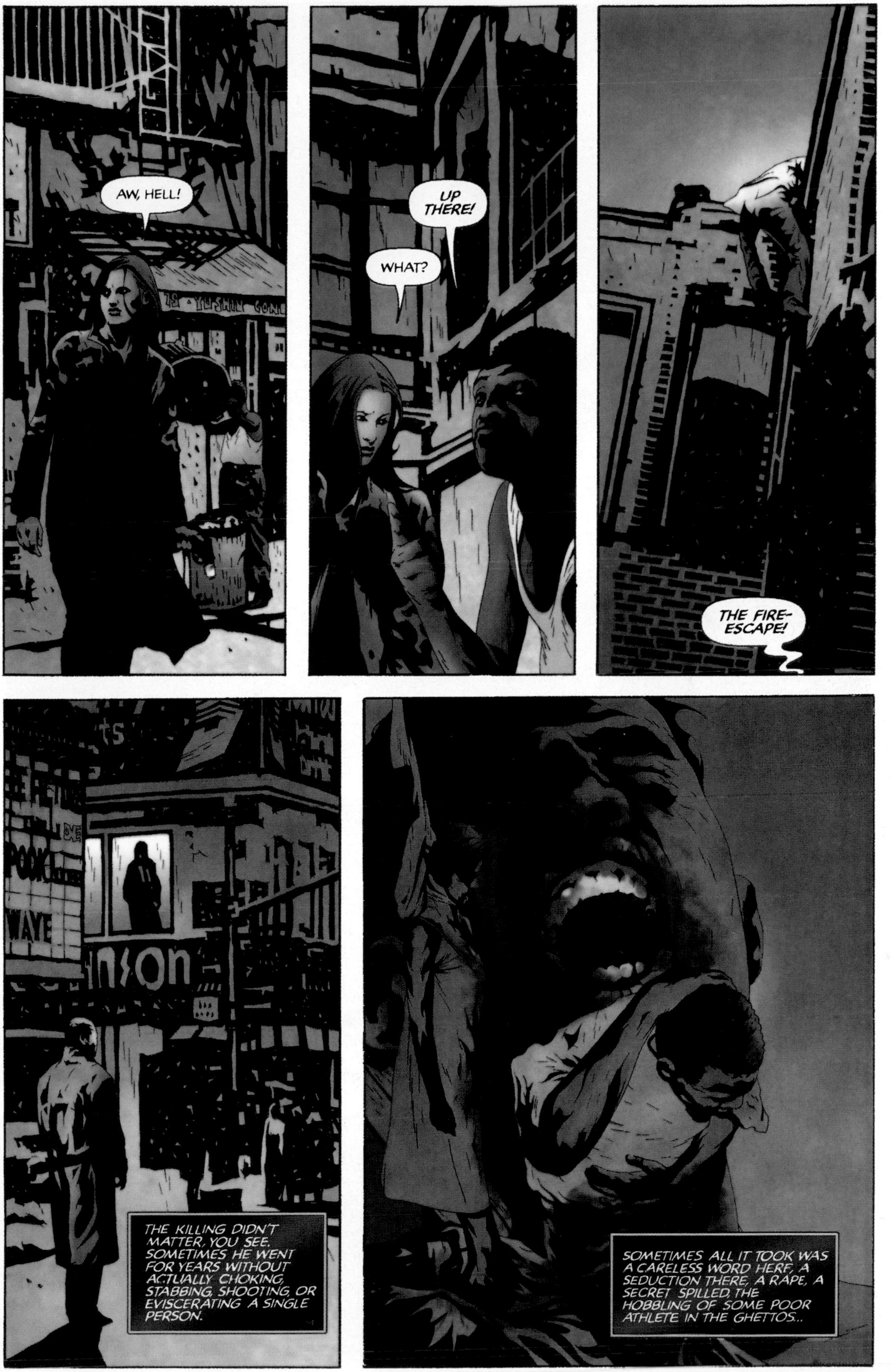
AW, HELL!
UP THERE!
WHAT?
THE FIRE-ESCAPE!
THE KILLING DIDN'T MATTER, YOU SEE. SOMETIMES HE WENT FOR YEARS WITHOUT ACTUALLY CHOKING, STABBING, SHOOTING, OR EVISCERATING A SINGLE PERSON.
SOMETIMES ALL IT TOOK WAS A CARELESS WORD HERE, A SEDUCTION THERE, A RAPE, A SECRET SPILLED, THE HOBBLING OF SOME POOR ATHLETE IN THE GHETTOS..

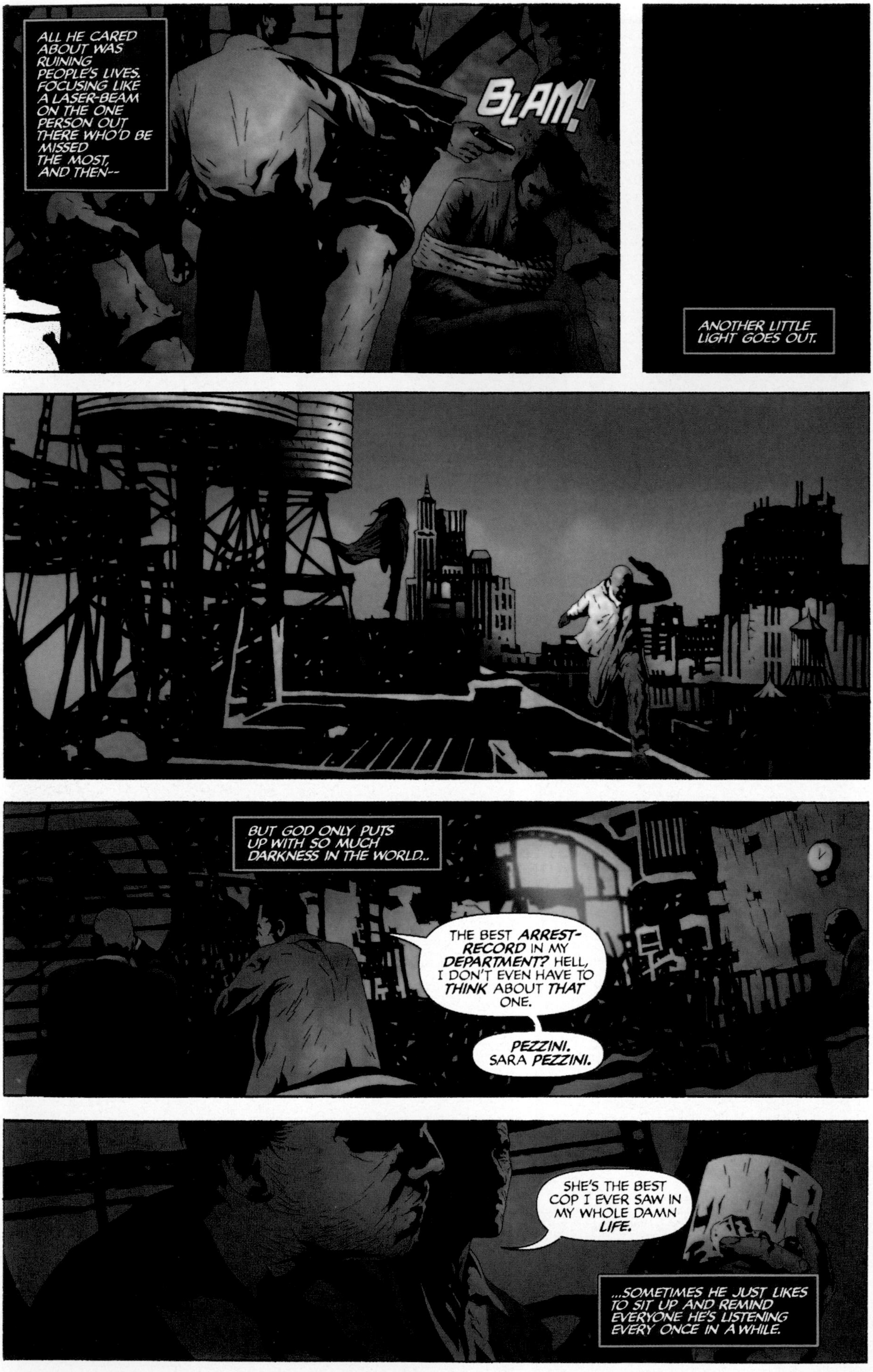
ALL HE CARED ABOUT WAS RUINING PEOPLE'S LIVES. FOCUSING LIKE A LASER-BEAM ON THE ONE PERSON OUT THERE WHO'D BE MISSED THE MOST, AND THEN--
BLAM!
ANOTHER LITTLE LIGHT GOES OUT.
BUT GOD ONLY PUTS UP WITH SO MUCH DARKNESS IN THE WORLD..
THE BEST ARREST-RECORD IN MY DEPARTMENT? HELL, I DON'T EVEN HAVE TO THINK ABOUT THAT ONE.
PEZZINI. SARA PEZZINI.
SHE'S THE BEST COP I EVER SAW IN MY WHOLE DAMN LIFE.
...SOMETIMES HE JUST LIKES TO SIT UP AND REMIND EVERYONE HE'S LISTENING EVERY ONCE IN A WHILE.

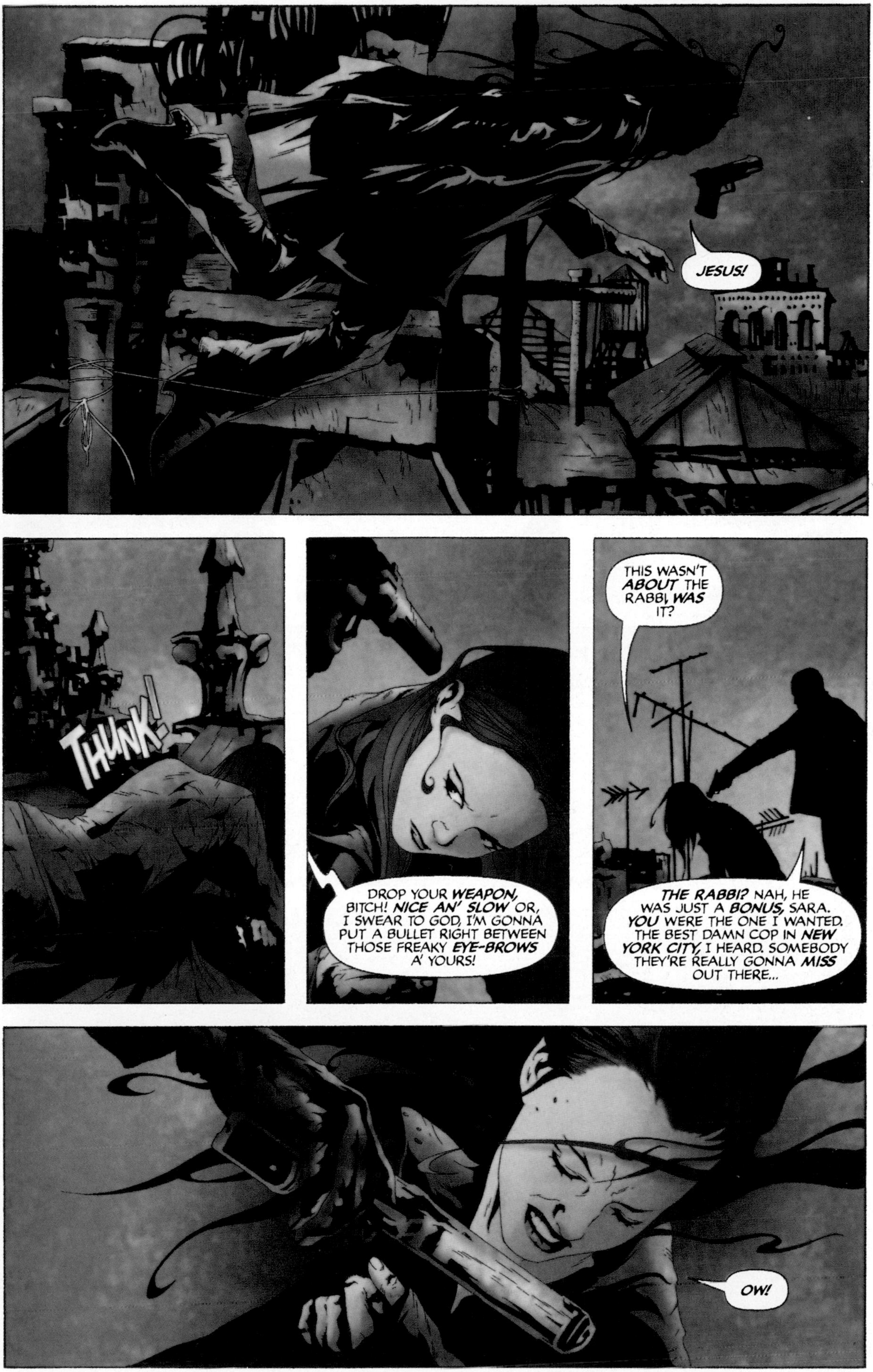
JESUS!
THUNK!
DROP YOUR WEAPON, BITCH! NICE AN' SLOW OR, I SWEAR TO GOD, I'M GONNA PUT A BULLET RIGHT BETWEEN THOSE FREAKY EYE-BROWS A' YOURS!
THIS WASN'T ABOUT THE RABBI, WAS IT?
THE RABBI? NAH, HE WAS JUST A BONUS, SARA. YOU WERE THE ONE I WANTED. THE BEST DAMN COP IN NEW YORK CITY, I HEARD. SOMEBODY THEY'RE REALLY GONNA MISS OUT THERE...
OW!

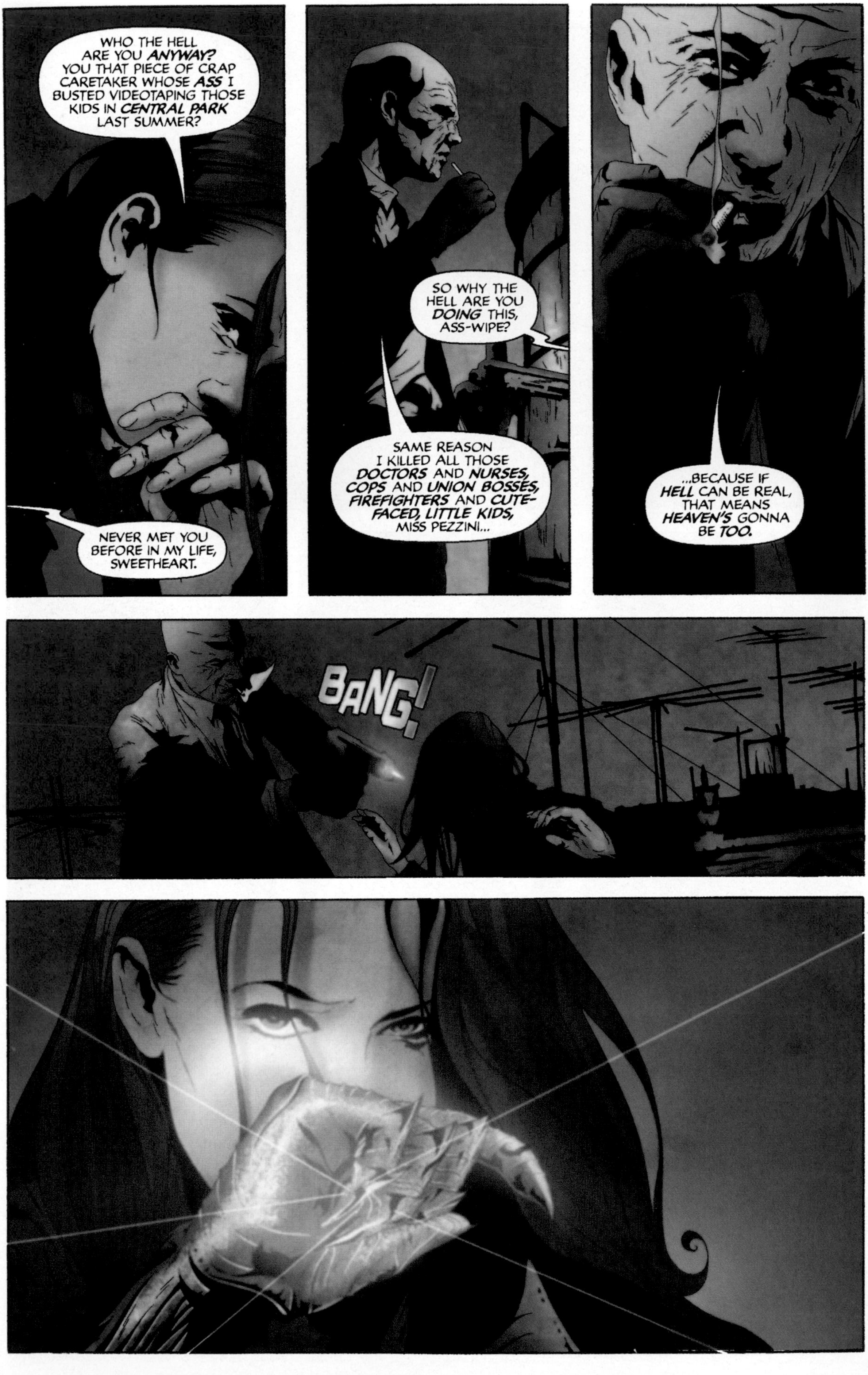
WHO THE HELL ARE YOU *ANYWAY?* YOU THAT PIECE OF CRAP CARETAKER WHOSE *ASS* I BUSTED VIDEOTAPING THOSE KIDS IN *CENTRAL PARK* LAST SUMMER?
NEVER MET YOU BEFORE IN MY LIFE, SWEETHEART.
SO WHY THE HELL ARE YOU *DOING* THIS, ASS-WIPE?
SAME REASON I KILLED ALL THOSE *DOCTORS* AND *NURSES, COPS* AND *UNION BOSSES, FIREFIGHTERS* AND *CUTE-FACED, LITTLE KIDS,* MISS PEZZINI...
...BECAUSE IF *HELL* CAN BE REAL, THAT MEANS *HEAVEN'S* GONNA BE *TOO.*
BANG!

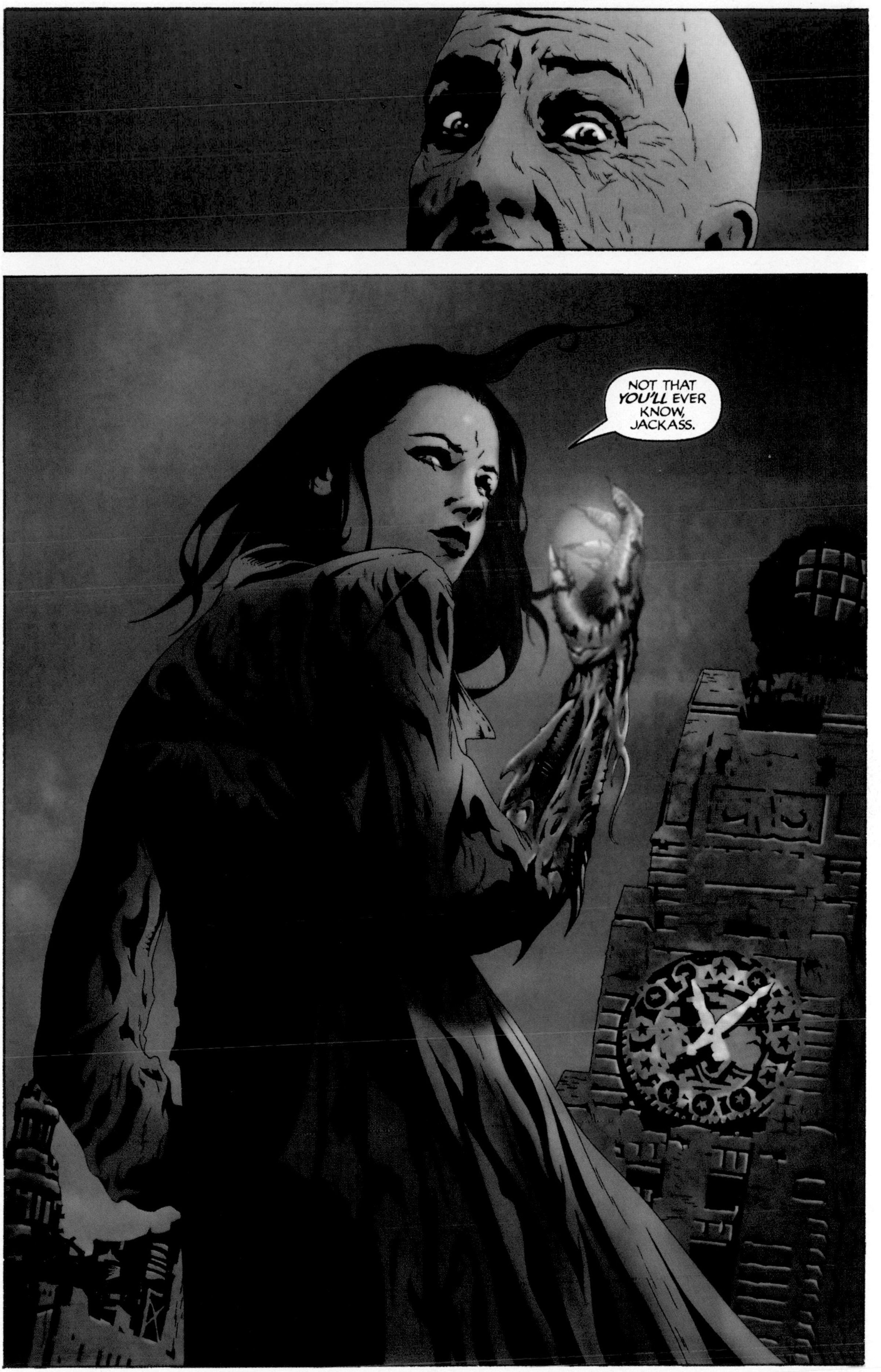
NOT THAT *YOU'LL* EVER KNOW, JACKASS.

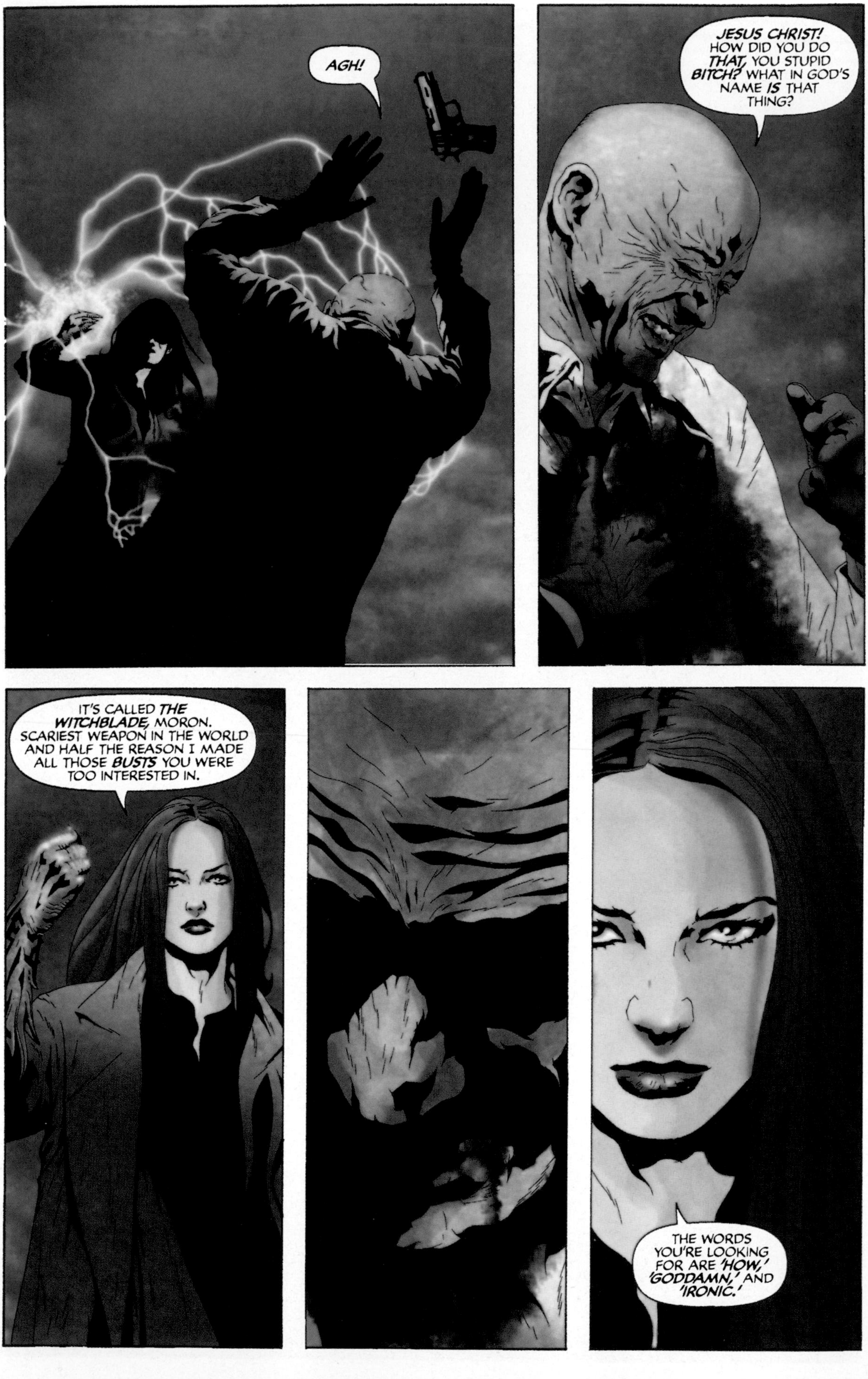
AGH!
JESUS CHRIST! HOW DID YOU DO THAT, YOU STUPID BITCH? WHAT IN GOD'S NAME IS THAT THING?
IT'S CALLED THE WITCHBLADE, MORON. SCARIEST WEAPON IN THE WORLD AND HALF THE REASON I MADE ALL THOSE BUSTS YOU WERE TOO INTERESTED IN.
THE WORDS YOU'RE LOOKING FOR ARE 'HOW,' 'GODDAMN,' AND 'IRONIC.'

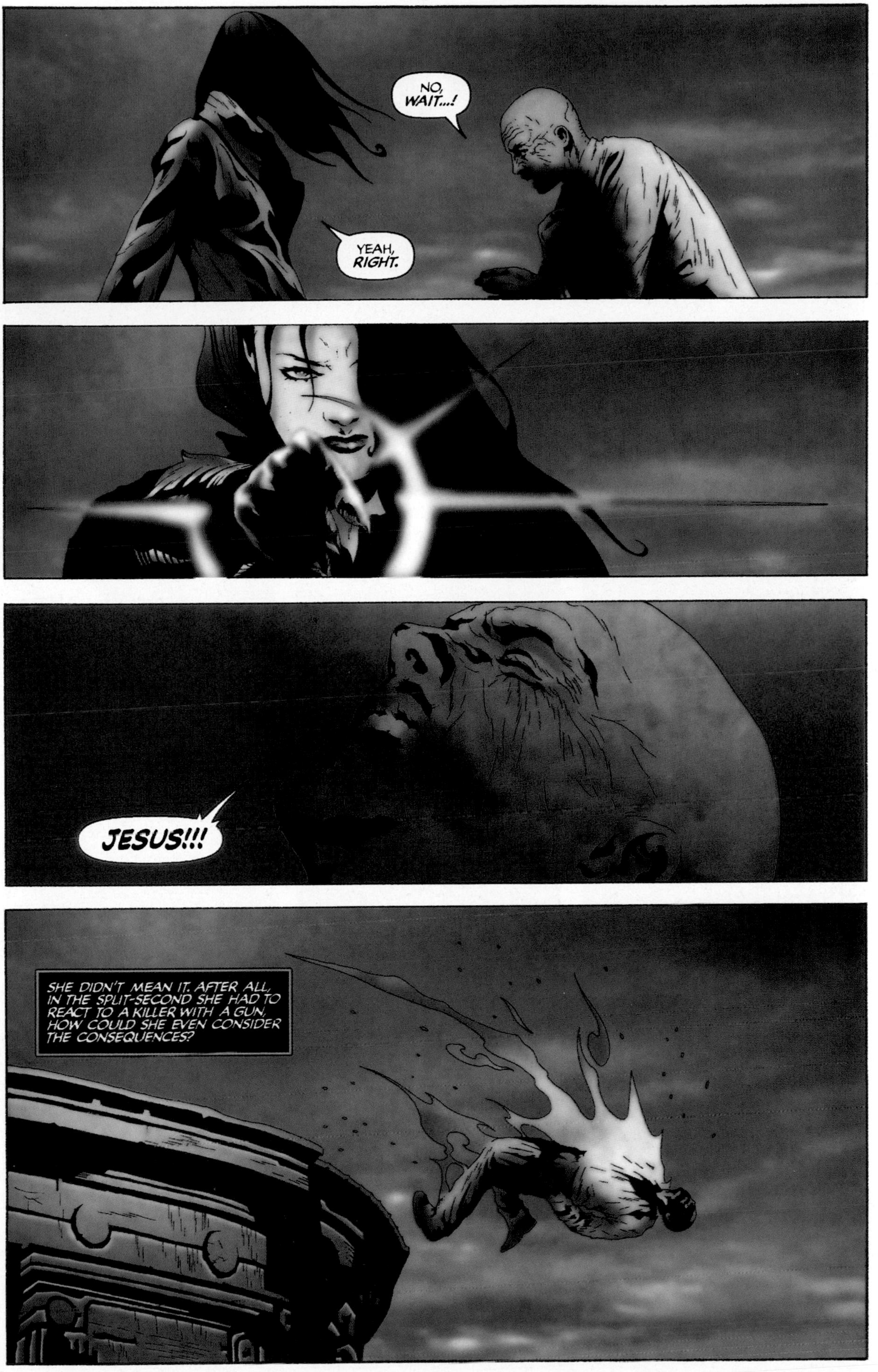
NO, WAIT...!
YEAH, RIGHT.
JESUS!!!
SHE DIDN'T MEAN IT. AFTER ALL, IN THE SPLIT-SECOND SHE HAD TO REACT TO A KILLER WITH A GUN, HOW COULD SHE EVEN CONSIDER THE CONSEQUENCES?

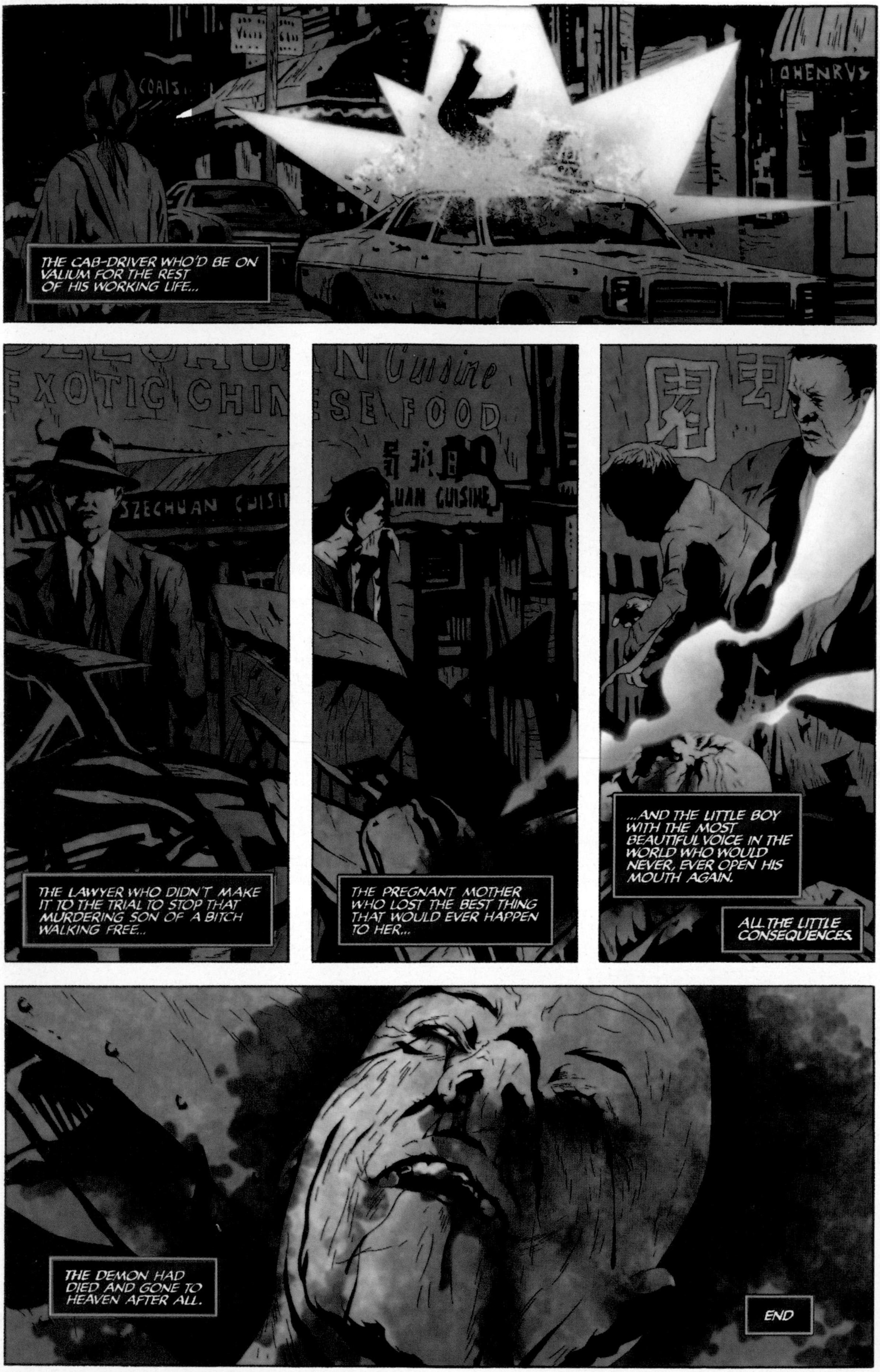
THE CAB-DRIVER WHO'D BE ON VALIUM FOR THE REST OF HIS WORKING LIFE...
THE LAWYER WHO DIDN'T MAKE IT TO THE TRIAL TO STOP THAT MURDERING SON OF A BITCH WALKING FREE...
THE PREGNANT MOTHER WHO LOST THE BEST THING THAT WOULD EVER HAPPEN TO HER...
...AND THE LITTLE BOY WITH THE MOST BEAUTIFUL VOICE IN THE WORLD WHO WOULD NEVER, EVER OPEN HIS MOUTH AGAIN.
ALL THE LITTLE CONSEQUENCES.
THE DEMON HAD DIED AND GONE TO HEAVEN AFTER ALL.
END

WITCHBLADE

DEMON REBORN

CHAPTER ONE

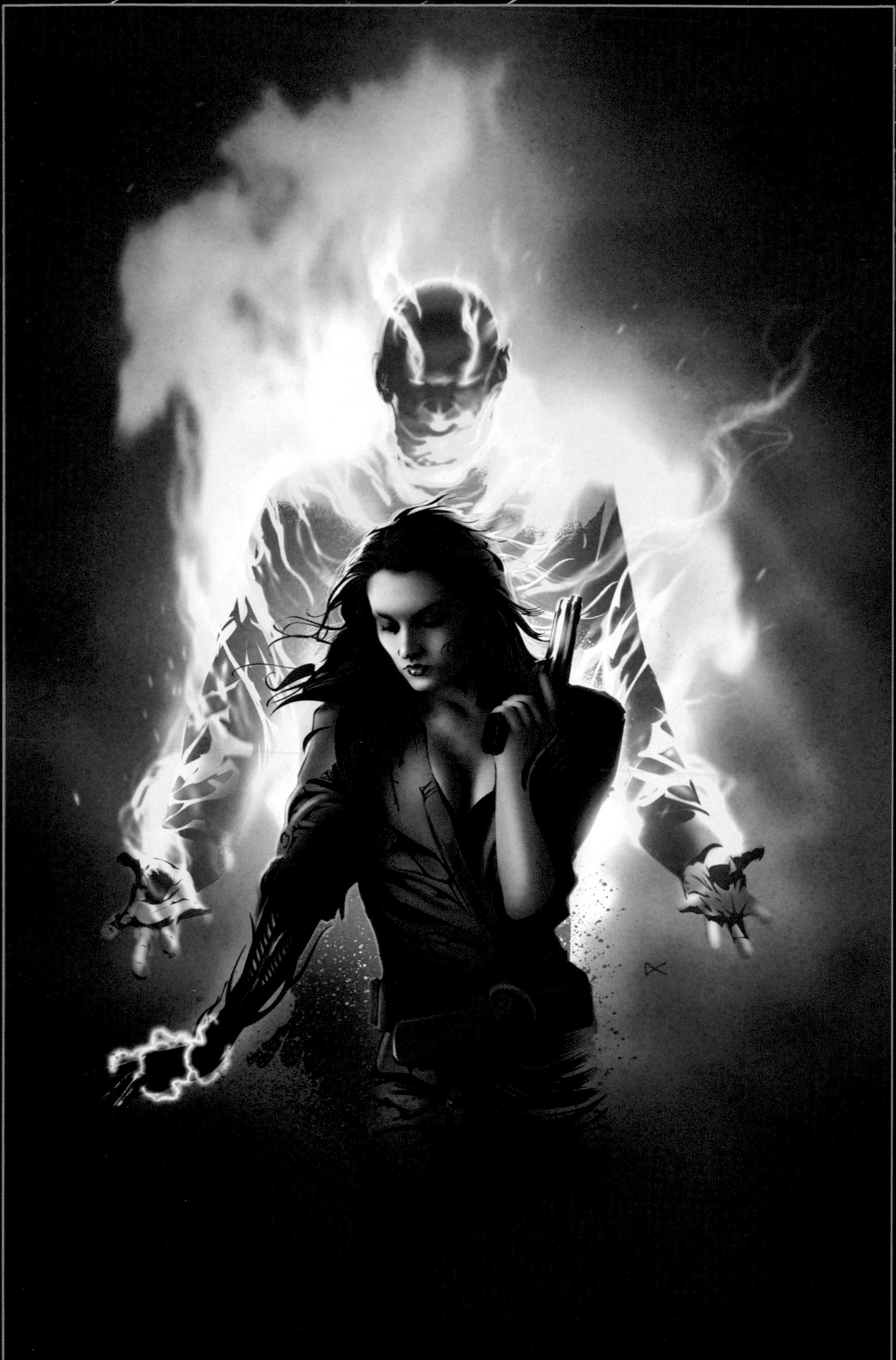

ISSUE #1 COVER BY DENNIS CALERO

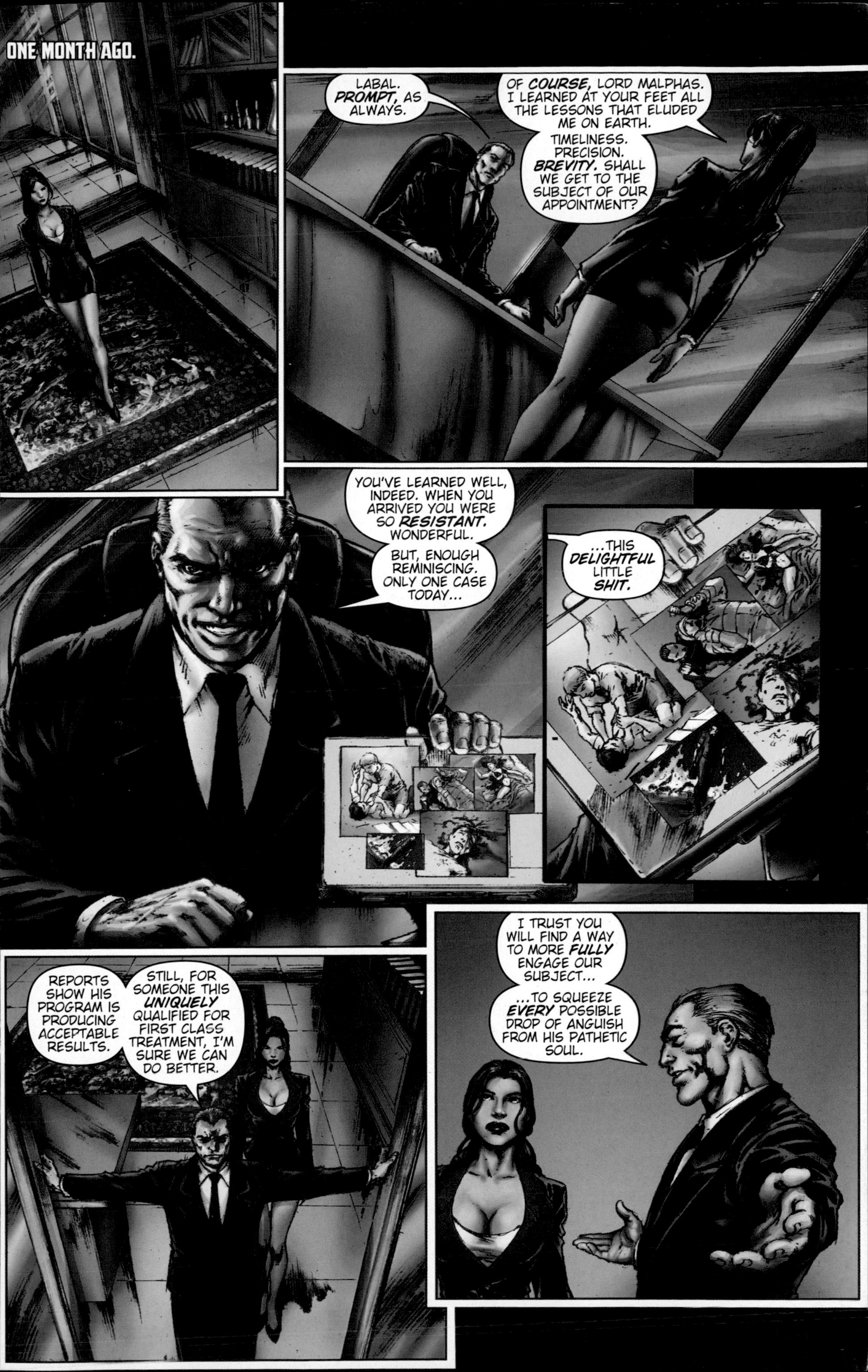
ONE MONTH AGO.
LABAL. PROMPT, AS ALWAYS.
OF COURSE, LORD MALPHAS. I LEARNED AT YOUR FEET ALL THE LESSONS THAT ELUDED ME ON EARTH.
TIMELINESS. PRECISION. BREVITY. SHALL WE GET TO THE SUBJECT OF OUR APPOINTMENT?
YOU'VE LEARNED WELL, INDEED. WHEN YOU ARRIVED YOU WERE SO RESISTANT. WONDERFUL.
BUT, ENOUGH REMINISCING. ONLY ONE CASE TODAY...
...THIS DELIGHTFUL LITTLE SHIT.
REPORTS SHOW HIS PROGRAM IS PRODUCING ACCEPTABLE RESULTS.
STILL, FOR SOMEONE THIS UNIQUELY QUALIFIED FOR FIRST CLASS TREATMENT, I'M SURE WE CAN DO BETTER.
I TRUST YOU WILL FIND A WAY TO MORE FULLY ENGAGE OUR SUBJECT...
...TO SQUEEZE EVERY POSSIBLE DROP OF ANGUISH FROM HIS PATHETIC SOUL.

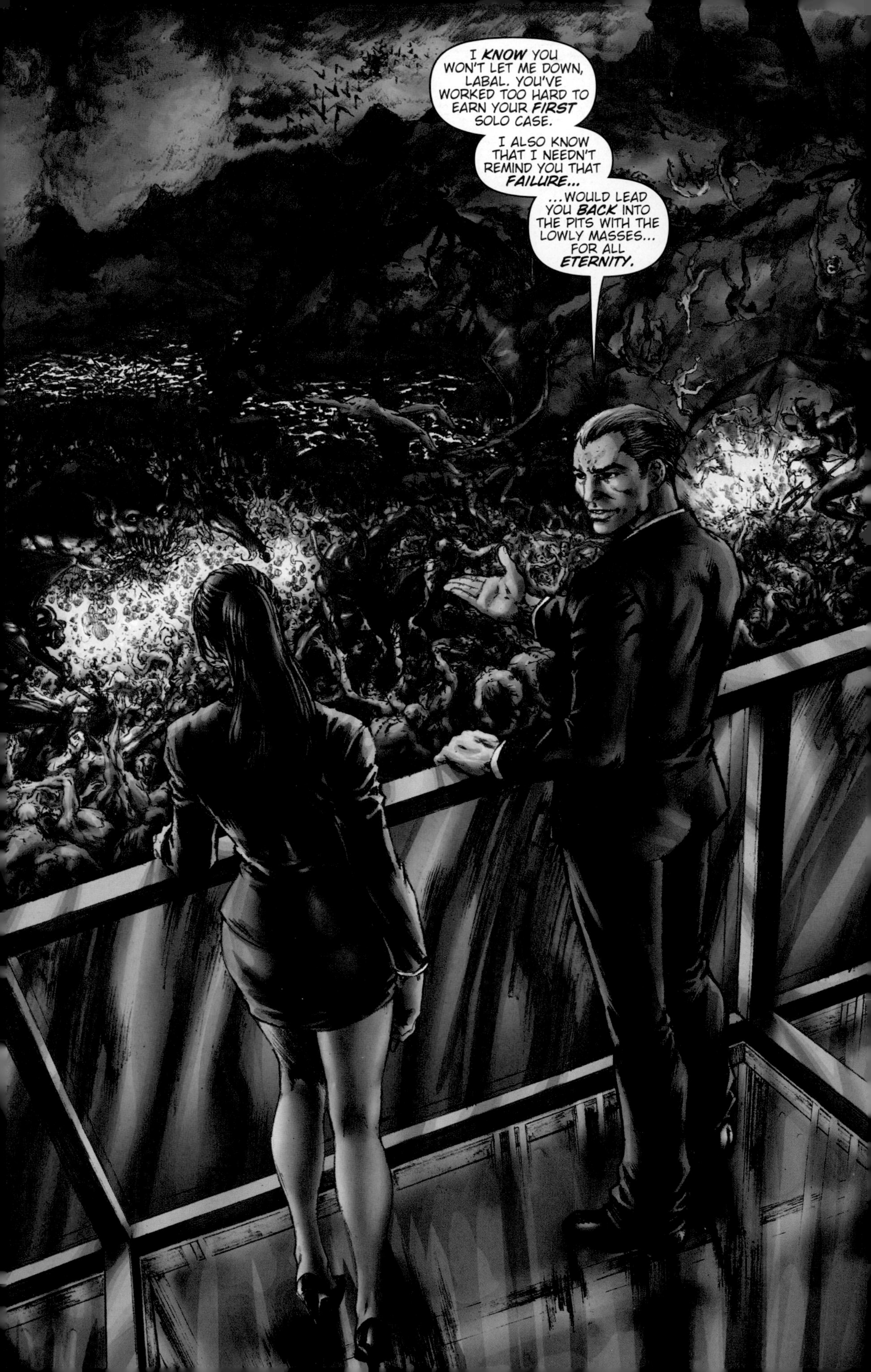
I KNOW YOU WON'T LET ME DOWN, LABAL. YOU'VE WORKED TOO HARD TO EARN YOUR FIRST SOLO CASE.
I ALSO KNOW THAT I NEEDN'T REMIND YOU THAT FAILURE...
...WOULD LEAD YOU BACK INTO THE PITS WITH THE LOWLY MASSES... FOR ALL ETERNITY.

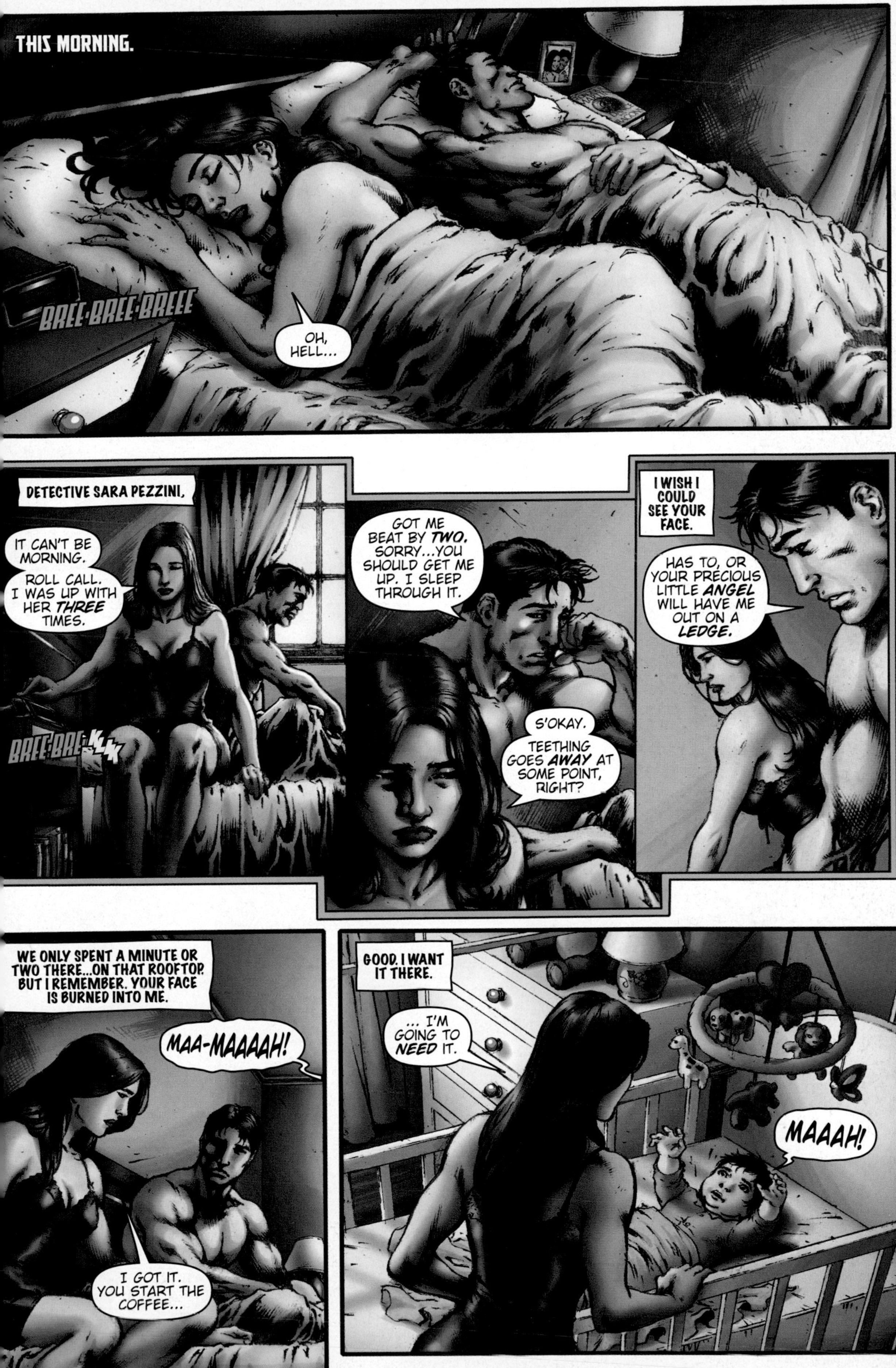
THIS MORNING.
BREE-BREE-BREEE
OH, HELL...
DETECTIVE SARA PEZZINI.
IT CAN'T BE MORNING.
ROLL CALL. I WAS UP WITH HER THREE TIMES.
BREE-BRE-KLIK
GOT ME BEAT BY TWO. SORRY...YOU SHOULD GET ME UP. I SLEEP THROUGH IT.
S'OKAY. TEETHING GOES AWAY AT SOME POINT, RIGHT?
I WISH I COULD SEE YOUR FACE.
HAS TO, OR YOUR PRECIOUS LITTLE ANGEL WILL HAVE ME OUT ON A LEDGE.
WE ONLY SPENT A MINUTE OR TWO THERE...ON THAT ROOFTOP. BUT I REMEMBER. YOUR FACE IS BURNED INTO ME.
MAA-MAAAAH!
I GOT IT. YOU START THE COFFEE...
GOOD. I WANT IT THERE.
... I'M GOING TO NEED IT.
MAAAH!

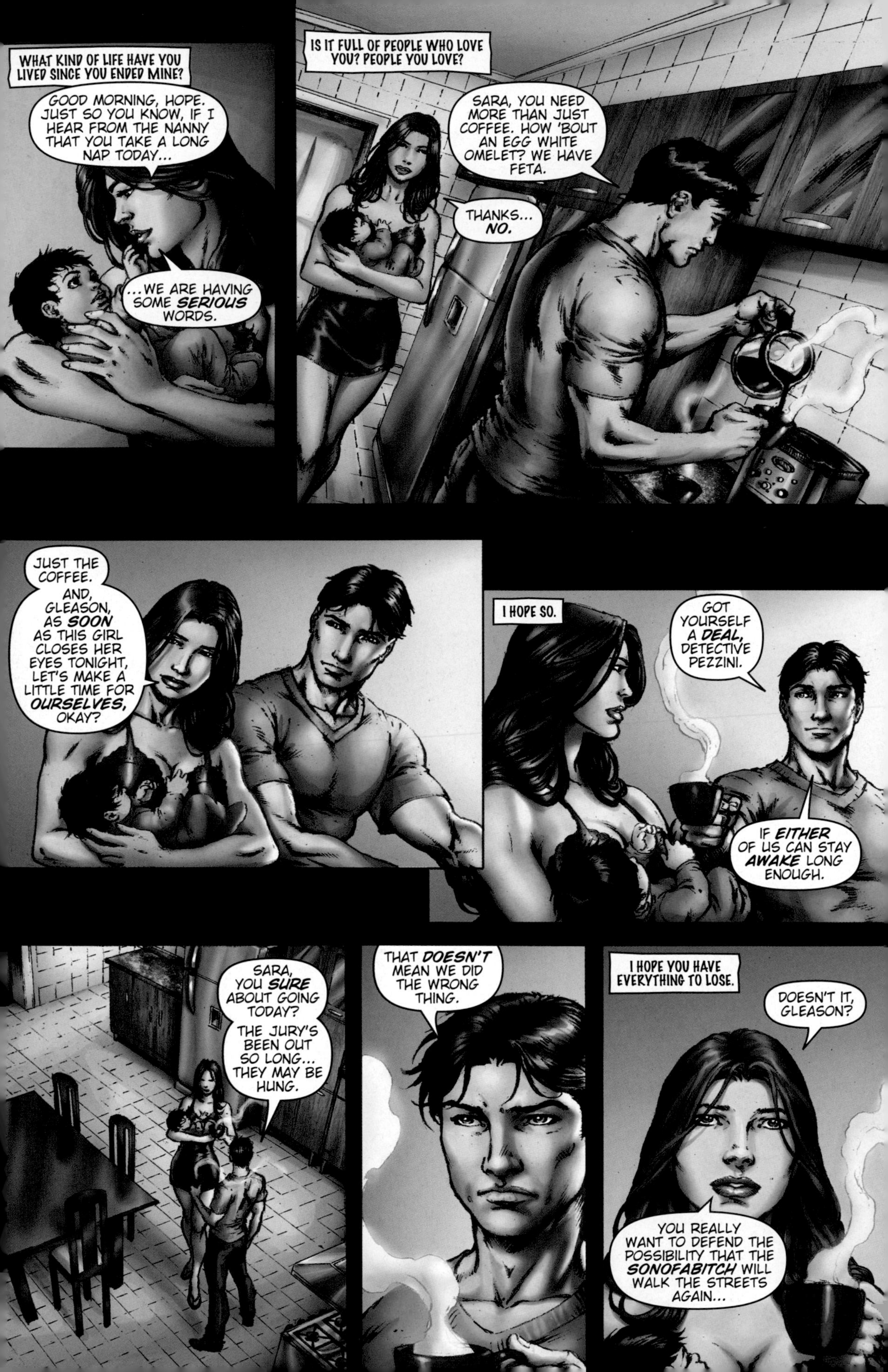
WHAT KIND OF LIFE HAVE YOU LIVED SINCE YOU ENDED MINE?
GOOD MORNING, HOPE. JUST SO YOU KNOW, IF I HEAR FROM THE NANNY THAT YOU TAKE A LONG NAP TODAY...
...WE ARE HAVING SOME SERIOUS WORDS.
IS IT FULL OF PEOPLE WHO LOVE YOU? PEOPLE YOU LOVE?
SARA, YOU NEED MORE THAN JUST COFFEE. HOW 'BOUT AN EGG WHITE OMELET? WE HAVE FETA.
THANKS... NO.
JUST THE COFFEE.
AND, GLEASON, AS SOON AS THIS GIRL CLOSES HER EYES TONIGHT, LET'S MAKE A LITTLE TIME FOR OURSELVES, OKAY?
I HOPE SO.
GOT YOURSELF A DEAL, DETECTIVE PEZZINI.
IF EITHER OF US CAN STAY AWAKE LONG ENOUGH.
SARA, YOU SURE ABOUT GOING TODAY?
THE JURY'S BEEN OUT SO LONG... THEY MAY BE HUNG.
THAT DOESN'T MEAN WE DID THE WRONG THING.
I HOPE YOU HAVE EVERYTHING TO LOSE.
DOESN'T IT, GLEASON?
YOU REALLY WANT TO DEFEND THE POSSIBILITY THAT THE SONOFABITCH WILL WALK THE STREETS AGAIN...

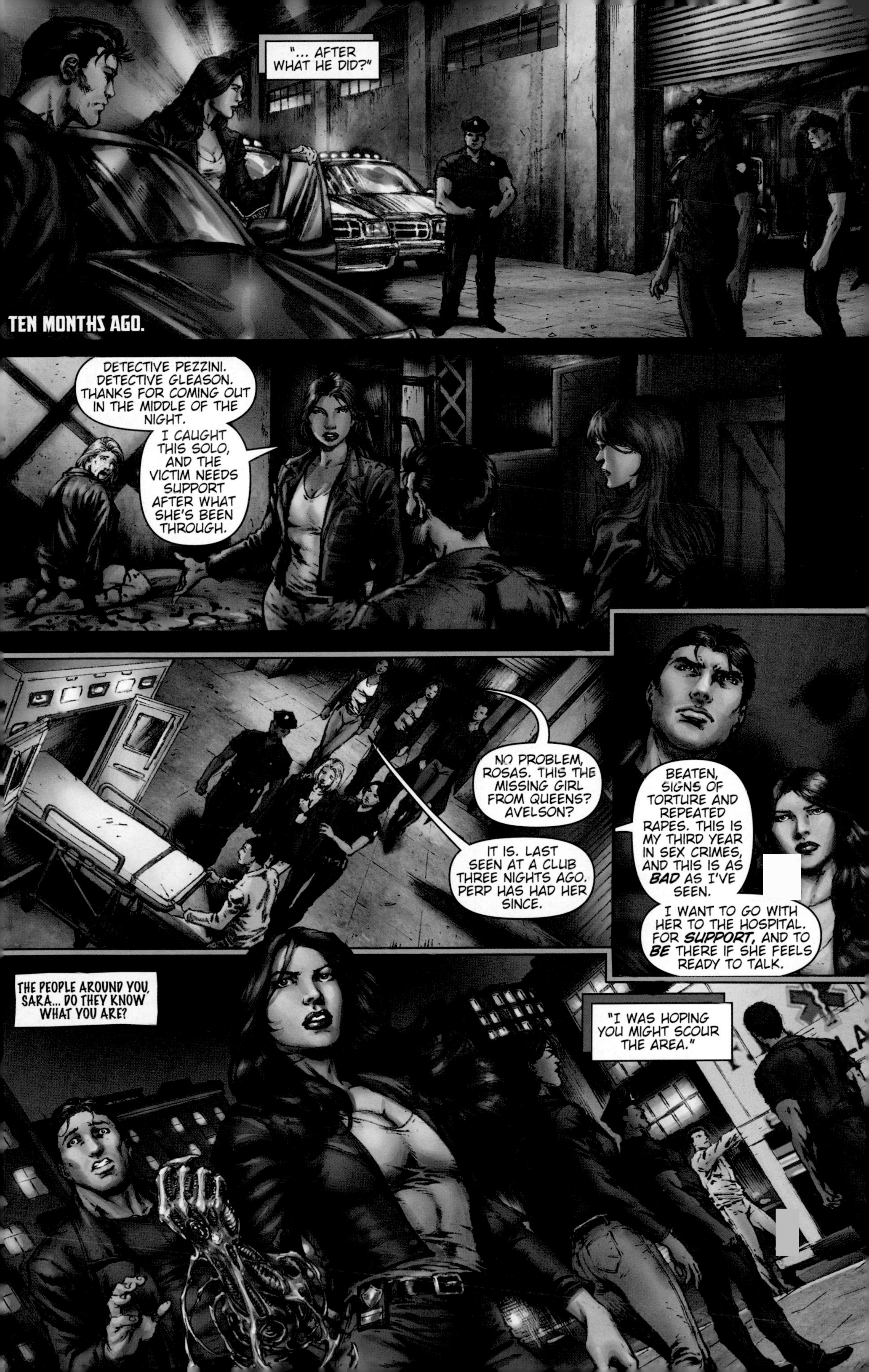
"... AFTER WHAT HE DID?"
TEN MONTHS AGO.
DETECTIVE PEZZINI. DETECTIVE GLEASON. THANKS FOR COMING OUT IN THE MIDDLE OF THE NIGHT.
I CAUGHT THIS SOLO, AND THE VICTIM NEEDS SUPPORT AFTER WHAT SHE'S BEEN THROUGH.
NO PROBLEM, ROSAS. THIS THE MISSING GIRL FROM QUEENS? AVELSON?
IT IS. LAST SEEN AT A CLUB THREE NIGHTS AGO. PERP HAS HAD HER SINCE.
BEATEN, SIGNS OF TORTURE AND REPEATED RAPES. THIS IS MY THIRD YEAR IN SEX CRIMES, AND THIS IS AS BAD AS I'VE SEEN.
I WANT TO GO WITH HER TO THE HOSPITAL. FOR SUPPORT, AND TO BE THERE IF SHE FEELS READY TO TALK.
THE PEOPLE AROUND YOU, SARA... DO THEY KNOW WHAT YOU ARE?
"I WAS HOPING YOU MIGHT SCOUR THE AREA."

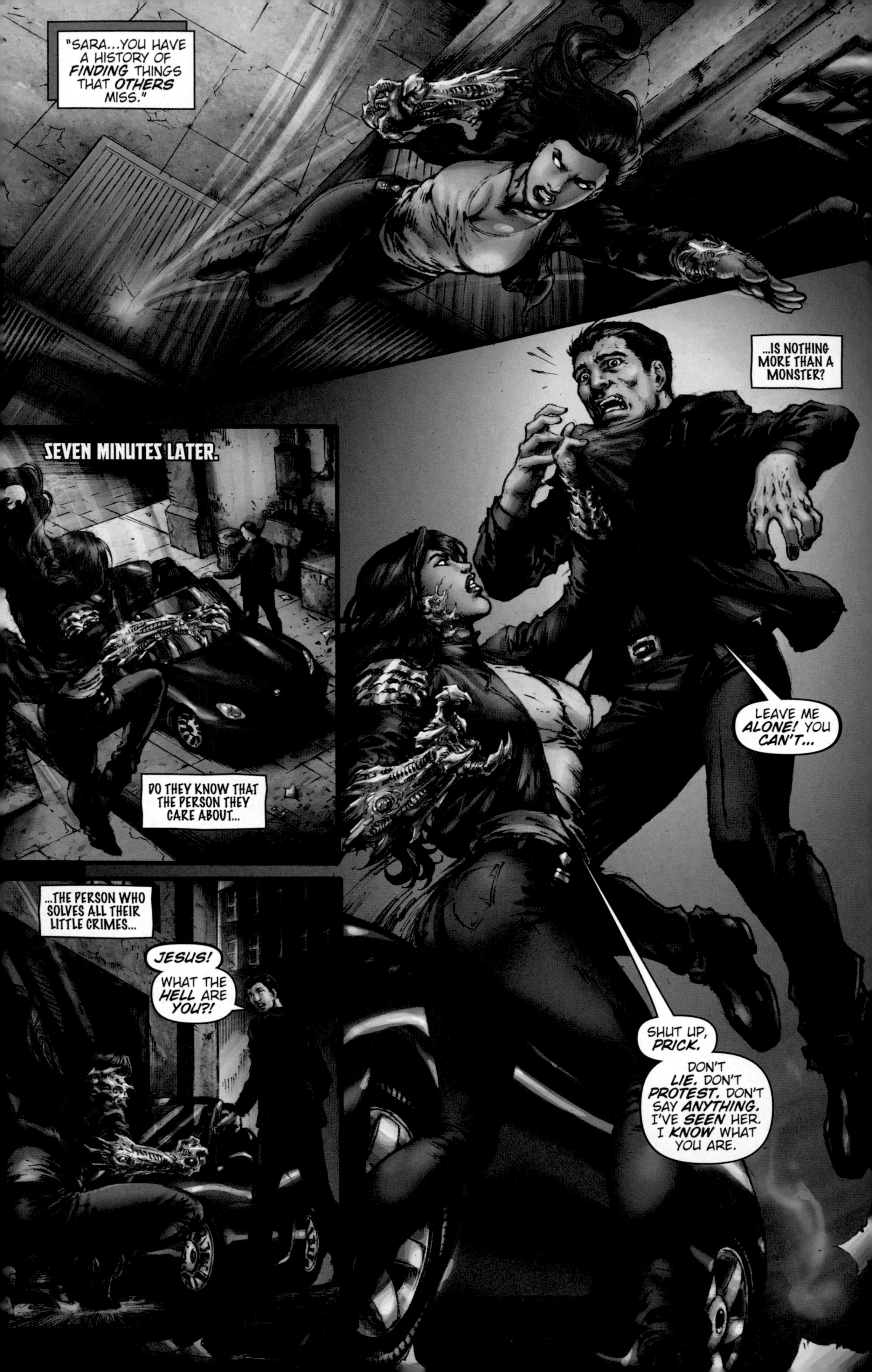
"SARA...YOU HAVE A HISTORY OF FINDING THINGS THAT OTHERS MISS."
SEVEN MINUTES LATER.
DO THEY KNOW THAT THE PERSON THEY CARE ABOUT...
...IS NOTHING MORE THAN A MONSTER?
LEAVE ME ALONE! YOU CAN'T...
...THE PERSON WHO SOLVES ALL THEIR LITTLE CRIMES...
JESUS!
WHAT THE HELL ARE YOU?!
SHUT UP, PRICK.
DON'T LIE. DON'T PROTEST. DON'T SAY ANYTHING. I'VE SEEN HER. I KNOW WHAT YOU ARE.

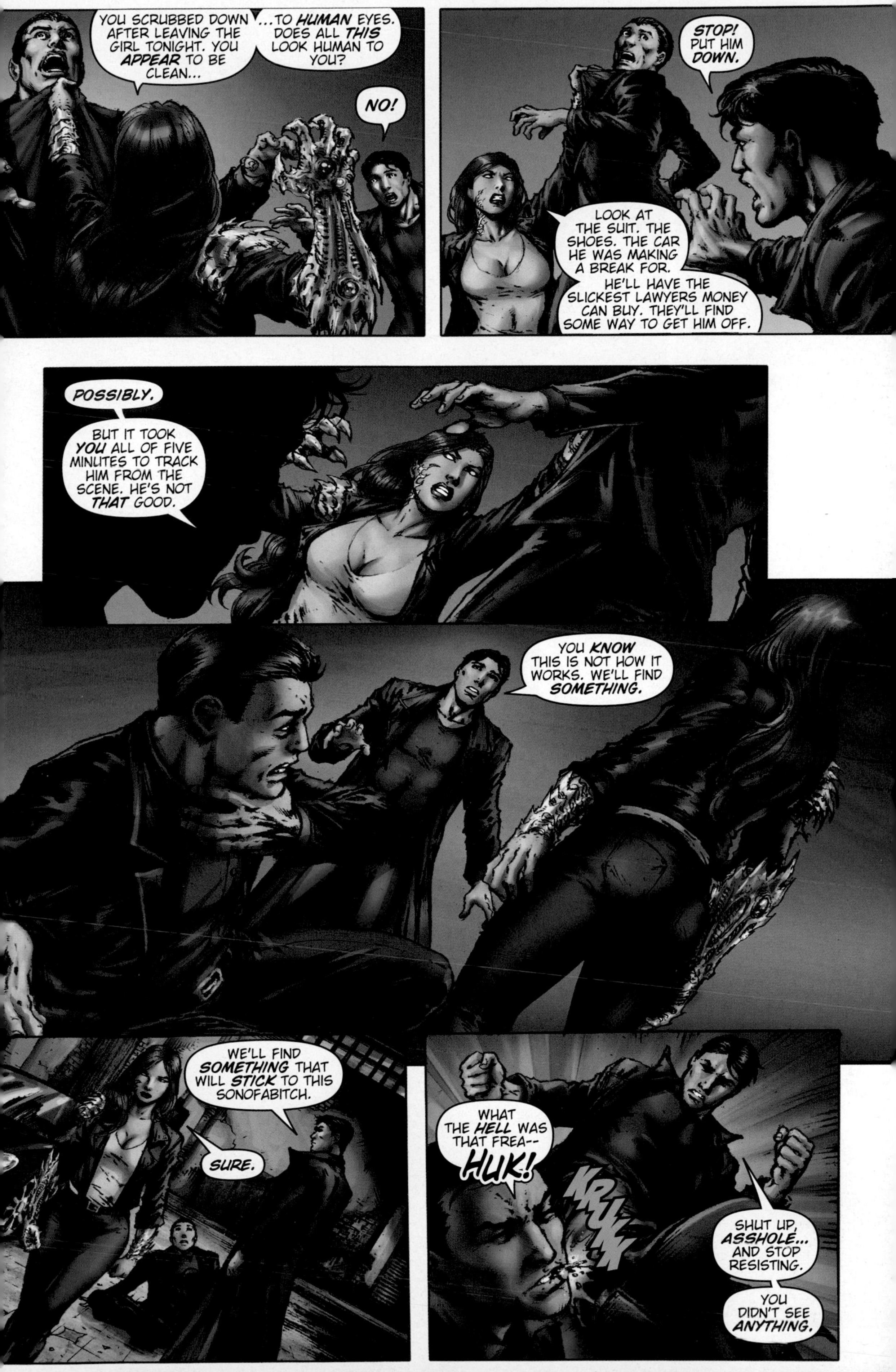
YOU SCRUBBED DOWN AFTER LEAVING THE GIRL TONIGHT. YOU APPEAR TO BE CLEAN...
...TO HUMAN EYES. DOES ALL THIS LOOK HUMAN TO YOU?
NO!
STOP! PUT HIM DOWN.
LOOK AT THE SUIT. THE SHOES. THE CAR HE WAS MAKING A BREAK FOR.
HE'LL HAVE THE SLICKEST LAWYERS MONEY CAN BUY. THEY'LL FIND SOME WAY TO GET HIM OFF.
POSSIBLY.
BUT IT TOOK YOU ALL OF FIVE MINUTES TO TRACK HIM FROM THE SCENE. HE'S NOT THAT GOOD.
YOU KNOW THIS IS NOT HOW IT WORKS. WE'LL FIND SOMETHING.
WE'LL FIND SOMETHING THAT WILL STICK TO THIS SONOFABITCH.
SURE.
WHAT THE HELL WAS THAT FREA--
HUK!
KRUNK
SHUT UP, ASSHOLE... AND STOP RESISTING.
YOU DIDN'T SEE ANYTHING.

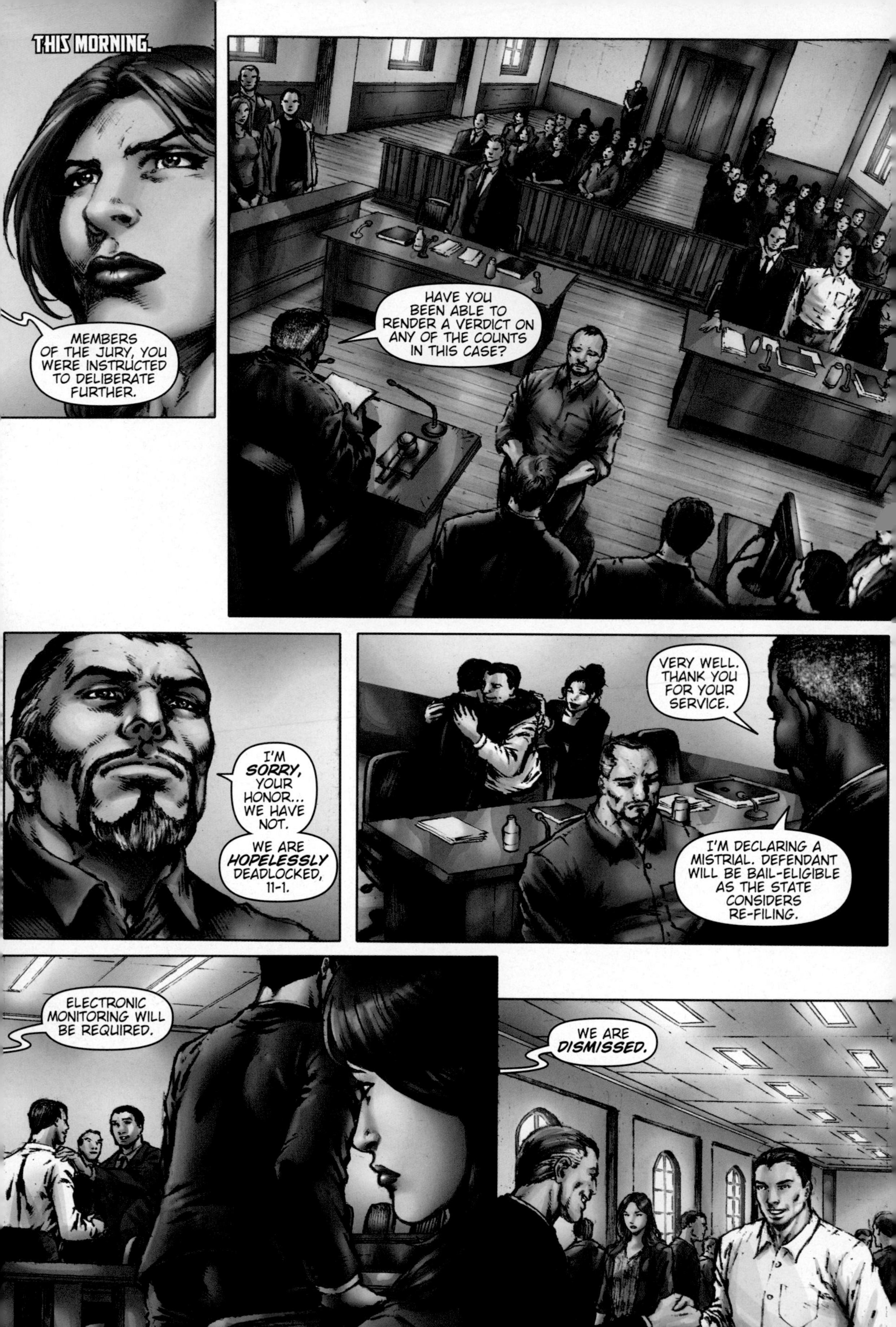
THIS MORNING.
MEMBERS OF THE JURY, YOU WERE INSTRUCTED TO DELIBERATE FURTHER.
HAVE YOU BEEN ABLE TO RENDER A VERDICT ON ANY OF THE COUNTS IN THIS CASE?
I'M SORRY, YOUR HONOR... WE HAVE NOT.
WE ARE HOPELESSLY DEADLOCKED, 11-1.
VERY WELL. THANK YOU FOR YOUR SERVICE.
I'M DECLARING A MISTRIAL. DEFENDANT WILL BE BAIL-ELIGIBLE AS THE STATE CONSIDERS RE-FILING.
ELECTRONIC MONITORING WILL BE REQUIRED.
WE ARE DISMISSED.

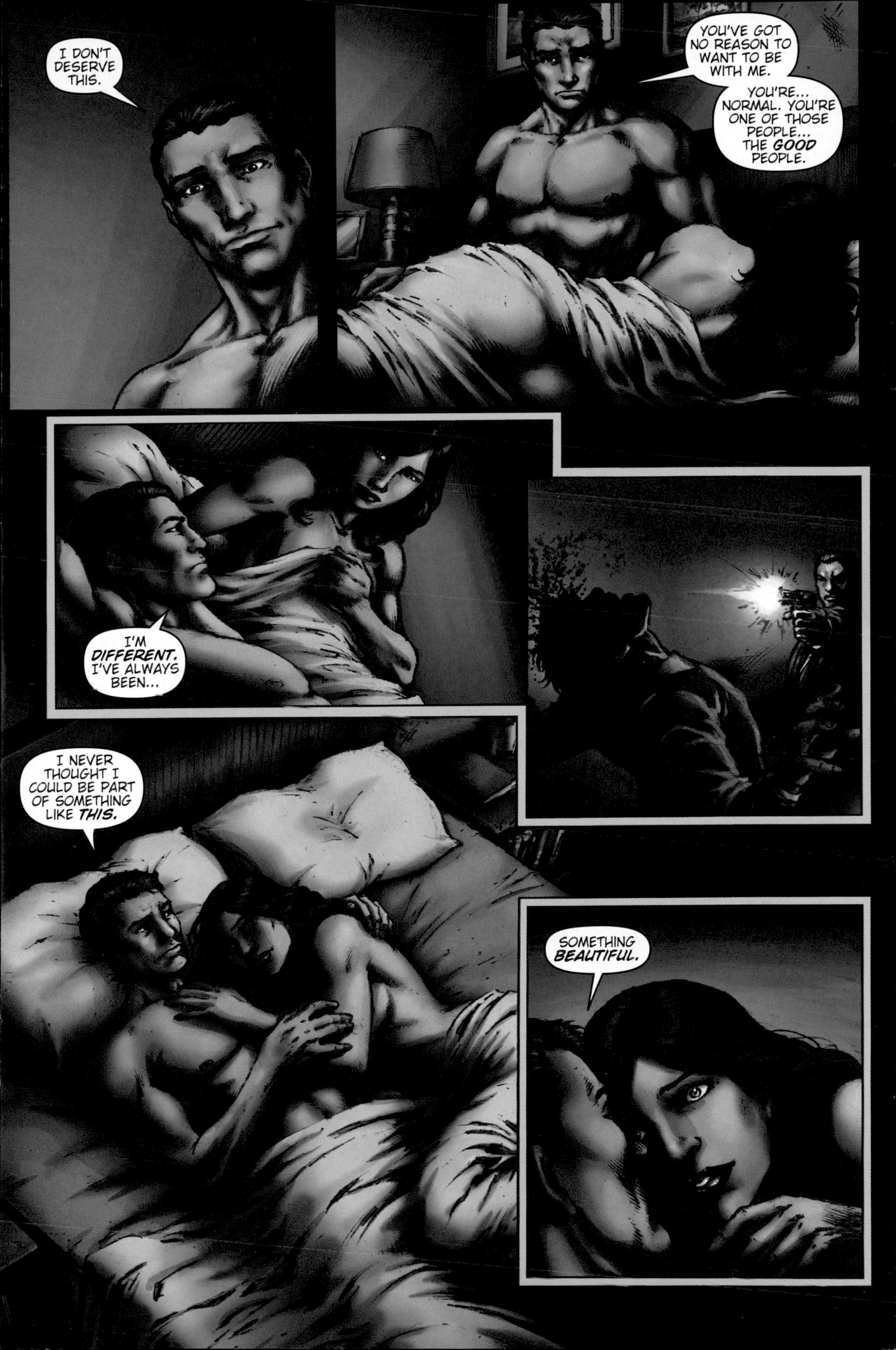
I DON'T DESERVE THIS.
YOU'VE GOT NO REASON TO WANT TO BE WITH ME.
YOU'RE... NORMAL. YOU'RE ONE OF THOSE PEOPLE... THE **GOOD** PEOPLE.
I'M ***DIFFERENT.*** I'VE ALWAYS BEEN...
I NEVER THOUGHT I COULD BE PART OF SOMETHING LIKE ***THIS.***
SOMETHING ***BEAUTIFUL.***

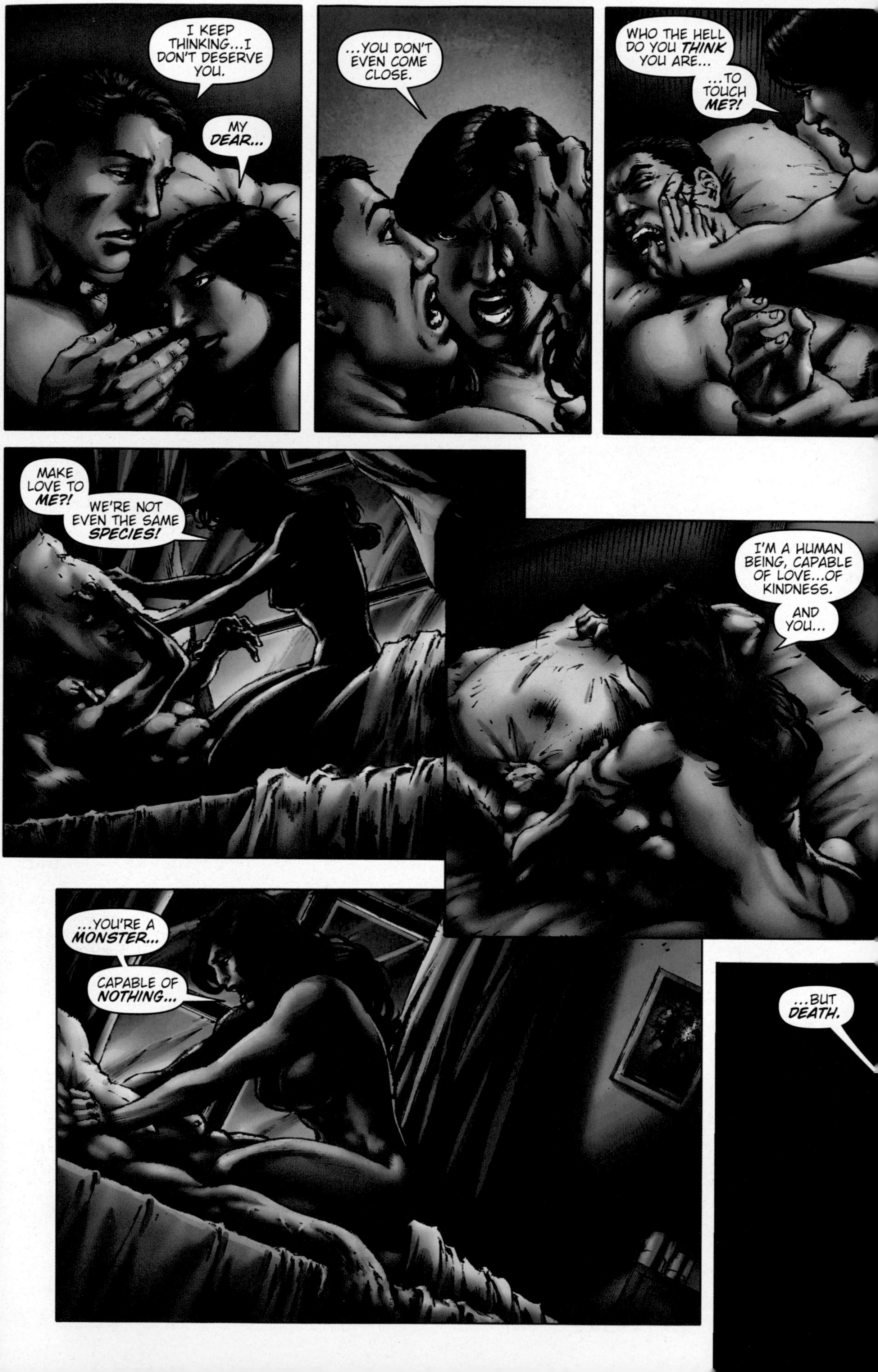
I KEEP THINKING...I DON'T DESERVE YOU.
MY *DEAR...*
...YOU DON'T EVEN COME CLOSE.
WHO THE HELL DO YOU *THINK* YOU ARE...
...TO TOUCH *ME?!*
MAKE LOVE TO *ME?!*
WE'RE NOT EVEN THE SAME *SPECIES!*
I'M A HUMAN BEING, CAPABLE OF LOVE...OF KINDNESS.
AND YOU...
...YOU'RE A *MONSTER...*
CAPABLE OF *NOTHING...*
...BUT *DEATH.*

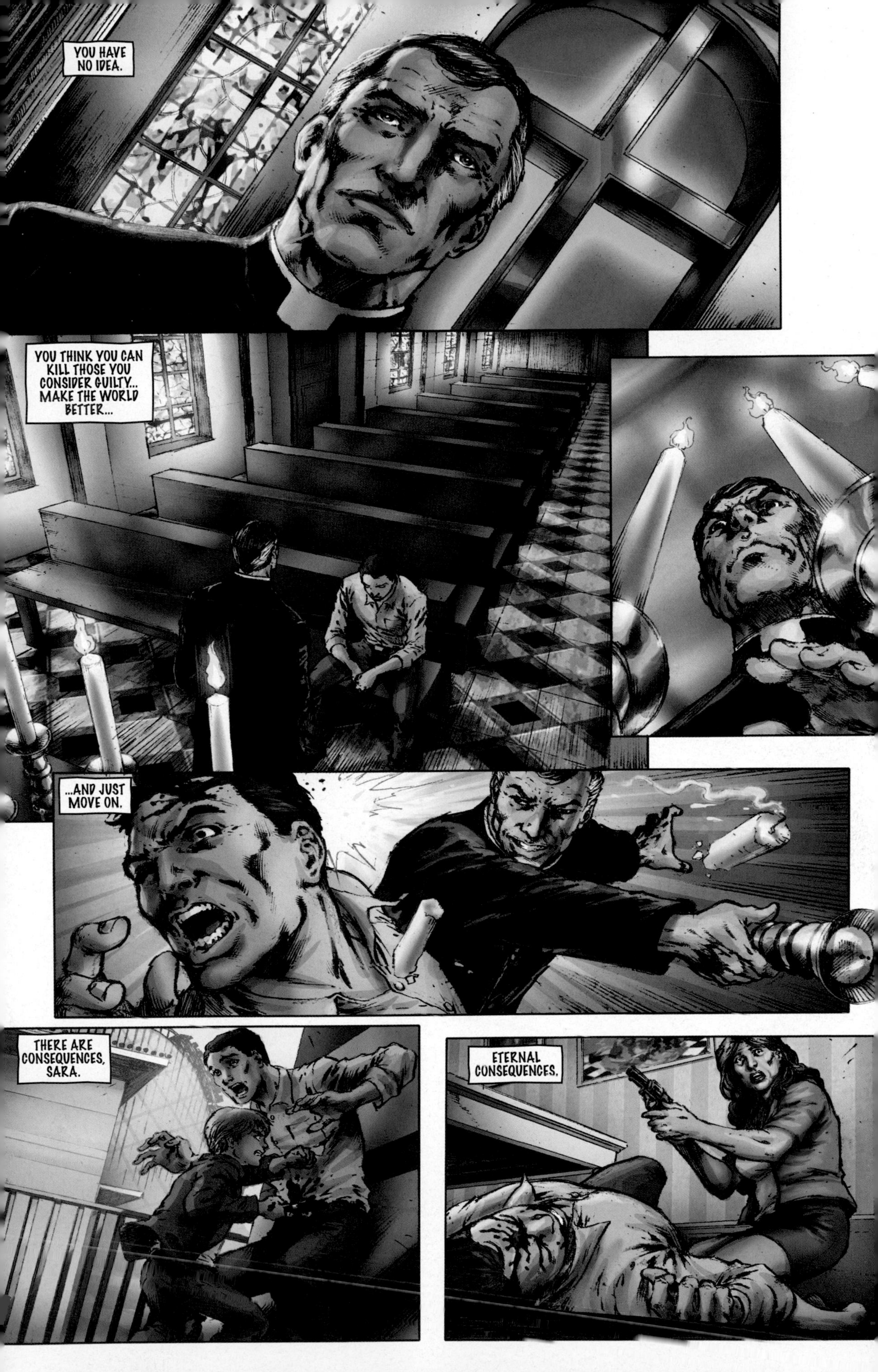
YOU HAVE NO IDEA.
YOU THINK YOU CAN KILL THOSE YOU CONSIDER GUILTY... MAKE THE WORLD BETTER...
...AND JUST MOVE ON.
THERE ARE CONSEQUENCES, SARA.
ETERNAL CONSEQUENCES.

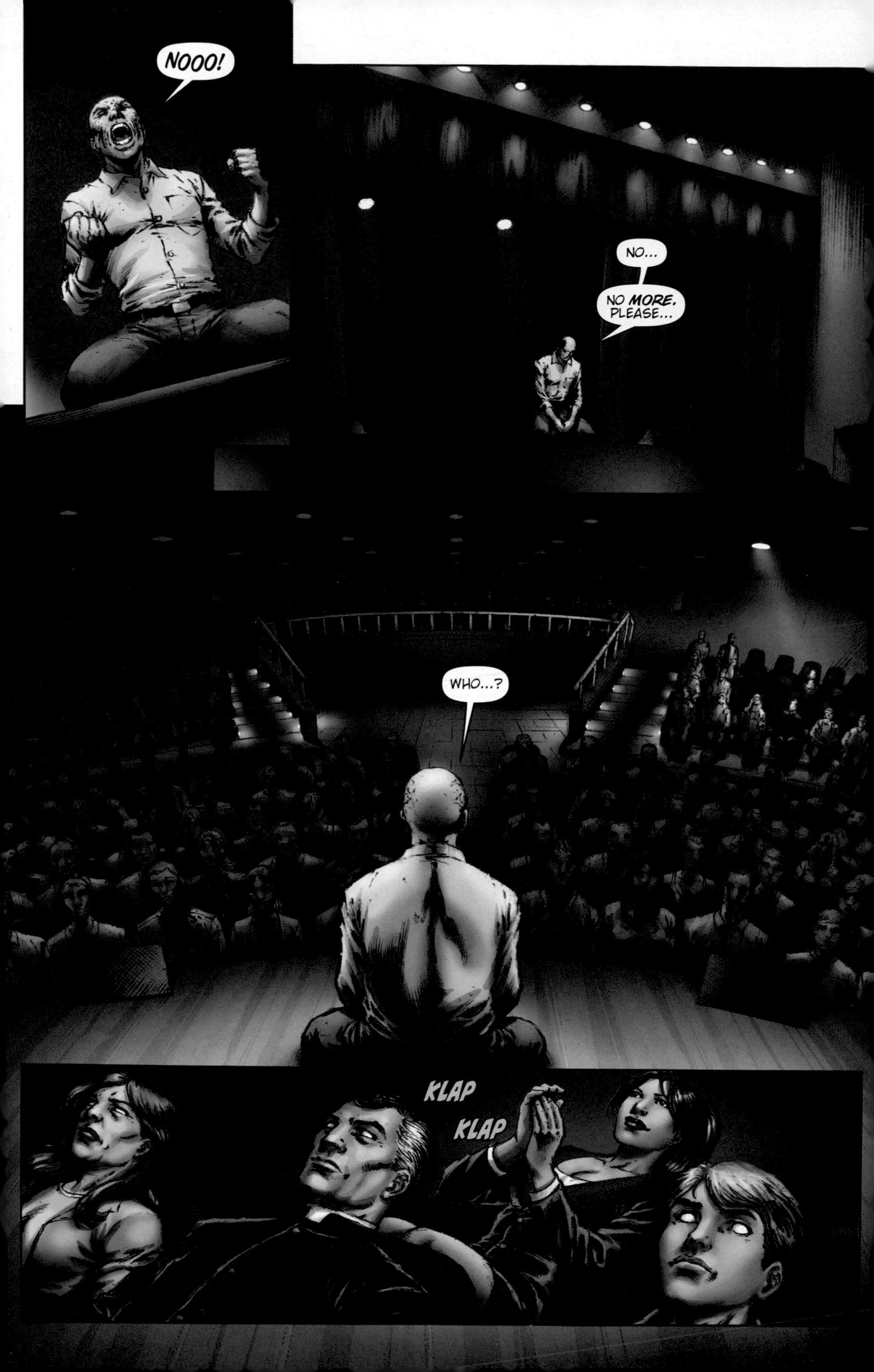
NOOO!
NO...
NO MORE. PLEASE...
WHO...?
KLAP
KLAP

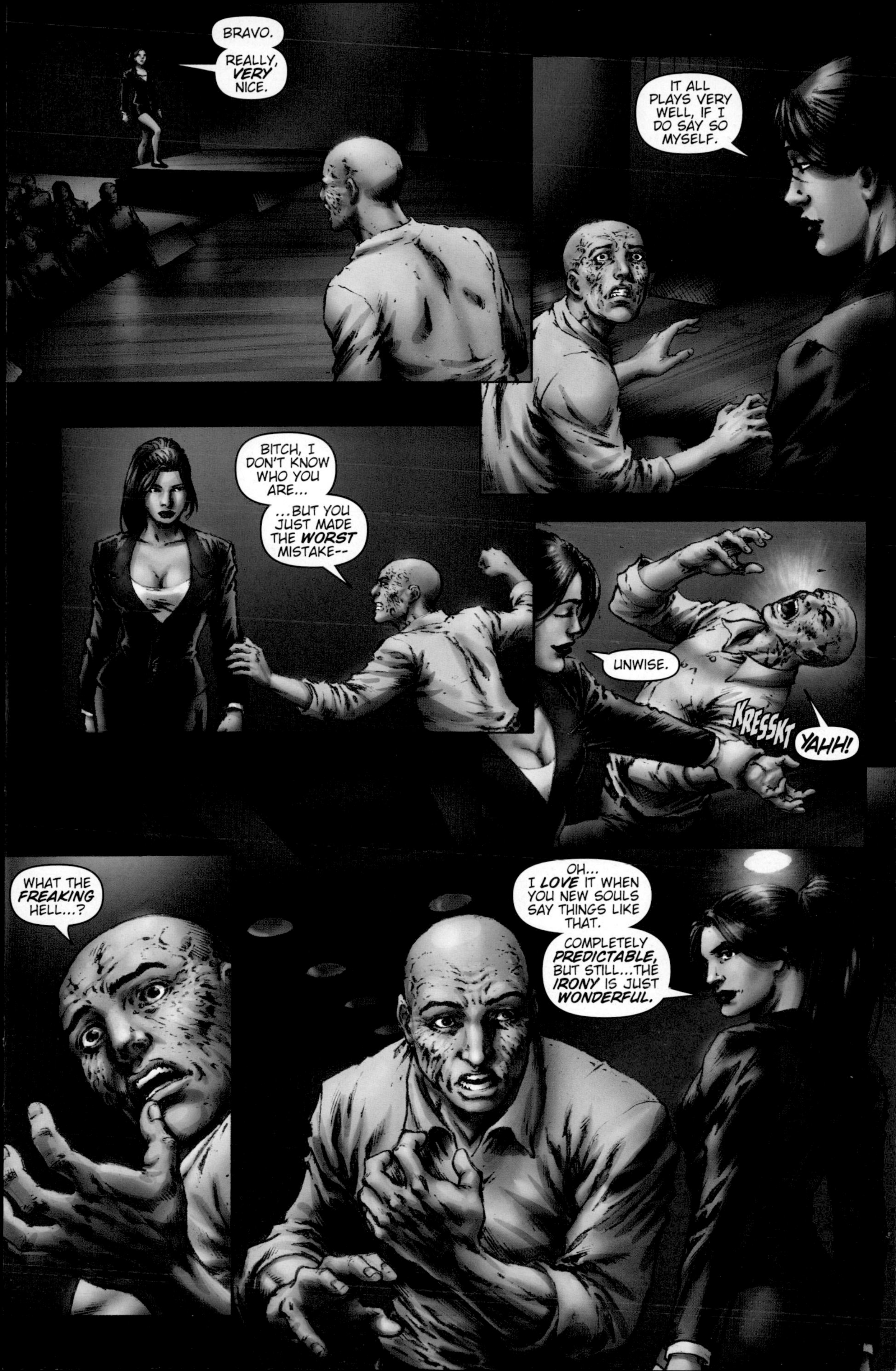
BRAVO.
REALLY, VERY NICE.
IT ALL PLAYS VERY WELL, IF I DO SAY SO MYSELF.
BITCH, I DON'T KNOW WHO YOU ARE...
...BUT YOU JUST MADE THE WORST MISTAKE--
UNWISE.
KRESSKT
YAHH!
WHAT THE FREAKING HELL...?
OH... I LOVE IT WHEN YOU NEW SOULS SAY THINGS LIKE THAT.
COMPLETELY PREDICTABLE, BUT STILL...THE IRONY IS JUST WONDERFUL.

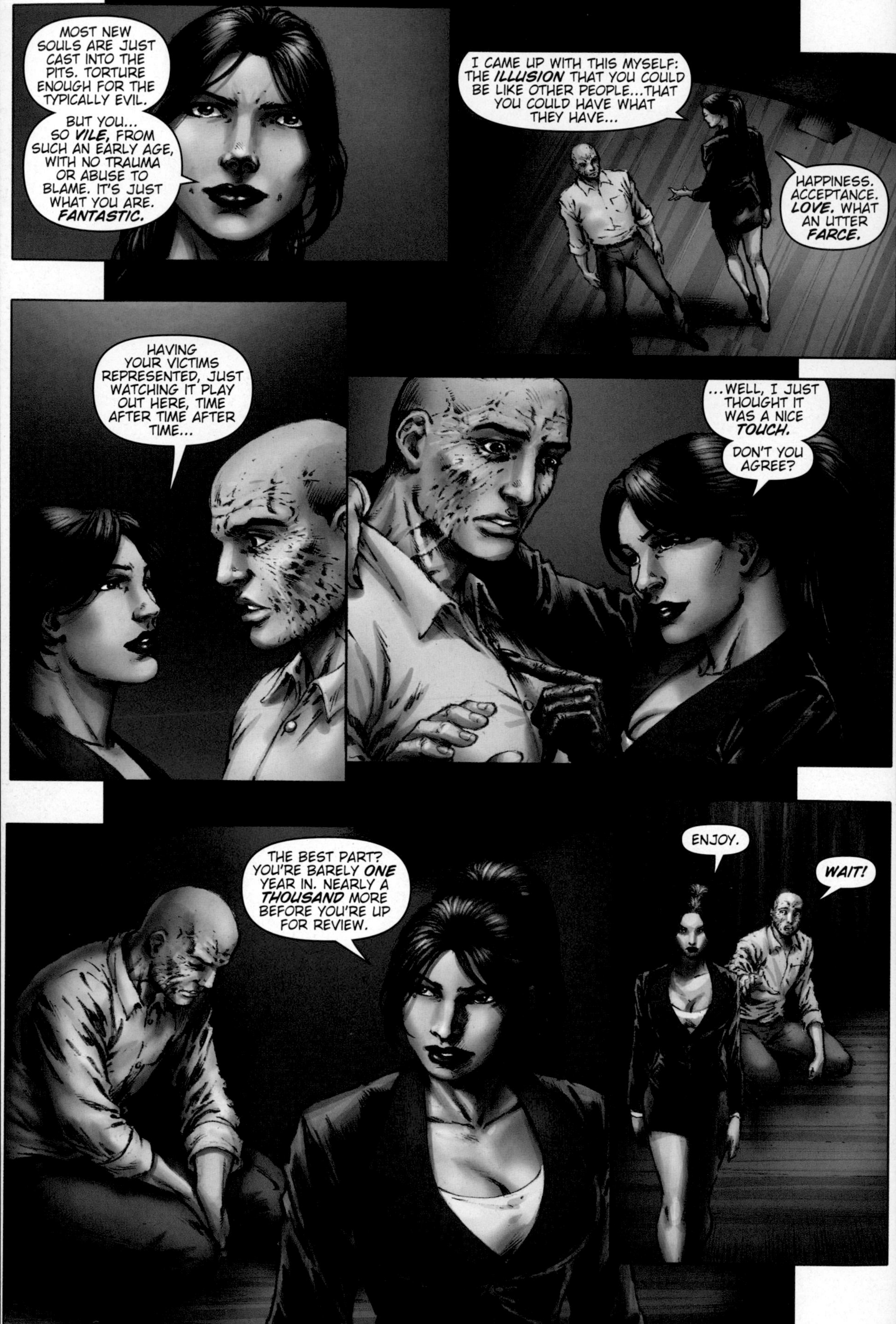
MOST NEW SOULS ARE JUST CAST INTO THE PITS. TORTURE ENOUGH FOR THE TYPICALLY EVIL.
BUT YOU... SO VILE, FROM SUCH AN EARLY AGE, WITH NO TRAUMA OR ABUSE TO BLAME. IT'S JUST WHAT YOU ARE. FANTASTIC.
I CAME UP WITH THIS MYSELF: THE ILLUSION THAT YOU COULD BE LIKE OTHER PEOPLE...THAT YOU COULD HAVE WHAT THEY HAVE...
HAPPINESS. ACCEPTANCE. LOVE. WHAT AN UTTER FARCE.
HAVING YOUR VICTIMS REPRESENTED, JUST WATCHING IT PLAY OUT HERE, TIME AFTER TIME AFTER TIME...
...WELL, I JUST THOUGHT IT WAS A NICE TOUCH.
DON'T YOU AGREE?
THE BEST PART? YOU'RE BARELY ONE YEAR IN. NEARLY A THOUSAND MORE BEFORE YOU'RE UP FOR REVIEW.
ENJOY.
WAIT!

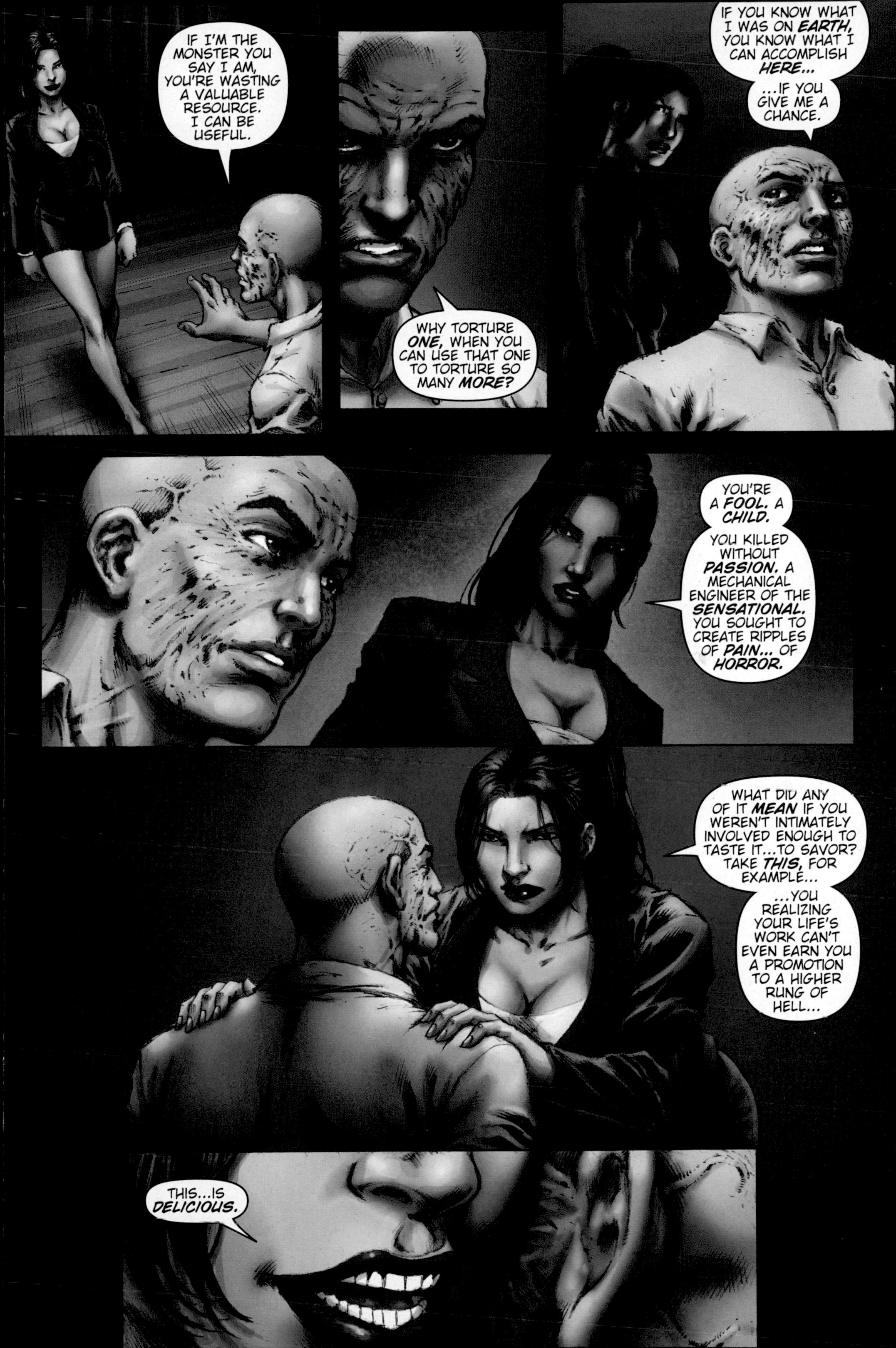
IF I'M THE MONSTER YOU SAY I AM, YOU'RE WASTING A VALUABLE RESOURCE. I CAN BE USEFUL.
WHY TORTURE ONE, WHEN YOU CAN USE THAT ONE TO TORTURE SO MANY MORE?
IF YOU KNOW WHAT I WAS ON EARTH, YOU KNOW WHAT I CAN ACCOMPLISH HERE...
...IF YOU GIVE ME A CHANCE.
YOU'RE A FOOL. A CHILD.
YOU KILLED WITHOUT PASSION. A MECHANICAL ENGINEER OF THE SENSATIONAL. YOU SOUGHT TO CREATE RIPPLES OF PAIN... OF HORROR.
WHAT DID ANY OF IT MEAN IF YOU WEREN'T INTIMATELY INVOLVED ENOUGH TO TASTE IT...TO SAVOR? TAKE THIS, FOR EXAMPLE...
...YOU REALIZING YOUR LIFE'S WORK CAN'T EVEN EARN YOU A PROMOTION TO A HIGHER RUNG OF HELL...
THIS...IS DELICIOUS.

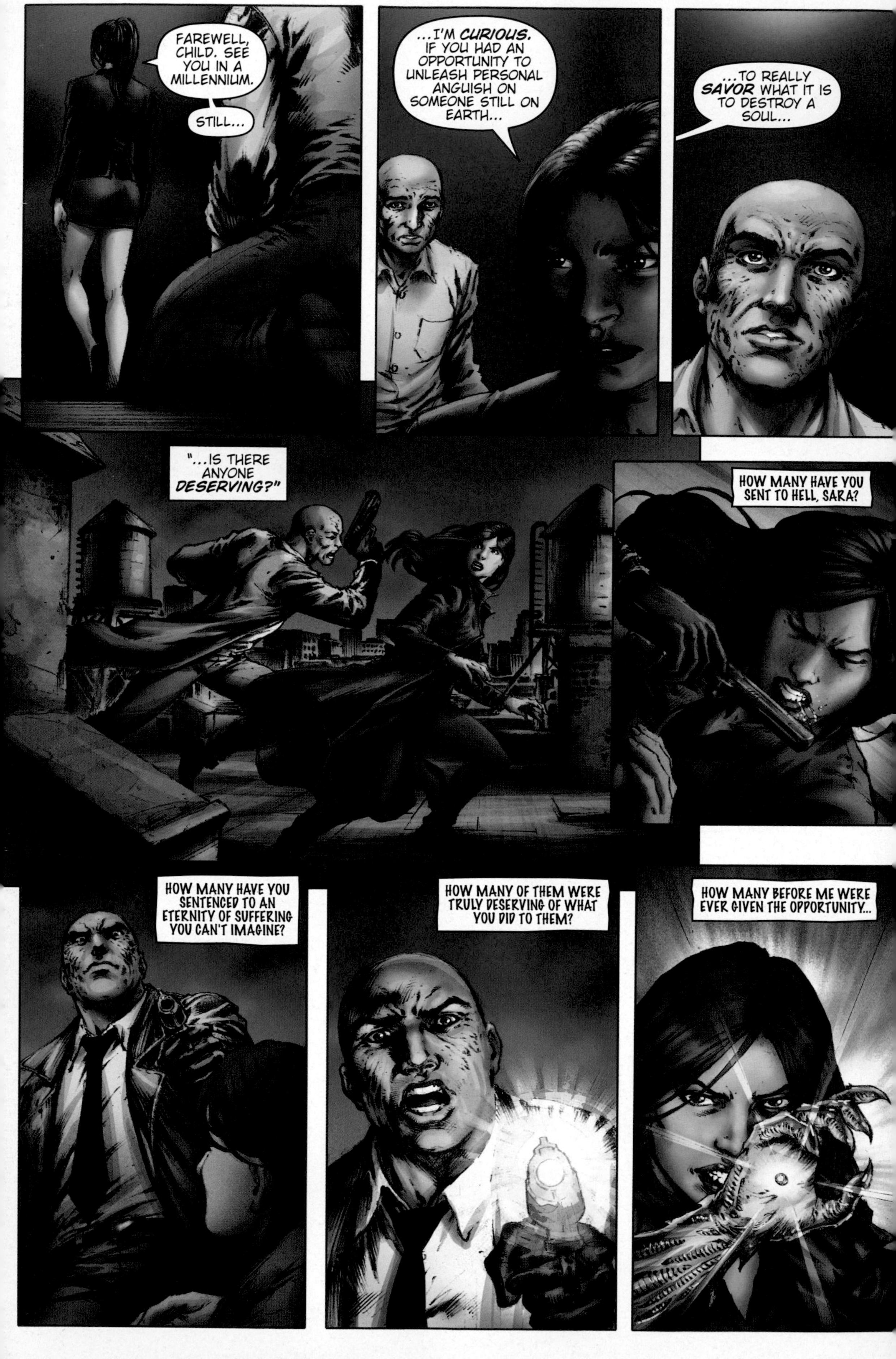
FAREWELL, CHILD. SEE YOU IN A MILLENNIUM.
STILL...
...I'M CURIOUS. IF YOU HAD AN OPPORTUNITY TO UNLEASH PERSONAL ANGUISH ON SOMEONE STILL ON EARTH...
...TO REALLY SAVOR WHAT IT IS TO DESTROY A SOUL...
"...IS THERE ANYONE DESERVING?"
HOW MANY HAVE YOU SENT TO HELL, SARA?
HOW MANY HAVE YOU SENTENCED TO AN ETERNITY OF SUFFERING YOU CAN'T IMAGINE?
HOW MANY OF THEM WERE TRULY DESERVING OF WHAT YOU DID TO THEM?
HOW MANY BEFORE ME WERE EVER GIVEN THE OPPORTUNITY...

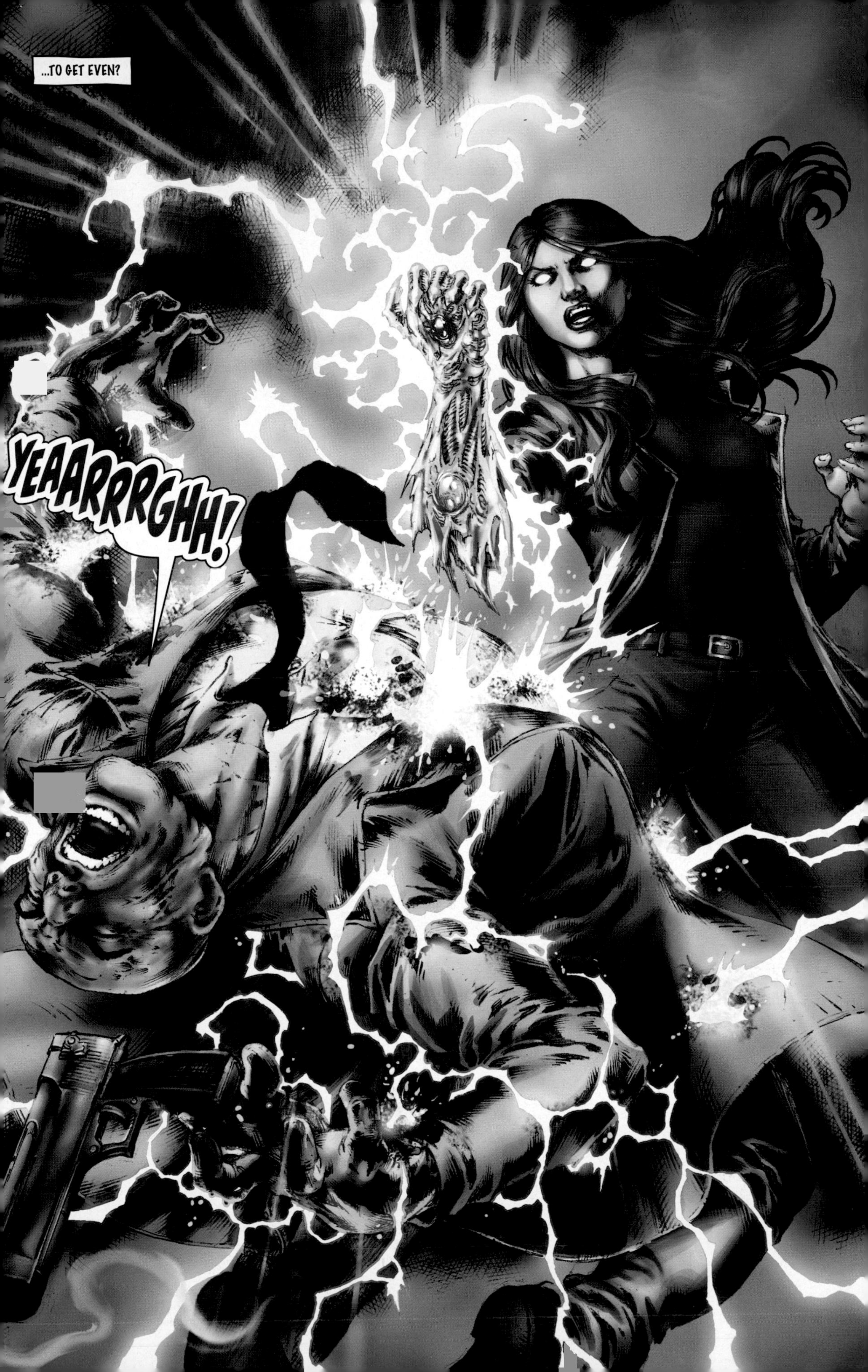
...TO GET EVEN?
YEAARRRGHH!

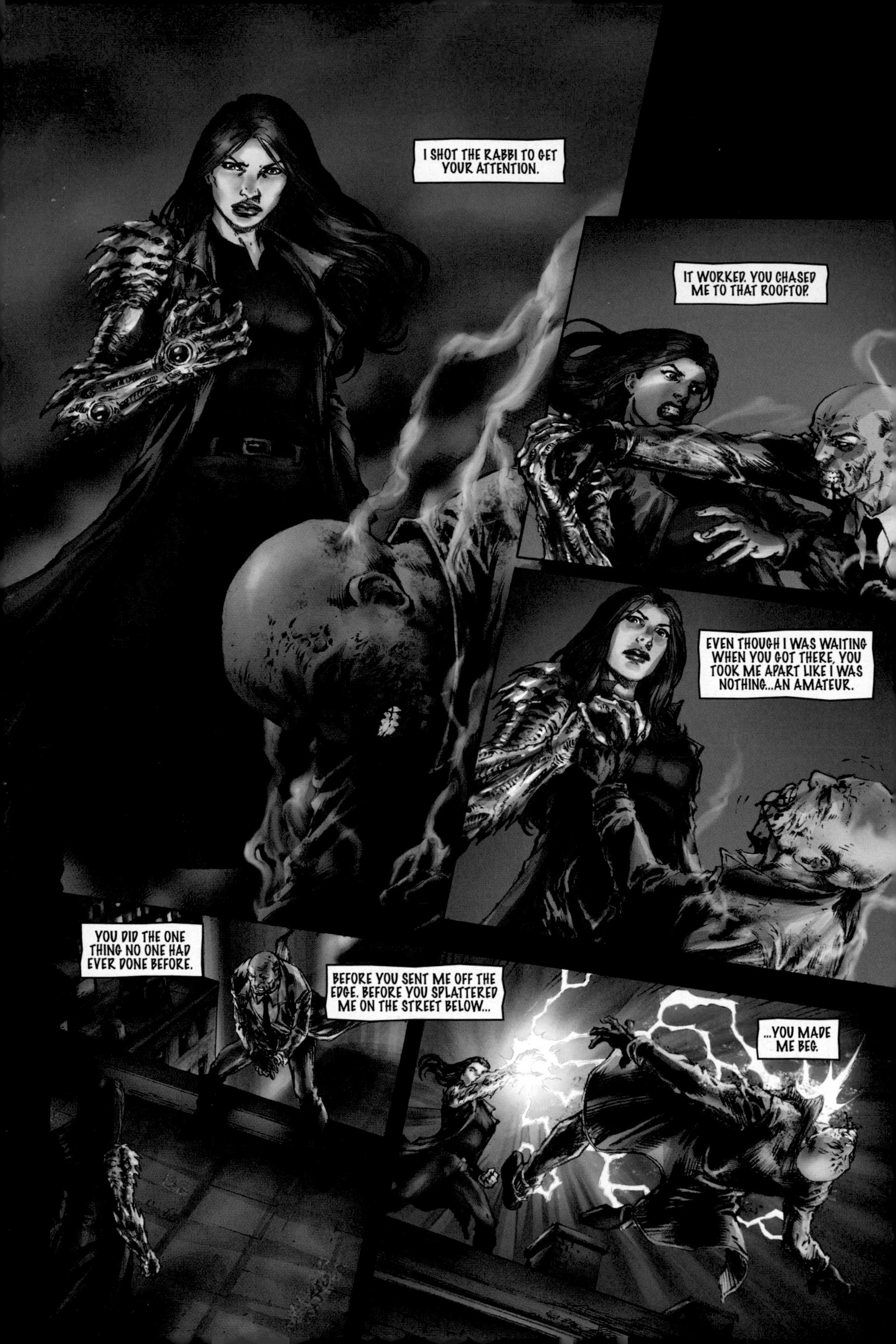
I SHOT THE RABBI TO GET YOUR ATTENTION.
IT WORKED. YOU CHASED ME TO THAT ROOFTOP.
EVEN THOUGH I WAS WAITING WHEN YOU GOT THERE, YOU TOOK ME APART LIKE I WAS NOTHING...AN AMATEUR.
YOU DID THE ONE THING NO ONE HAD EVER DONE BEFORE.
BEFORE YOU SENT ME OFF THE EDGE. BEFORE YOU SPLATTERED ME ON THE STREET BELOW...
...YOU MADE ME BEG.

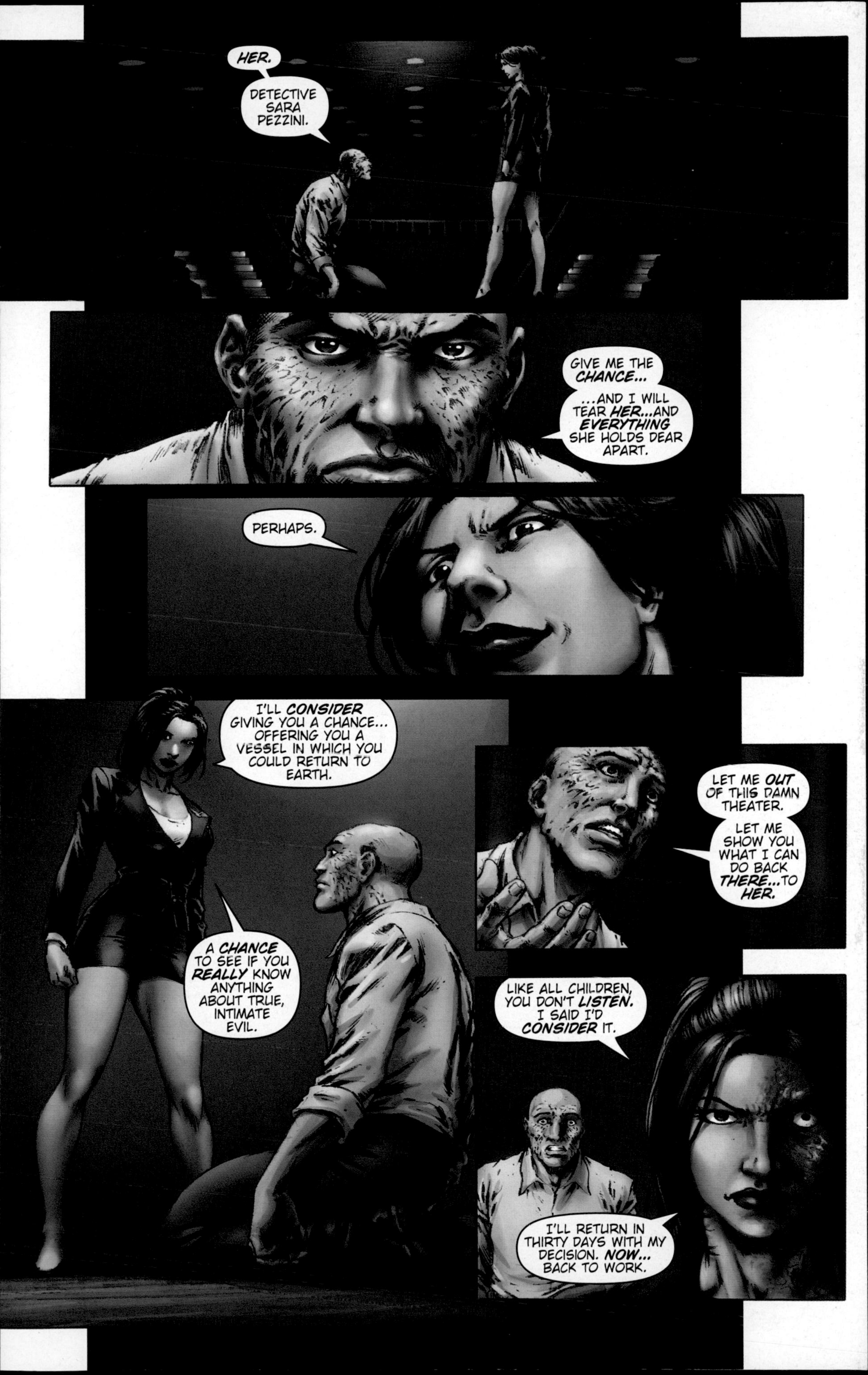
HER.
DETECTIVE SARA PEZZINI.
GIVE ME THE CHANCE...
...AND I WILL TEAR HER...AND EVERYTHING SHE HOLDS DEAR APART.
PERHAPS.
I'LL CONSIDER GIVING YOU A CHANCE... OFFERING YOU A VESSEL IN WHICH YOU COULD RETURN TO EARTH.
A CHANCE TO SEE IF YOU REALLY KNOW ANYTHING ABOUT TRUE, INTIMATE EVIL.
LET ME OUT OF THIS DAMN THEATER.
LET ME SHOW YOU WHAT I CAN DO BACK THERE...TO HER.
LIKE ALL CHILDREN, YOU DON'T LISTEN. I SAID I'D CONSIDER IT.
I'LL RETURN IN THIRTY DAYS WITH MY DECISION. NOW... BACK TO WORK.

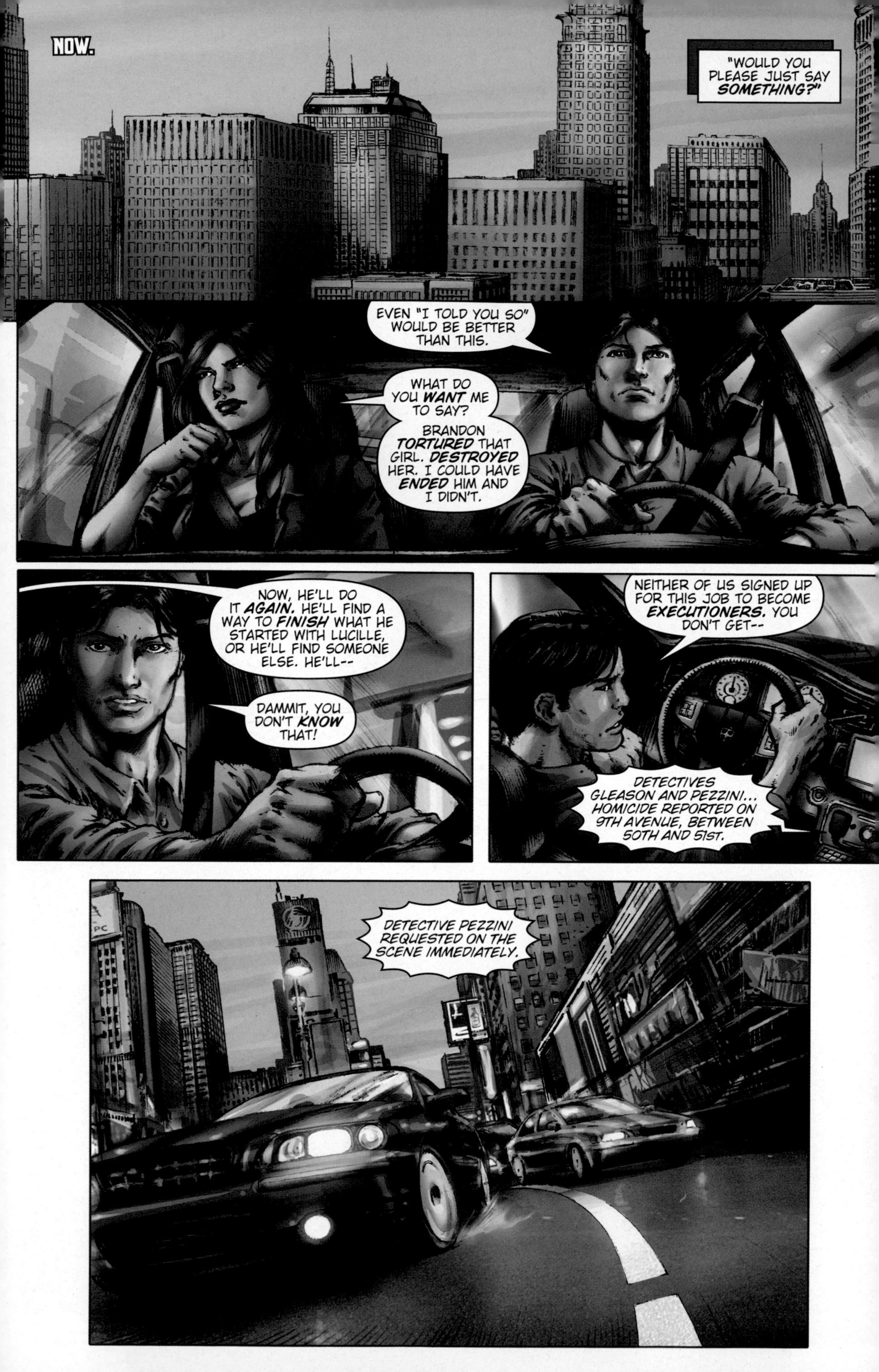
NOW.
"WOULD YOU PLEASE JUST SAY *SOMETHING?*"
EVEN "I TOLD YOU SO" WOULD BE BETTER THAN THIS.
WHAT DO YOU *WANT* ME TO SAY?
BRANDON *TORTURED* THAT GIRL. *DESTROYED* HER. I COULD HAVE *ENDED* HIM AND I DIDN'T.
NOW, HE'LL DO IT *AGAIN.* HE'LL FIND A WAY TO *FINISH* WHAT HE STARTED WITH LUCILLE, OR HE'LL FIND SOMEONE ELSE. HE'LL--
DAMMIT, YOU DON'T *KNOW* THAT!
NEITHER OF US SIGNED UP FOR THIS JOB TO BECOME *EXECUTIONERS.* YOU DON'T GET--
DETECTIVES GLEASON AND PEZZINI... HOMICIDE REPORTED ON 9TH AVENUE, BETWEEN 50TH AND 51ST.
DETECTIVE PEZZINI REQUESTED ON THE SCENE IMMEDIATELY.

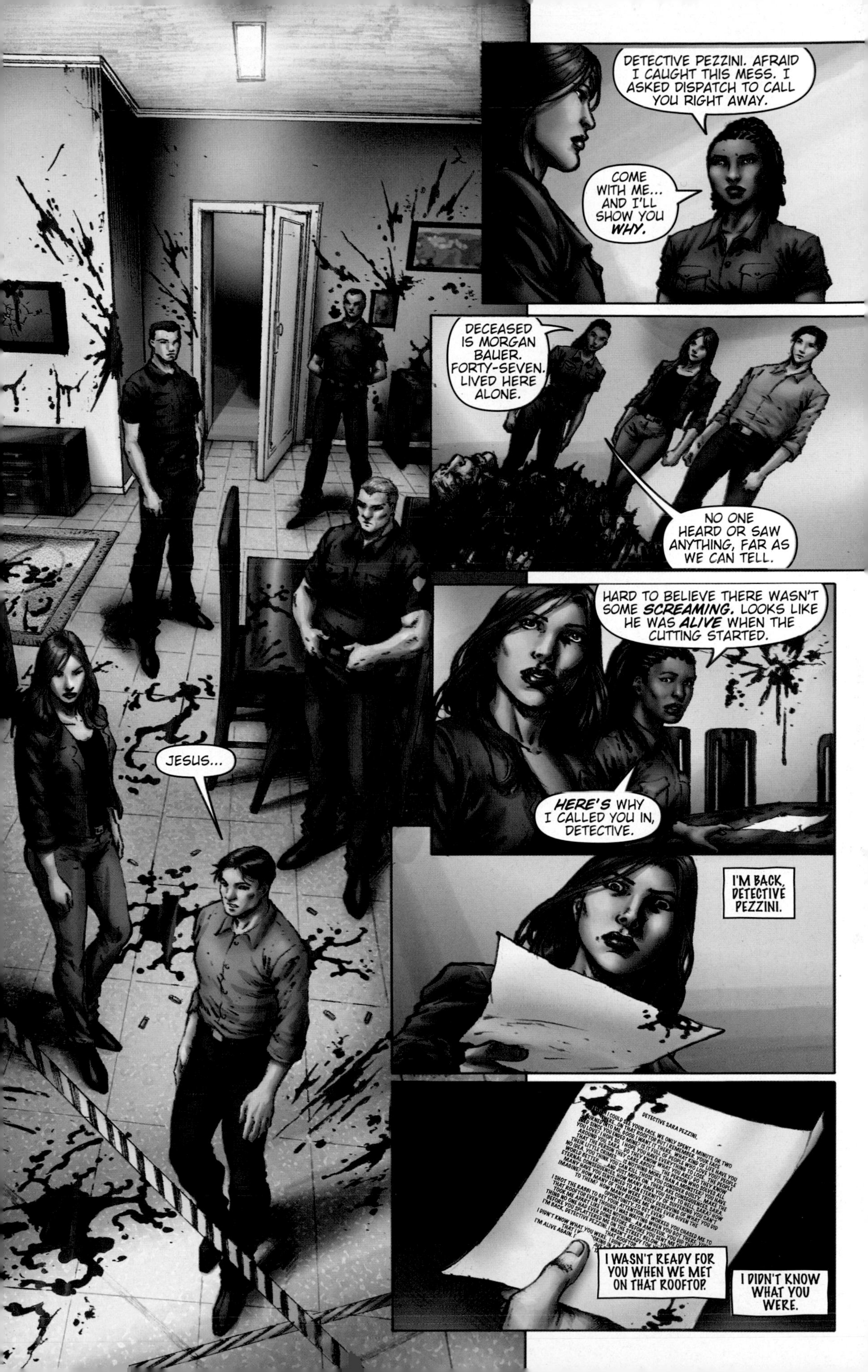
JESUS...
DETECTIVE PEZZINI. AFRAID I CAUGHT THIS MESS. I ASKED DISPATCH TO CALL YOU RIGHT AWAY.
COME WITH ME... AND I'LL SHOW YOU WHY.
DECEASED IS MORGAN BAUER. FORTY-SEVEN. LIVED HERE ALONE.
NO ONE HEARD OR SAW ANYTHING, FAR AS WE CAN TELL.
HARD TO BELIEVE THERE WASN'T SOME SCREAMING. LOOKS LIKE HE WAS ALIVE WHEN THE CUTTING STARTED.
HERE'S WHY I CALLED YOU IN, DETECTIVE.
I'M BACK, DETECTIVE PEZZINI.
DETECTIVE SARA PEZZINI
I WASN'T READY FOR YOU WHEN WE MET ON THAT ROOFTOP.
I DIDN'T KNOW WHAT YOU WERE.

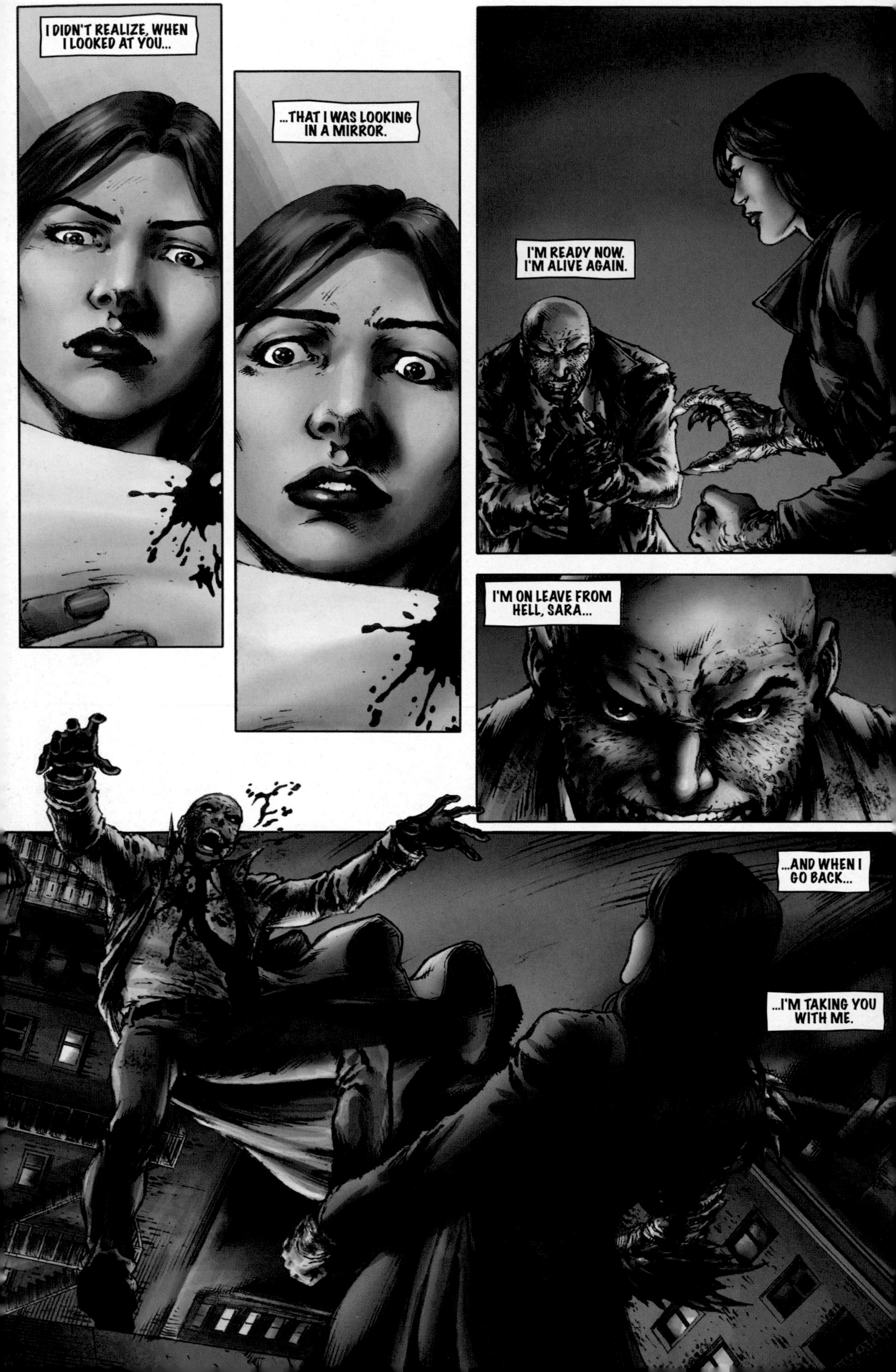
I DIDN'T REALIZE, WHEN I LOOKED AT YOU...
...THAT I WAS LOOKING IN A MIRROR.
I'M READY NOW. I'M ALIVE AGAIN.
I'M ON LEAVE FROM HELL, SARA...
...AND WHEN I GO BACK...
...I'M TAKING YOU WITH ME.

WITCHBLADE
DEMON REBORN

CHAPTER TWO

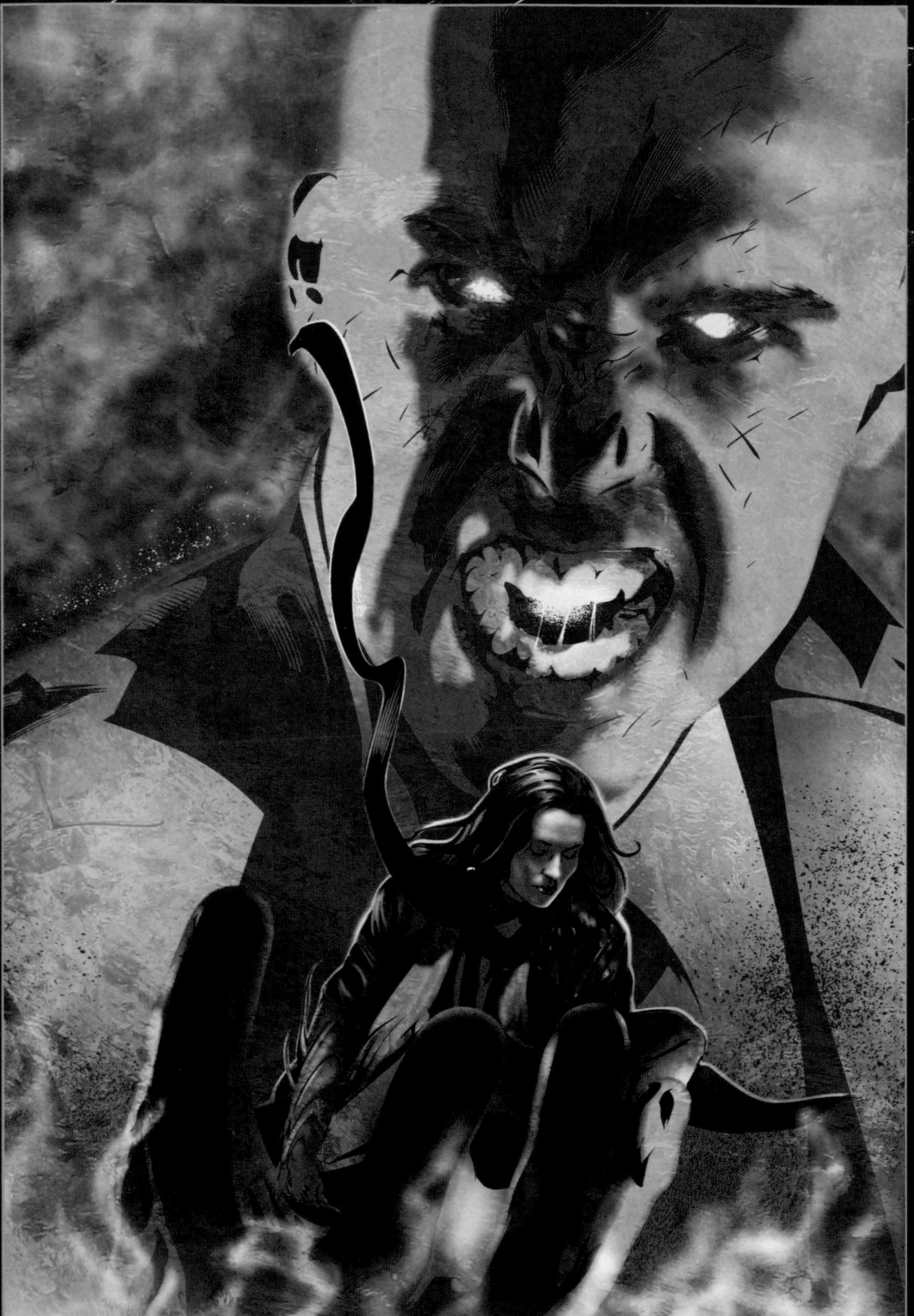

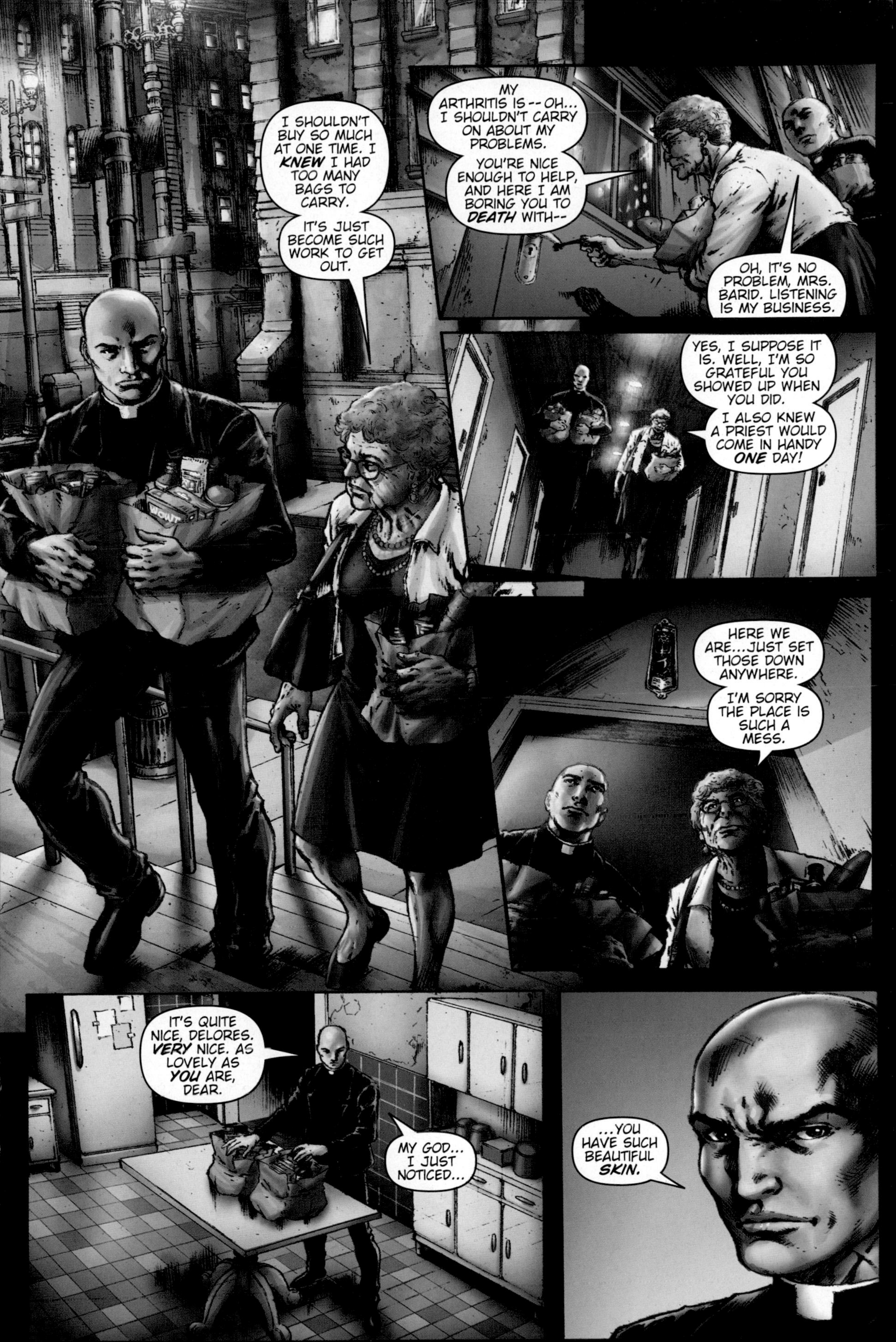
I SHOULDN'T BUY SO MUCH AT ONE TIME. I KNEW I HAD TOO MANY BAGS TO CARRY.
IT'S JUST BECOME SUCH WORK TO GET OUT.
MY ARTHRITIS IS -- OH... I SHOULDN'T CARRY ON ABOUT MY PROBLEMS.
YOU'RE NICE ENOUGH TO HELP, AND HERE I AM BORING YOU TO DEATH WITH--
OH, IT'S NO PROBLEM, MRS. BARID. LISTENING IS MY BUSINESS.
YES, I SUPPOSE IT IS. WELL, I'M SO GRATEFUL YOU SHOWED UP WHEN YOU DID.
I ALSO KNEW A PRIEST WOULD COME IN HANDY ONE DAY!
HERE WE ARE...JUST SET THOSE DOWN ANYWHERE.
I'M SORRY THE PLACE IS SUCH A MESS.
IT'S QUITE NICE, DELORES. VERY NICE. AS LOVELY AS YOU ARE, DEAR.
MY GOD... I JUST NOTICED...
...YOU HAVE SUCH BEAUTIFUL SKIN.

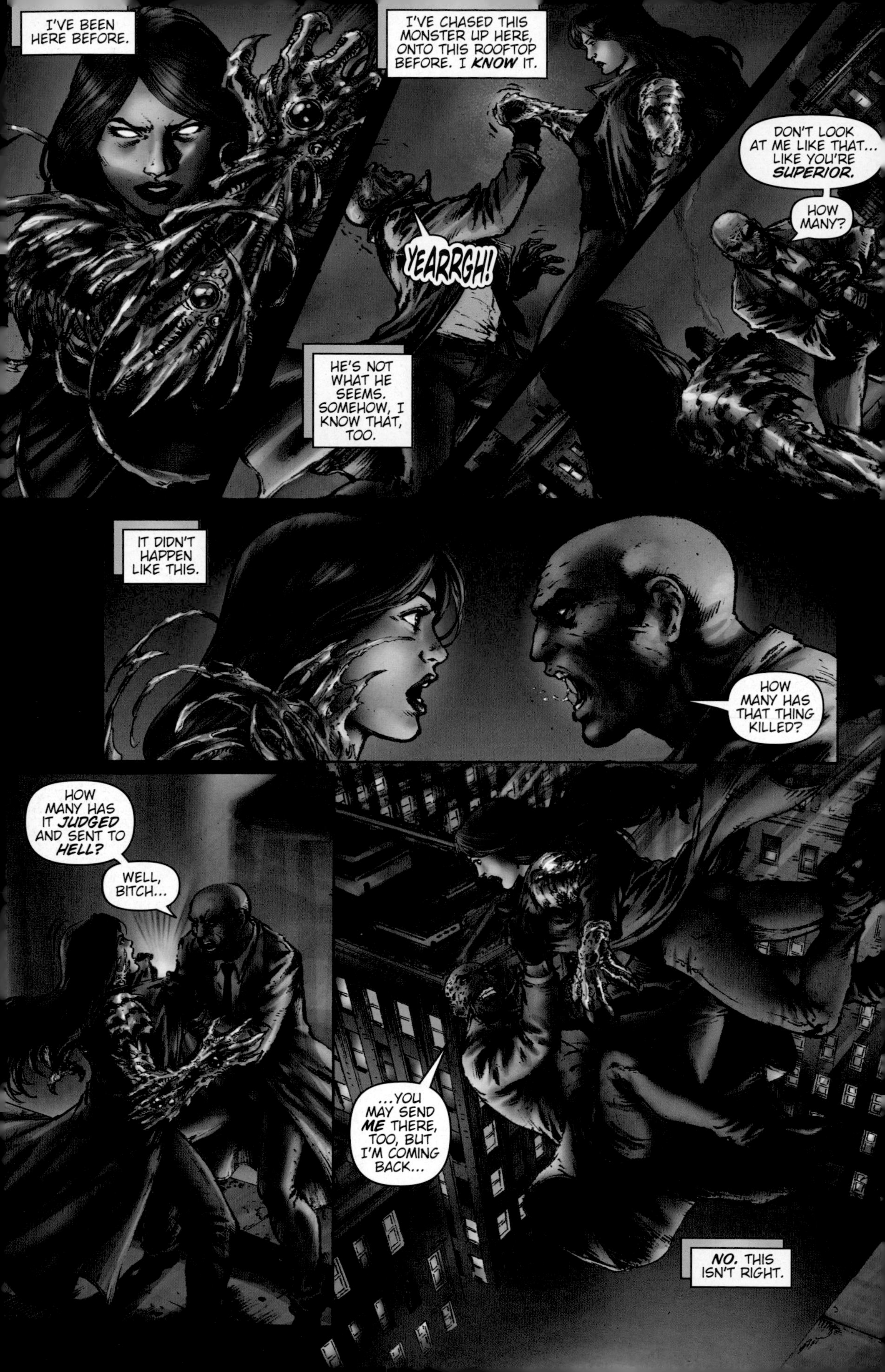
I'VE BEEN HERE BEFORE.
I'VE CHASED THIS MONSTER UP HERE, ONTO THIS ROOFTOP BEFORE. I KNOW IT.
YEARRGH!
HE'S NOT WHAT HE SEEMS. SOMEHOW, I KNOW THAT, TOO.
DON'T LOOK AT ME LIKE THAT... LIKE YOU'RE SUPERIOR.
HOW MANY?
IT DIDN'T HAPPEN LIKE THIS.
HOW MANY HAS THAT THING KILLED?
HOW MANY HAS IT JUDGED AND SENT TO HELL?
WELL, BITCH...
...YOU MAY SEND ME THERE, TOO, BUT I'M COMING BACK...
NO. THIS ISN'T RIGHT.

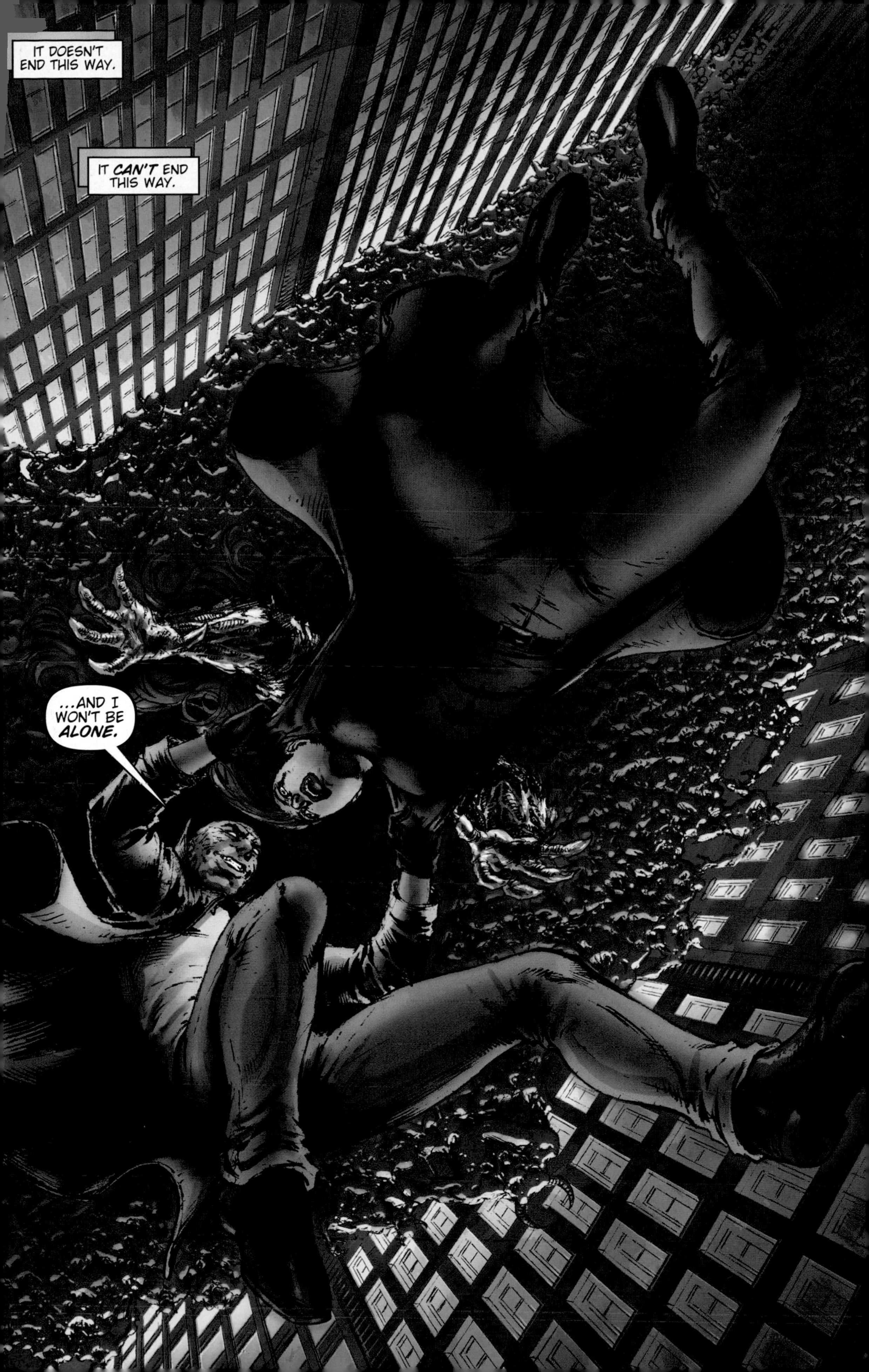
IT DOESN'T END THIS WAY.
IT CAN'T END THIS WAY.
...AND I WON'T BE ALONE.

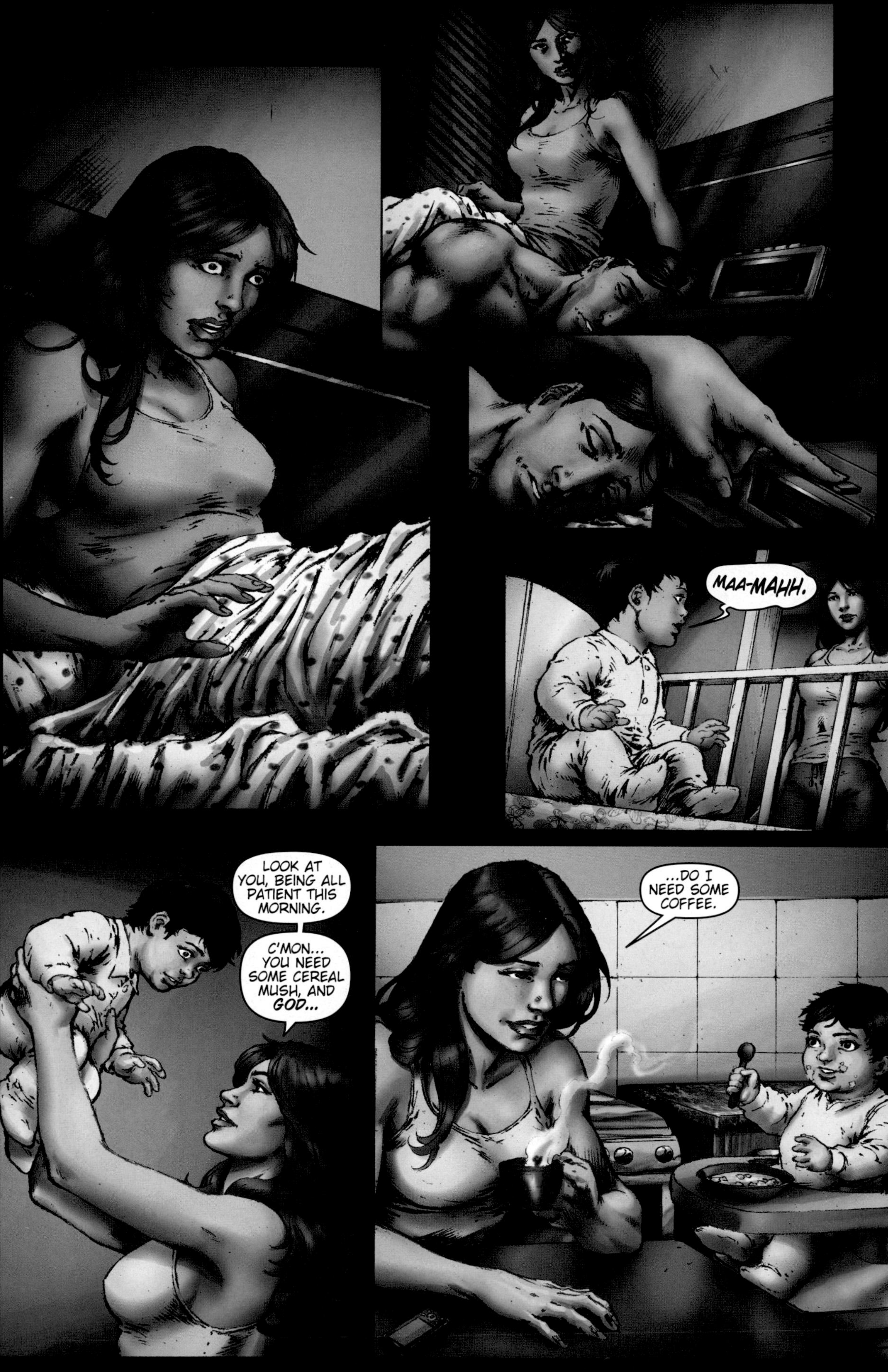
MAA-MAHH.
LOOK AT YOU, BEING ALL PATIENT THIS MORNING.
C'MON... YOU NEED SOME CEREAL MUSH, AND GOD...
...DO I NEED SOME COFFEE.

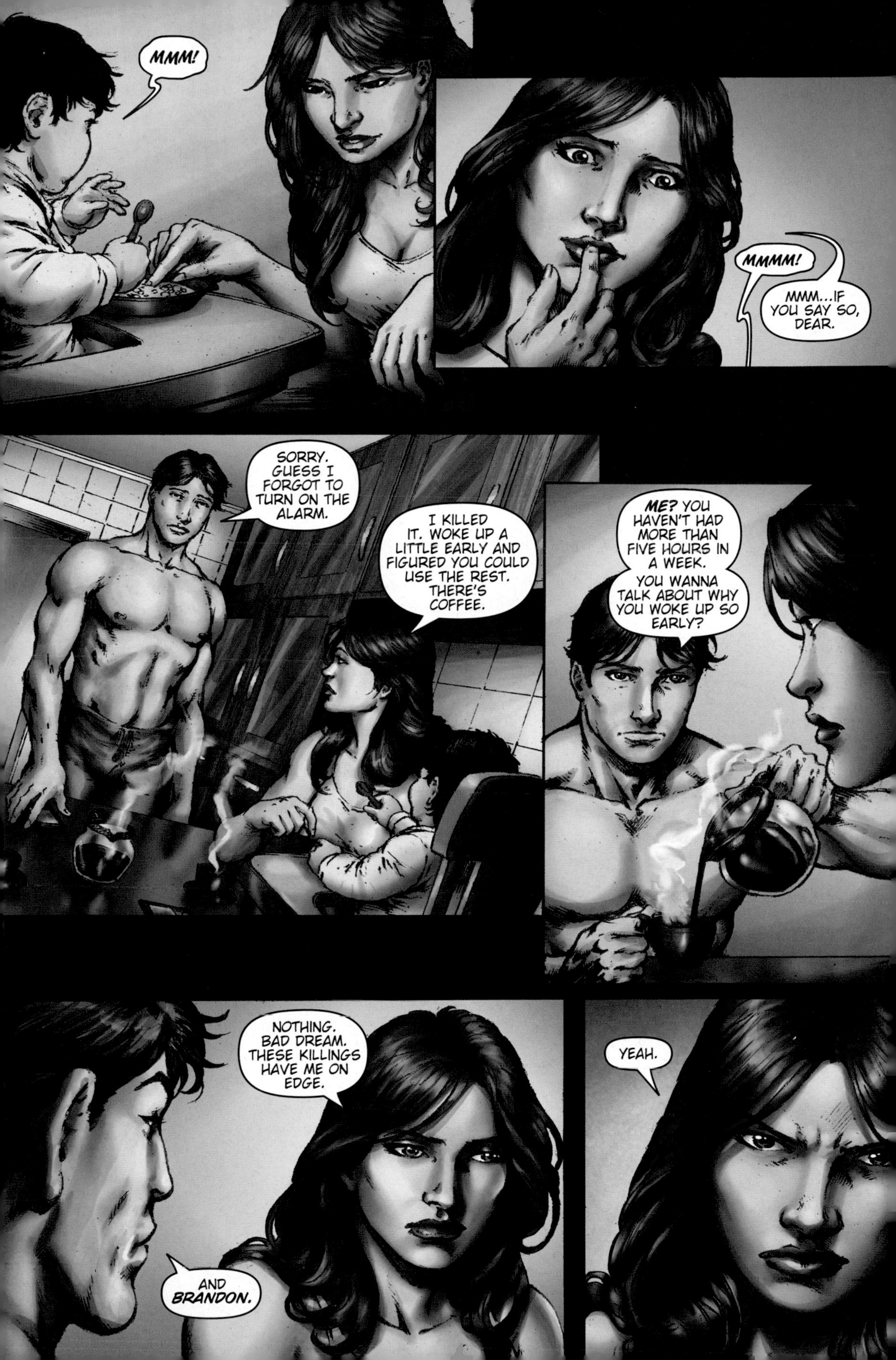
MMM!
MMMM!
MMM...IF YOU SAY SO, DEAR.
SORRY. GUESS I FORGOT TO TURN ON THE ALARM.
I KILLED IT. WOKE UP A LITTLE EARLY AND FIGURED YOU COULD USE THE REST. THERE'S COFFEE.
ME? YOU HAVEN'T HAD MORE THAN FIVE HOURS IN A WEEK.
YOU WANNA TALK ABOUT WHY YOU WOKE UP SO EARLY?
NOTHING. BAD DREAM. THESE KILLINGS HAVE ME ON EDGE.
AND BRANDON.
YEAH.

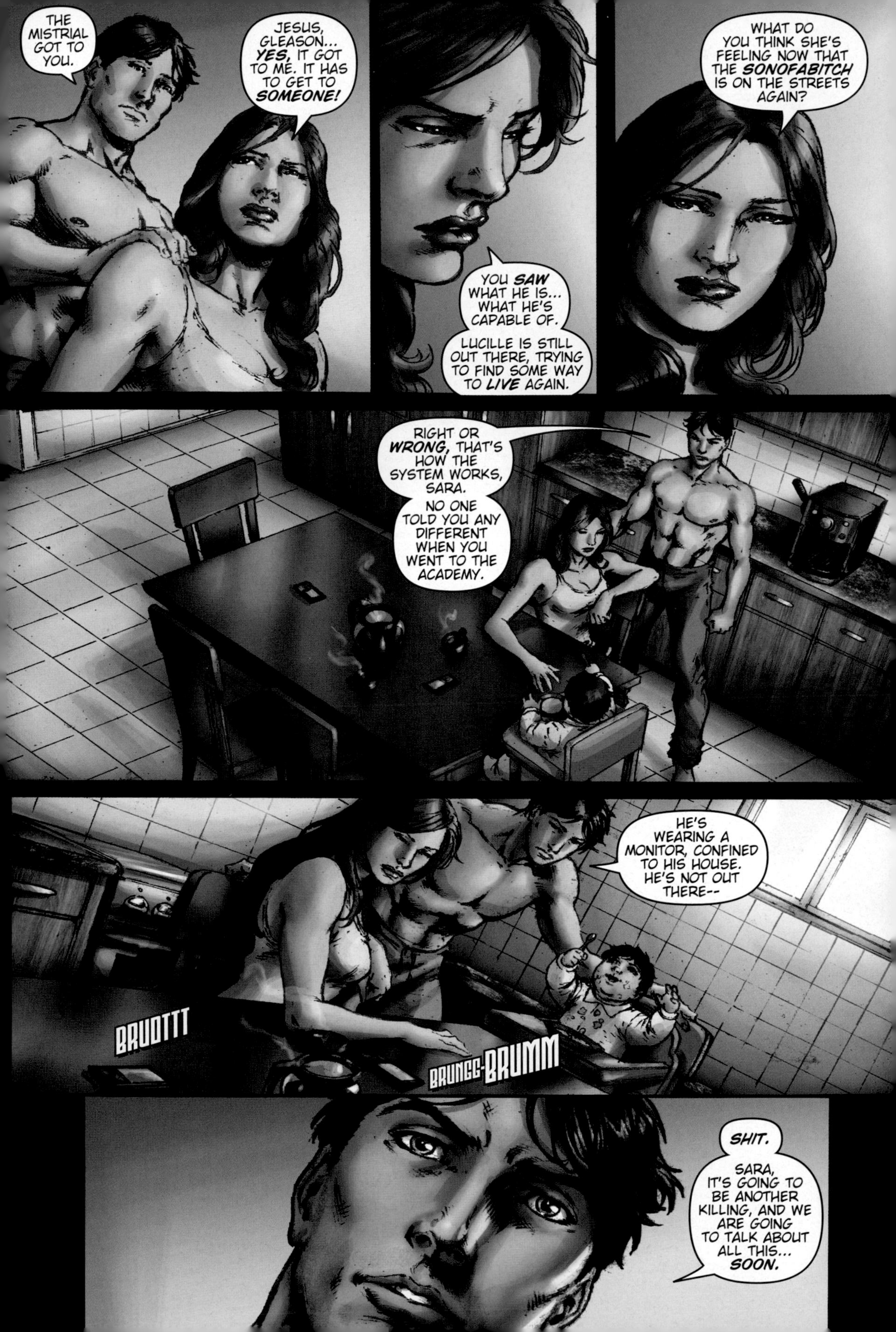
THE MISTRIAL GOT TO YOU.
JESUS, GLEASON... YES, IT GOT TO ME. IT HAS TO GET TO SOMEONE!
YOU SAW WHAT HE IS... WHAT HE'S CAPABLE OF.
LUCILLE IS STILL OUT THERE, TRYING TO FIND SOME WAY TO LIVE AGAIN.
WHAT DO YOU THINK SHE'S FEELING NOW THAT THE SONOFABITCH IS ON THE STREETS AGAIN?
RIGHT OR WRONG, THAT'S HOW THE SYSTEM WORKS, SARA.
NO ONE TOLD YOU ANY DIFFERENT WHEN YOU WENT TO THE ACADEMY.
HE'S WEARING A MONITOR, CONFINED TO HIS HOUSE. HE'S NOT OUT THERE--
BRUDTTT
BRUNGG-BRUMM
SHIT.
SARA, IT'S GOING TO BE ANOTHER KILLING, AND WE ARE GOING TO TALK ABOUT ALL THIS... SOON.

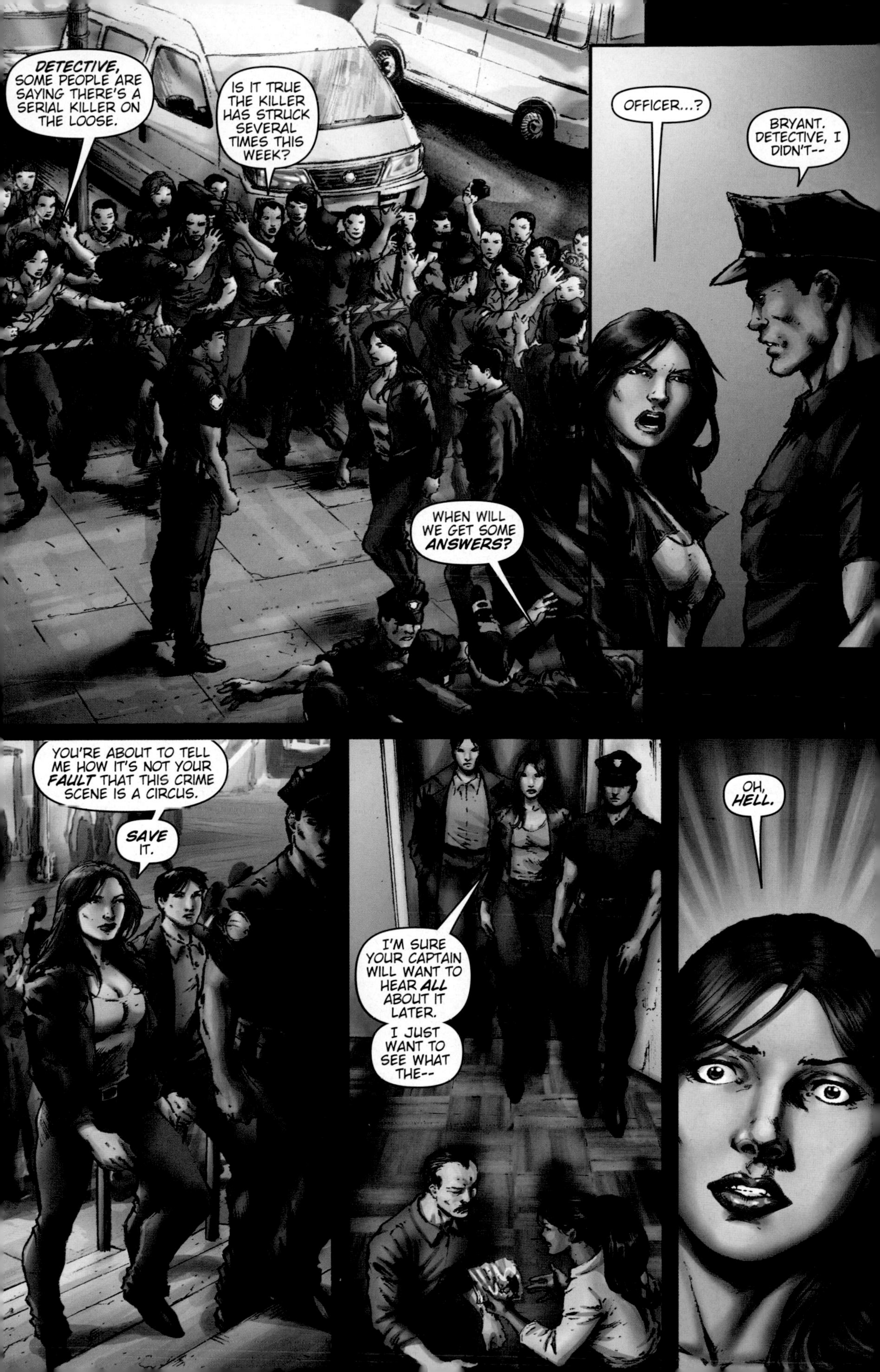
DETECTIVE, SOME PEOPLE ARE SAYING THERE'S A SERIAL KILLER ON THE LOOSE.
IS IT TRUE THE KILLER HAS STRUCK SEVERAL TIMES THIS WEEK?
WHEN WILL WE GET SOME ANSWERS?
OFFICER...?
BRYANT. DETECTIVE, I DIDN'T--
YOU'RE ABOUT TO TELL ME HOW IT'S NOT YOUR FAULT THAT THIS CRIME SCENE IS A CIRCUS.
SAVE IT.
I'M SURE YOUR CAPTAIN WILL WANT TO HEAR ALL ABOUT IT LATER.
I JUST WANT TO SEE WHAT THE--
OH, HELL.

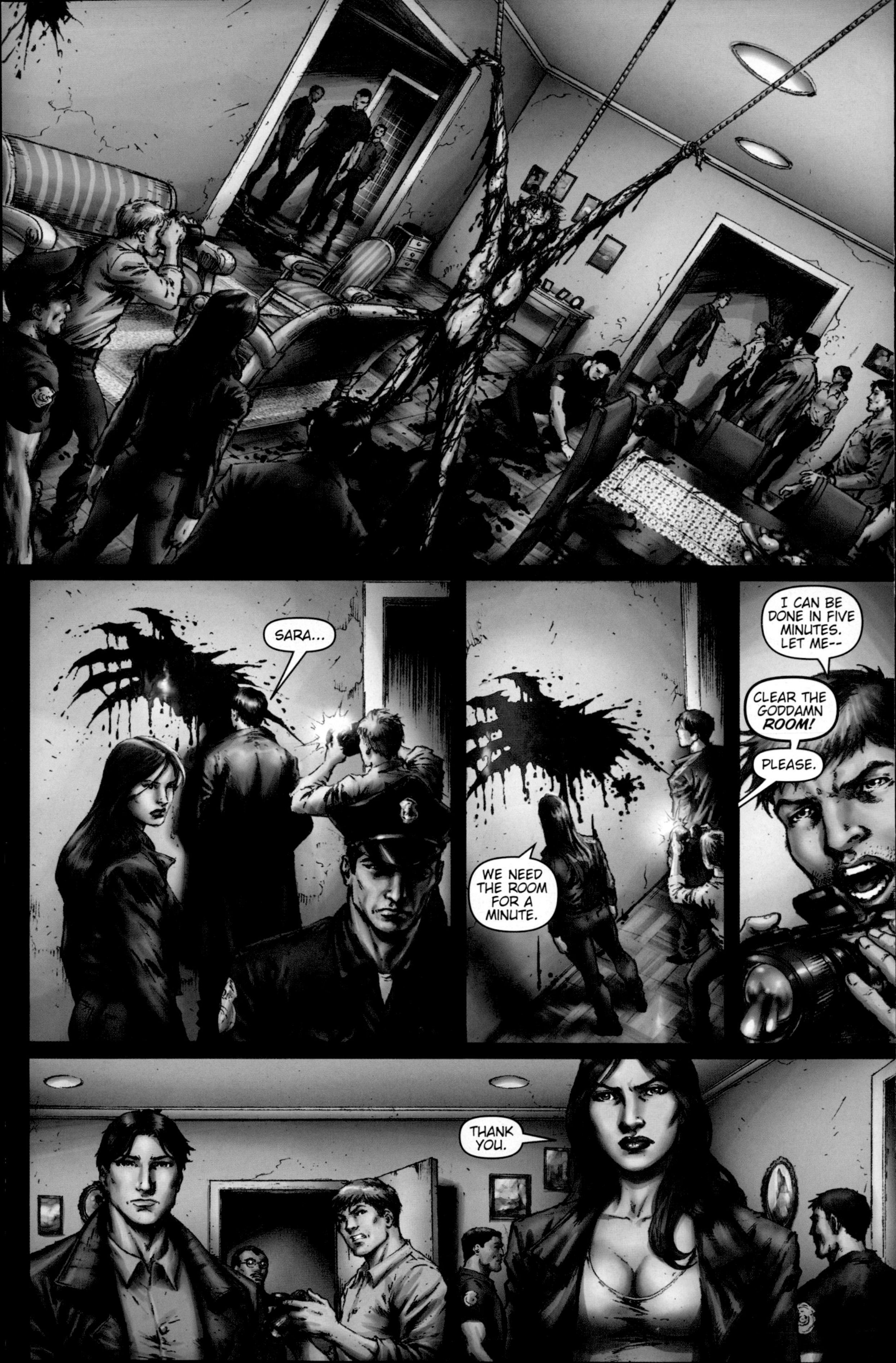
SARA...
WE NEED THE ROOM FOR A MINUTE.
I CAN BE DONE IN FIVE MINUTES. LET ME--
CLEAR THE GODDAMN *ROOM!*
PLEASE.
THANK YOU.

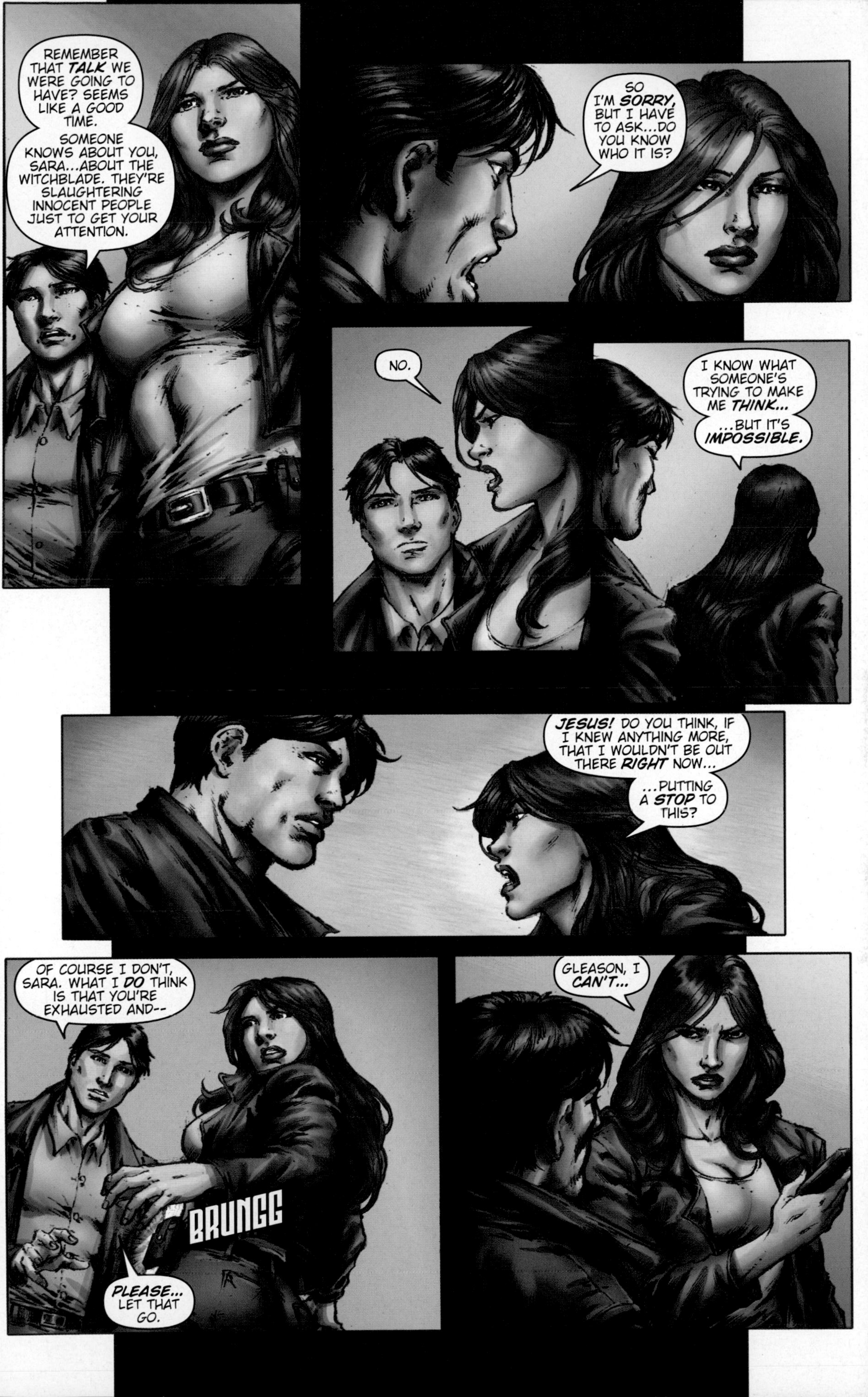
REMEMBER THAT TALK WE WERE GOING TO HAVE? SEEMS LIKE A GOOD TIME.
SOMEONE KNOWS ABOUT YOU, SARA...ABOUT THE WITCHBLADE. THEY'RE SLAUGHTERING INNOCENT PEOPLE JUST TO GET YOUR ATTENTION.
SO I'M SORRY, BUT I HAVE TO ASK...DO YOU KNOW WHO IT IS?
NO.
I KNOW WHAT SOMEONE'S TRYING TO MAKE ME THINK...
...BUT IT'S IMPOSSIBLE.
JESUS! DO YOU THINK, IF I KNEW ANYTHING MORE, THAT I WOULDN'T BE OUT THERE RIGHT NOW...
...PUTTING A STOP TO THIS?
OF COURSE I DON'T, SARA. WHAT I DO THINK IS THAT YOU'RE EXHAUSTED AND--
BRUNGG
PLEASE... LET THAT GO.
GLEASON, I CAN'T...

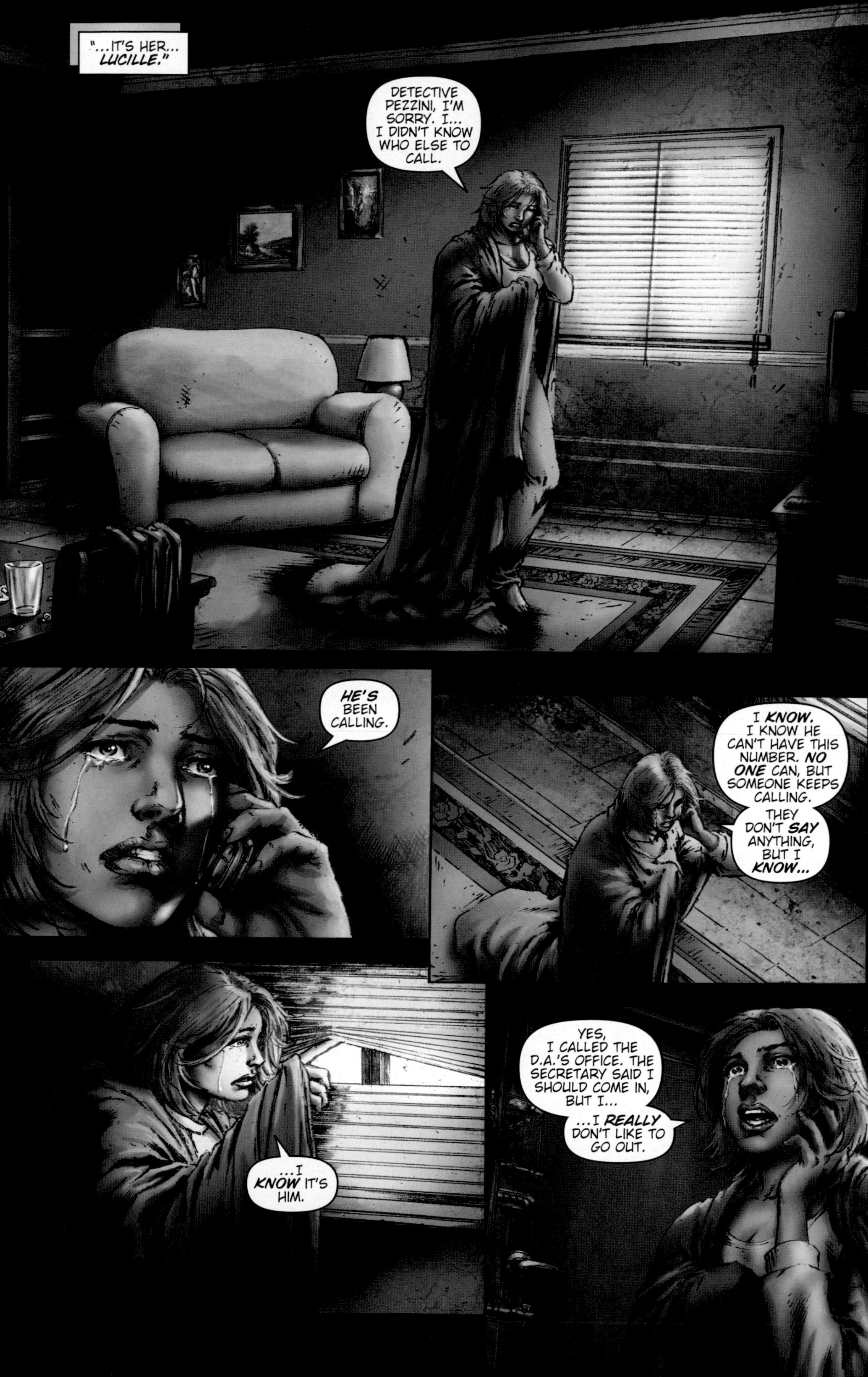
"...IT'S HER... LUCILLE."
DETECTIVE PEZZINI, I'M SORRY. I... I DIDN'T KNOW WHO ELSE TO CALL.
HE'S BEEN CALLING.
I KNOW. I KNOW HE CAN'T HAVE THIS NUMBER. NO ONE CAN, BUT SOMEONE KEEPS CALLING.
THEY DON'T SAY ANYTHING, BUT I KNOW...
...I KNOW IT'S HIM.
YES, I CALLED THE D.A.'S OFFICE. THE SECRETARY SAID I SHOULD COME IN, BUT I...
...I REALLY DON'T LIKE TO GO OUT.

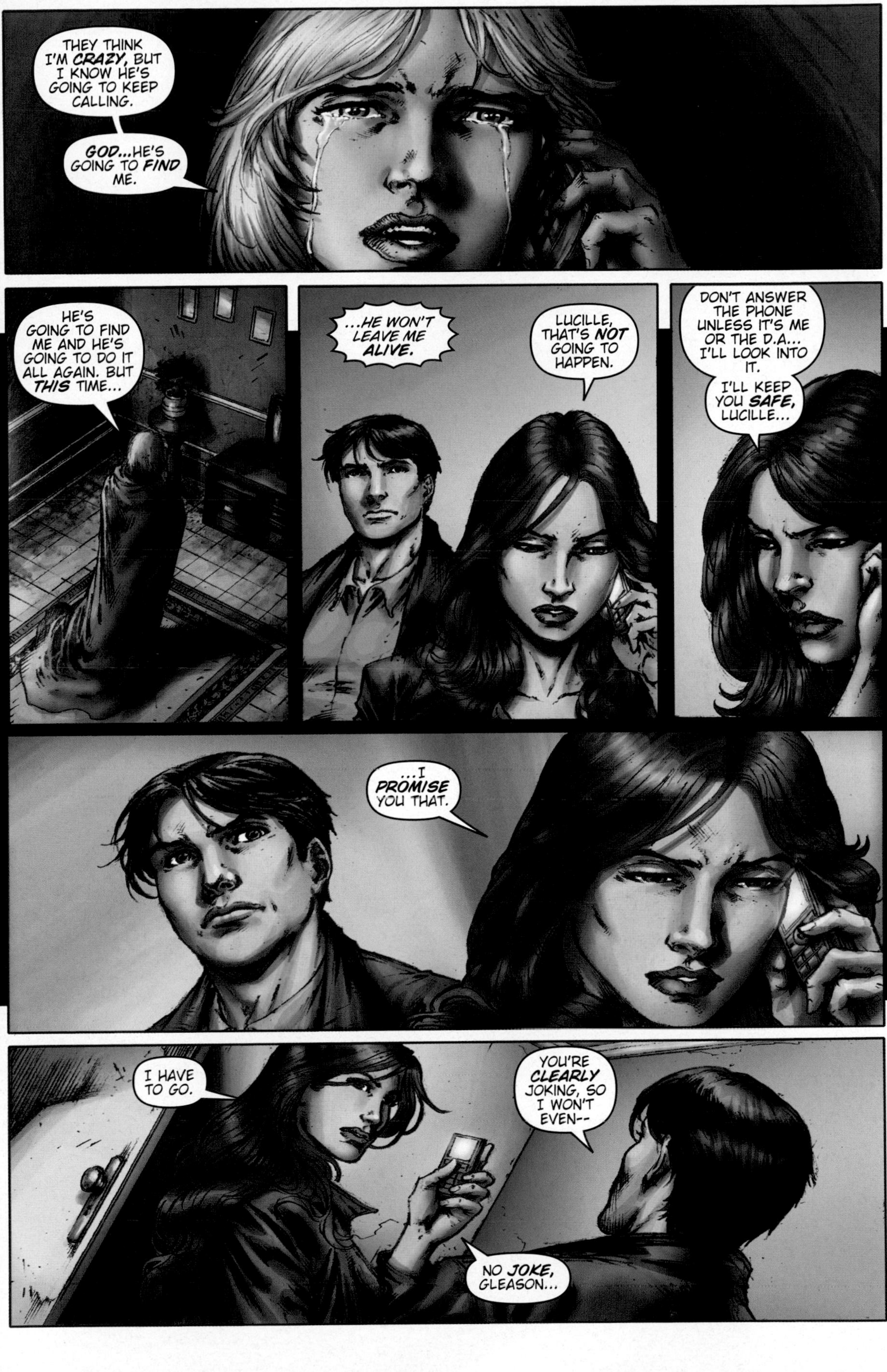
THEY THINK I'M CRAZY, BUT I KNOW HE'S GOING TO KEEP CALLING.
GOD...HE'S GOING TO FIND ME.
HE'S GOING TO FIND ME AND HE'S GOING TO DO IT ALL AGAIN. BUT THIS TIME...
...HE WON'T LEAVE ME ALIVE.
LUCILLE, THAT'S NOT GOING TO HAPPEN.
DON'T ANSWER THE PHONE UNLESS IT'S ME OR THE D.A... I'LL LOOK INTO IT.
I'LL KEEP YOU SAFE, LUCILLE...
...I PROMISE YOU THAT.
I HAVE TO GO.
YOU'RE CLEARLY JOKING, SO I WON'T EVEN--
NO JOKE, GLEASON...

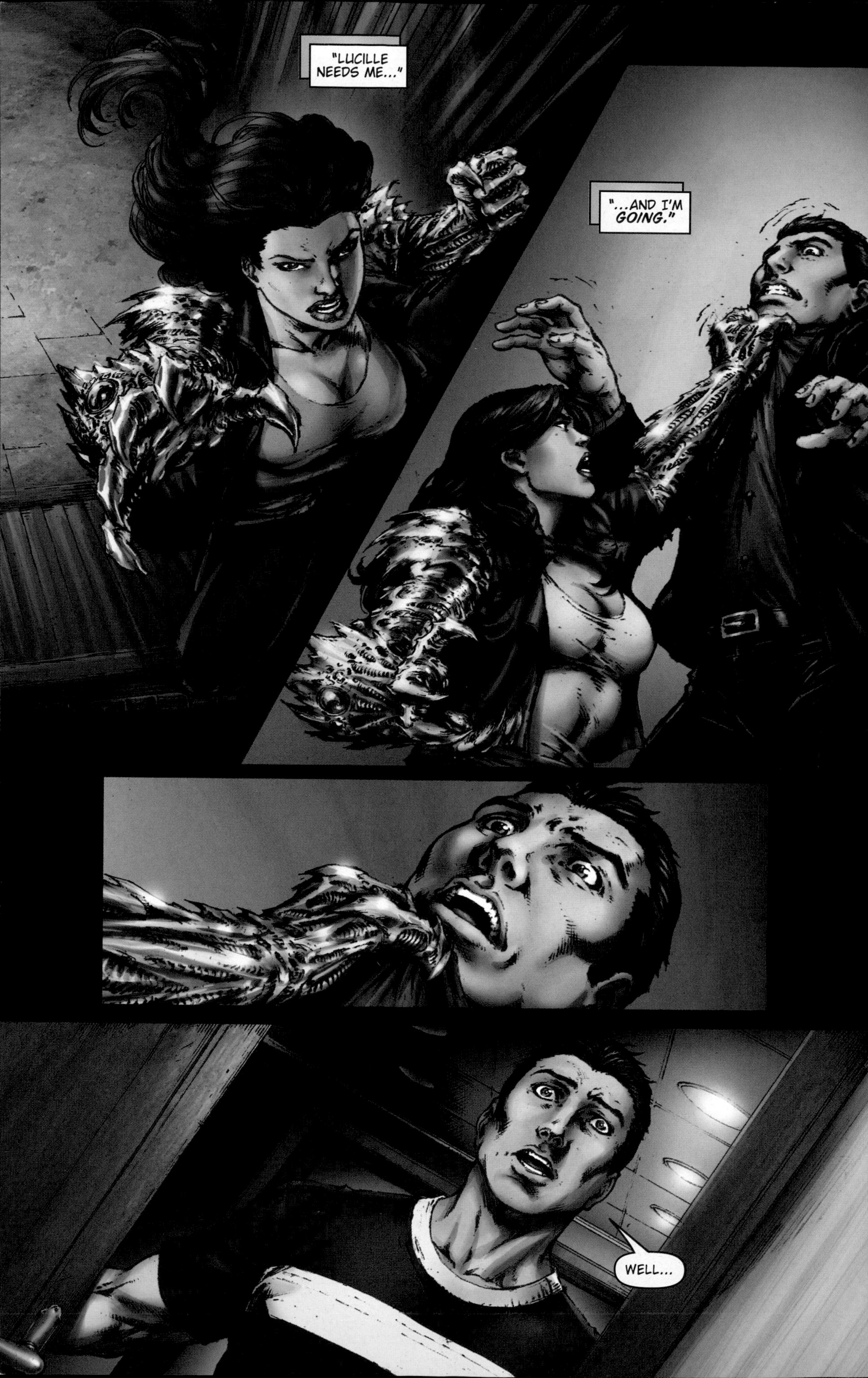
"LUCILLE NEEDS ME..."
"...AND I'M GOING."
WELL...

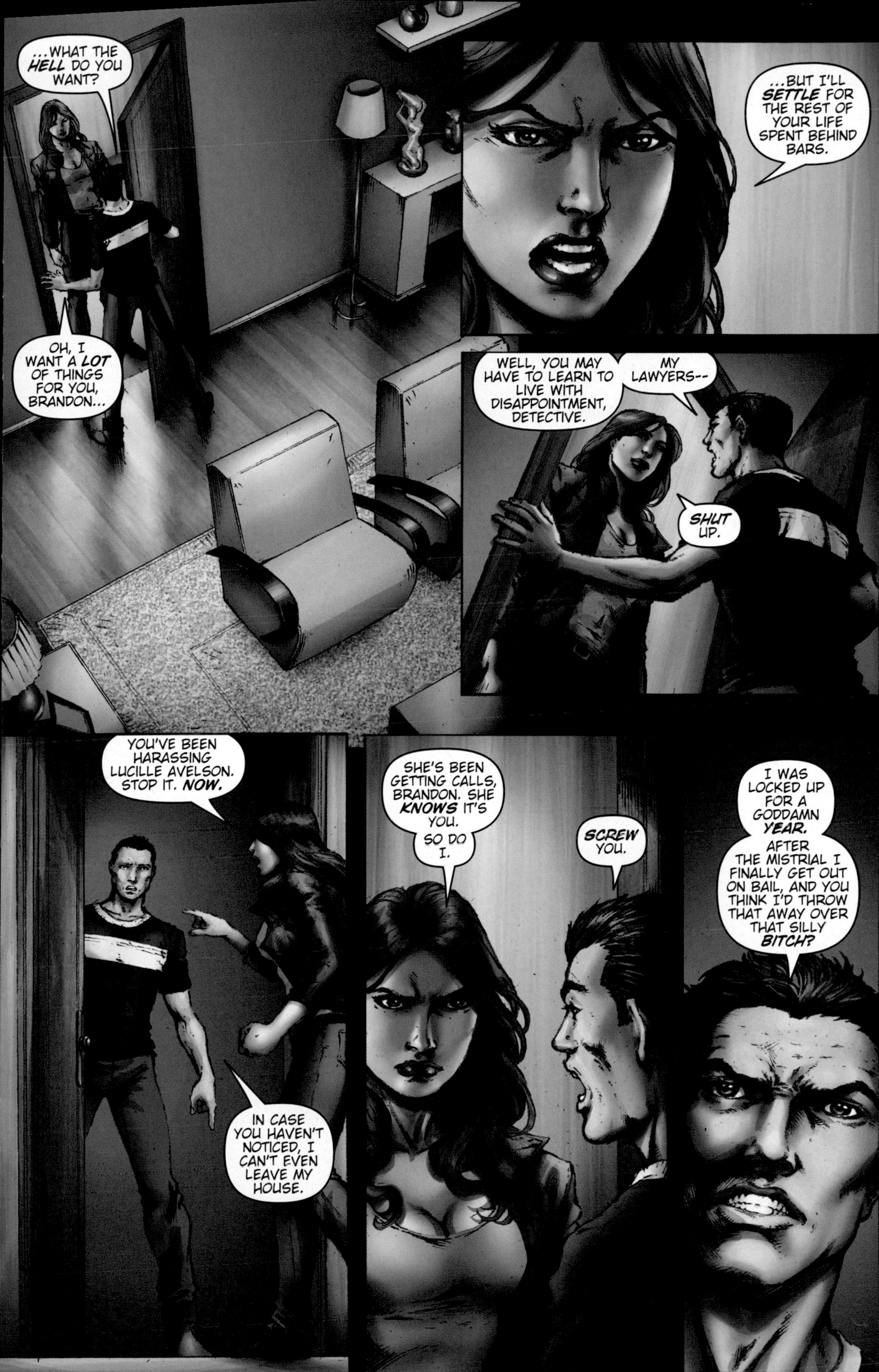
...WHAT THE HELL DO YOU WANT?
OH, I WANT A LOT OF THINGS FOR YOU, BRANDON...
...BUT I'LL SETTLE FOR THE REST OF YOUR LIFE SPENT BEHIND BARS.
WELL, YOU MAY HAVE TO LEARN TO LIVE WITH DISAPPOINTMENT, DETECTIVE.
MY LAWYERS--
SHUT UP.
YOU'VE BEEN HARASSING LUCILLE AVELSON. STOP IT. NOW.
IN CASE YOU HAVEN'T NOTICED, I CAN'T EVEN LEAVE MY HOUSE.
SHE'S BEEN GETTING CALLS, BRANDON. SHE KNOWS IT'S YOU.
SO DO I.
SCREW YOU.
I WAS LOCKED UP FOR A GODDAMN YEAR.
AFTER THE MISTRIAL I FINALLY GET OUT ON BAIL, AND YOU THINK I'D THROW THAT AWAY OVER THAT SILLY BITCH?

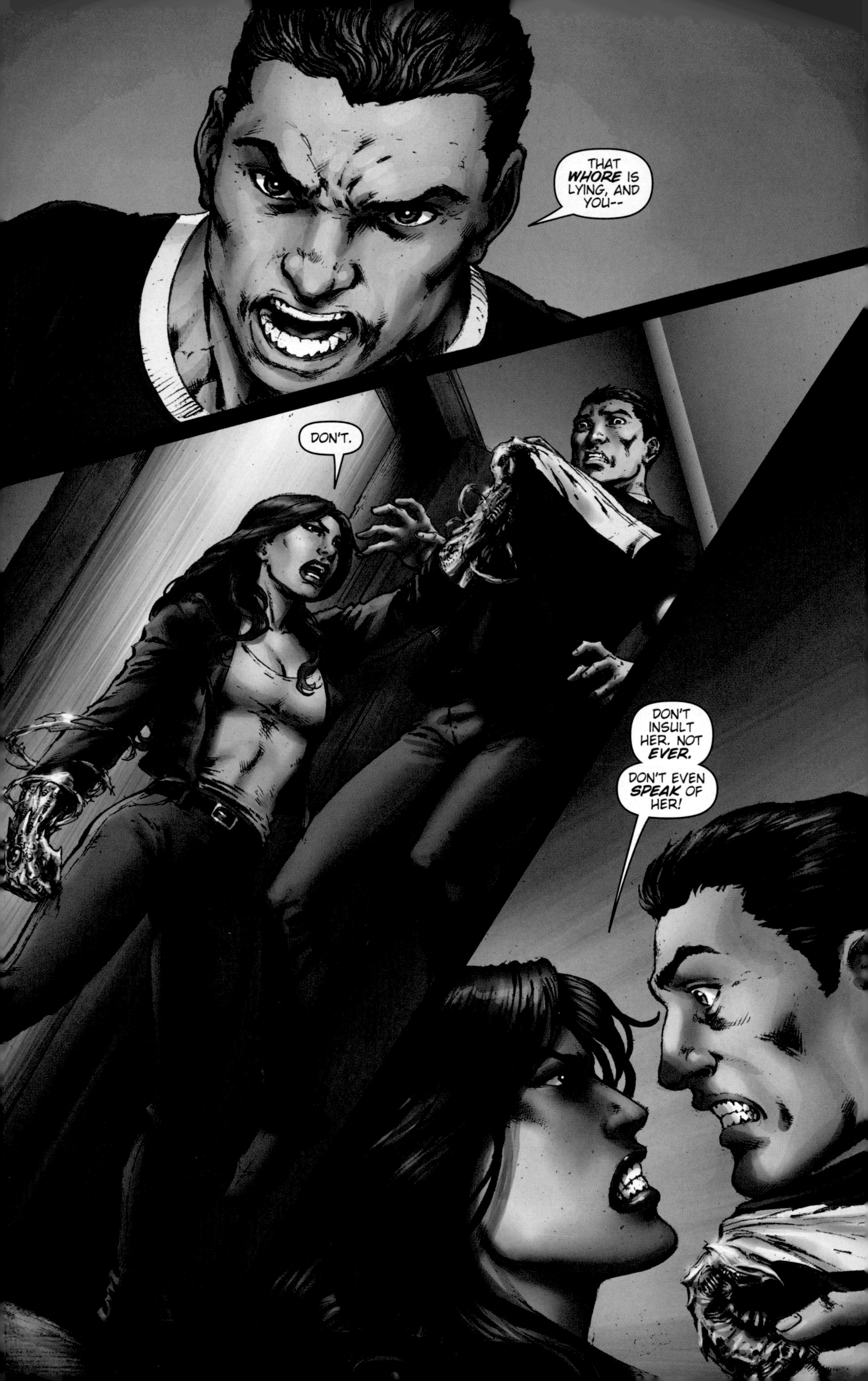
THAT **WHORE** IS LYING, AND YOU--
DON'T.
DON'T INSULT HER. NOT **EVER.**
DON'T EVEN **SPEAK** OF HER!

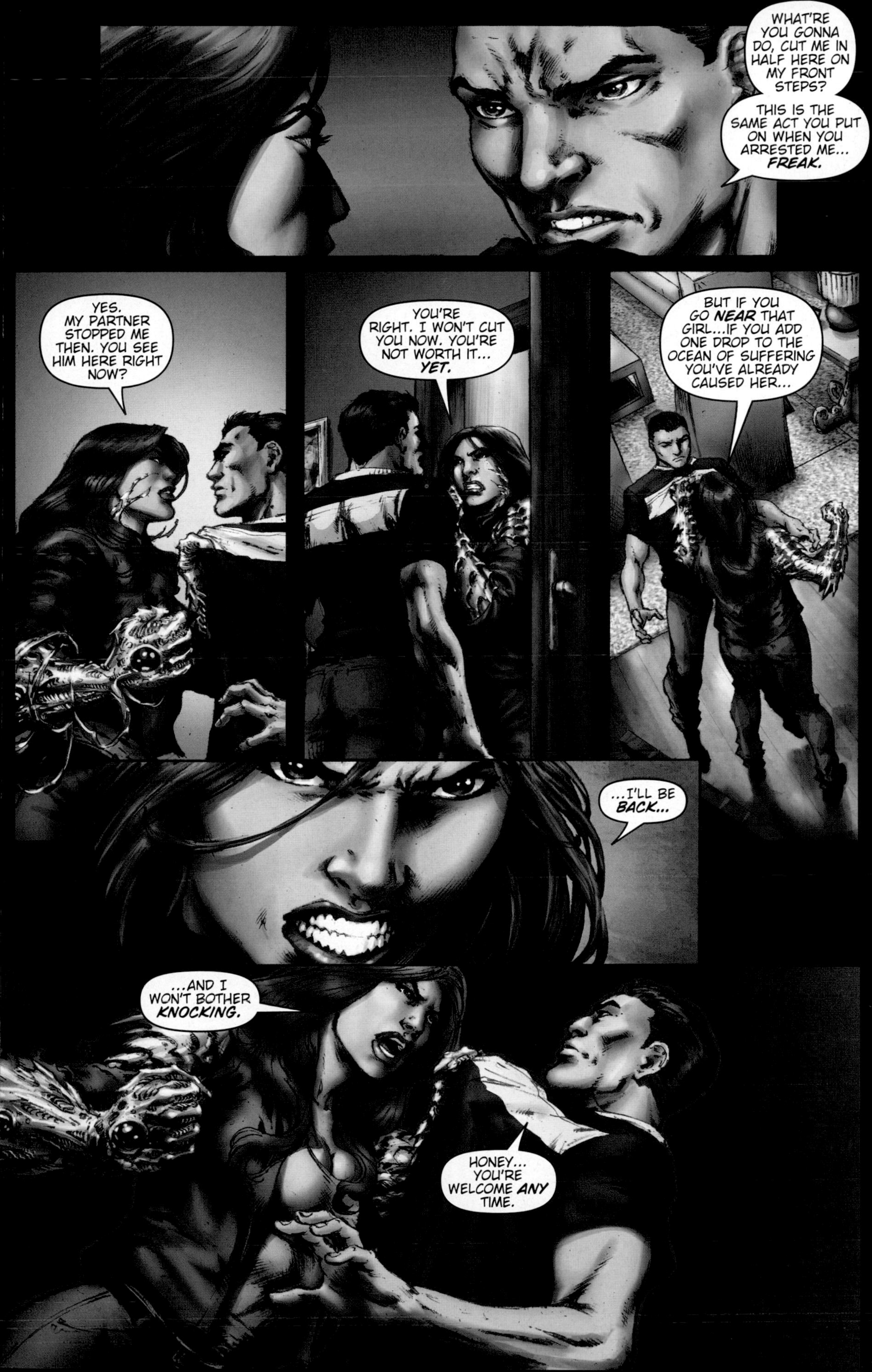
WHAT'RE YOU GONNA DO, CUT ME IN HALF HERE ON MY FRONT STEPS?
THIS IS THE SAME ACT YOU PUT ON WHEN YOU ARRESTED ME... **FREAK.**
YES. MY PARTNER STOPPED ME THEN. YOU SEE HIM HERE RIGHT NOW?
YOU'RE RIGHT. I WON'T CUT YOU NOW. YOU'RE NOT WORTH IT... **YET.**
BUT IF YOU GO **NEAR** THAT GIRL...IF YOU ADD ONE DROP TO THE OCEAN OF SUFFERING YOU'VE ALREADY CAUSED HER...
...I'LL BE **BACK...**
...AND I WON'T BOTHER **KNOCKING.**
HONEY... YOU'RE WELCOME **ANY** TIME.

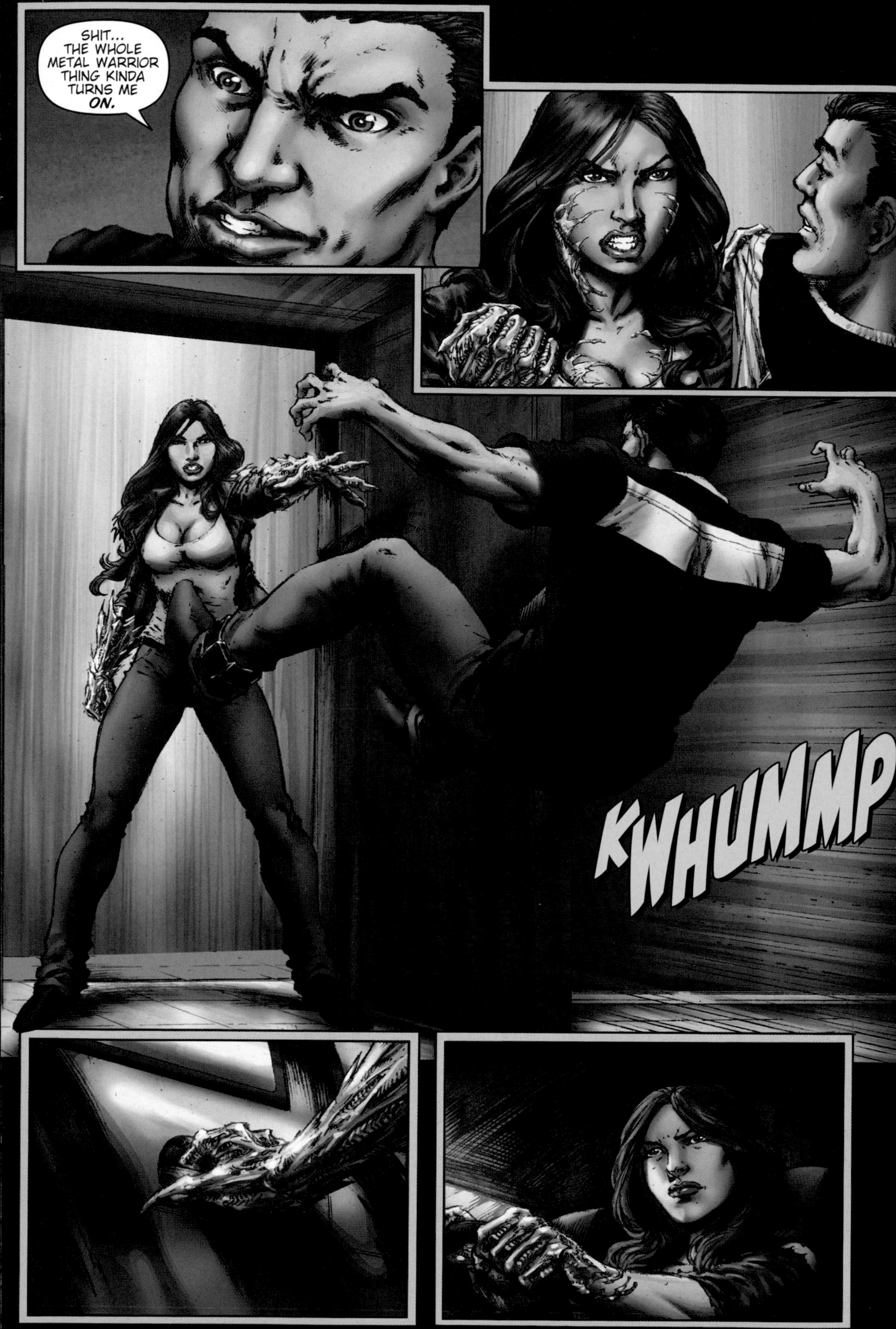
SHIT... THE WHOLE METAL WARRIOR THING KINDA TURNS ME ON.
KWHUMMP

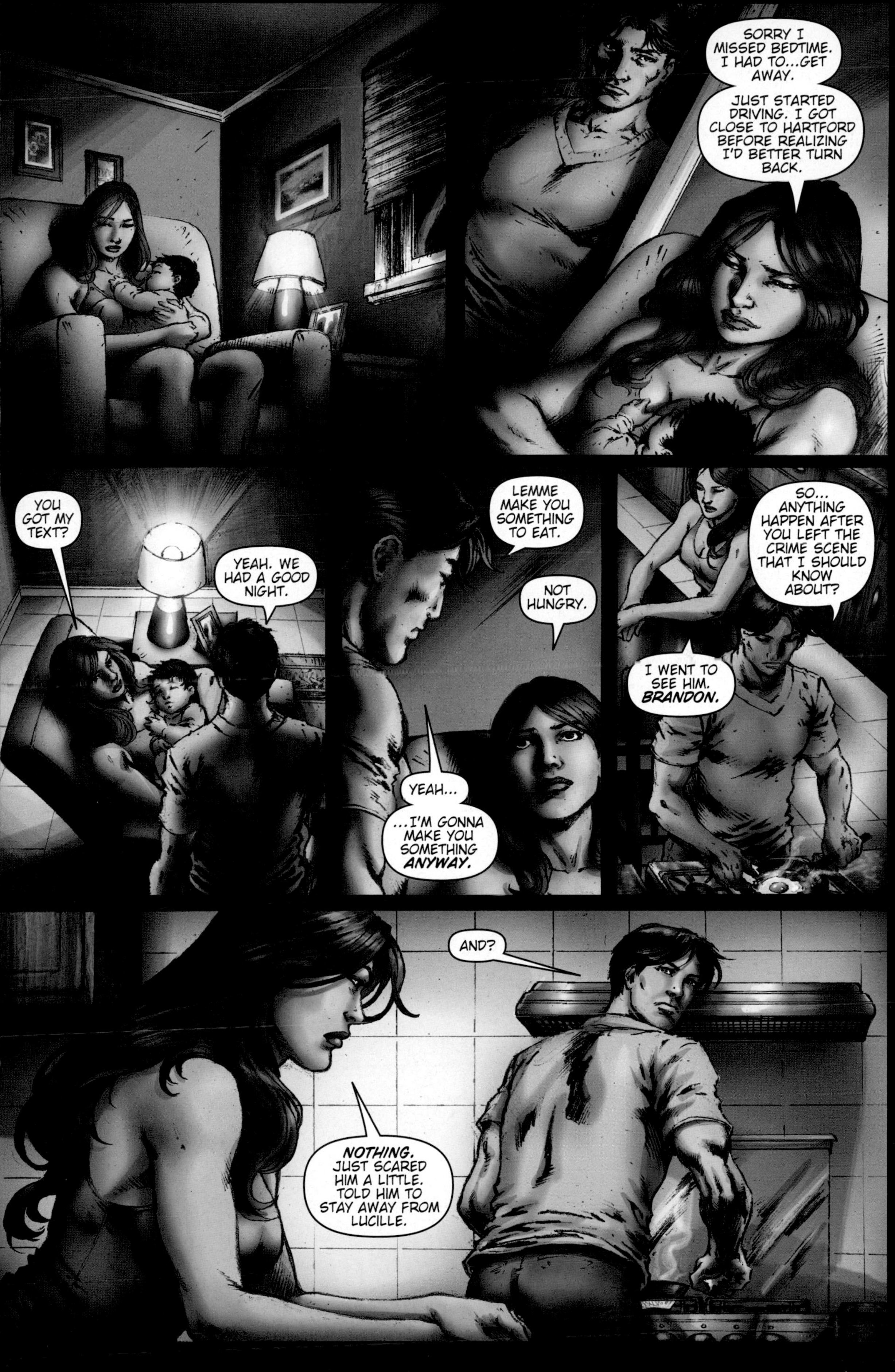
SORRY I MISSED BEDTIME. I HAD TO...GET AWAY.
JUST STARTED DRIVING. I GOT CLOSE TO HARTFORD BEFORE REALIZING I'D BETTER TURN BACK.
YOU GOT MY TEXT?
YEAH. WE HAD A GOOD NIGHT.
LEMME MAKE YOU SOMETHING TO EAT.
NOT HUNGRY.
YEAH...
...I'M GONNA MAKE YOU SOMETHING *ANYWAY.*
SO... ANYTHING HAPPEN AFTER YOU LEFT THE CRIME SCENE THAT I SHOULD KNOW ABOUT?
I WENT TO SEE HIM. ***BRANDON.***
AND?
NOTHING. JUST SCARED HIM A LITTLE. TOLD HIM TO STAY AWAY FROM LUCILLE.

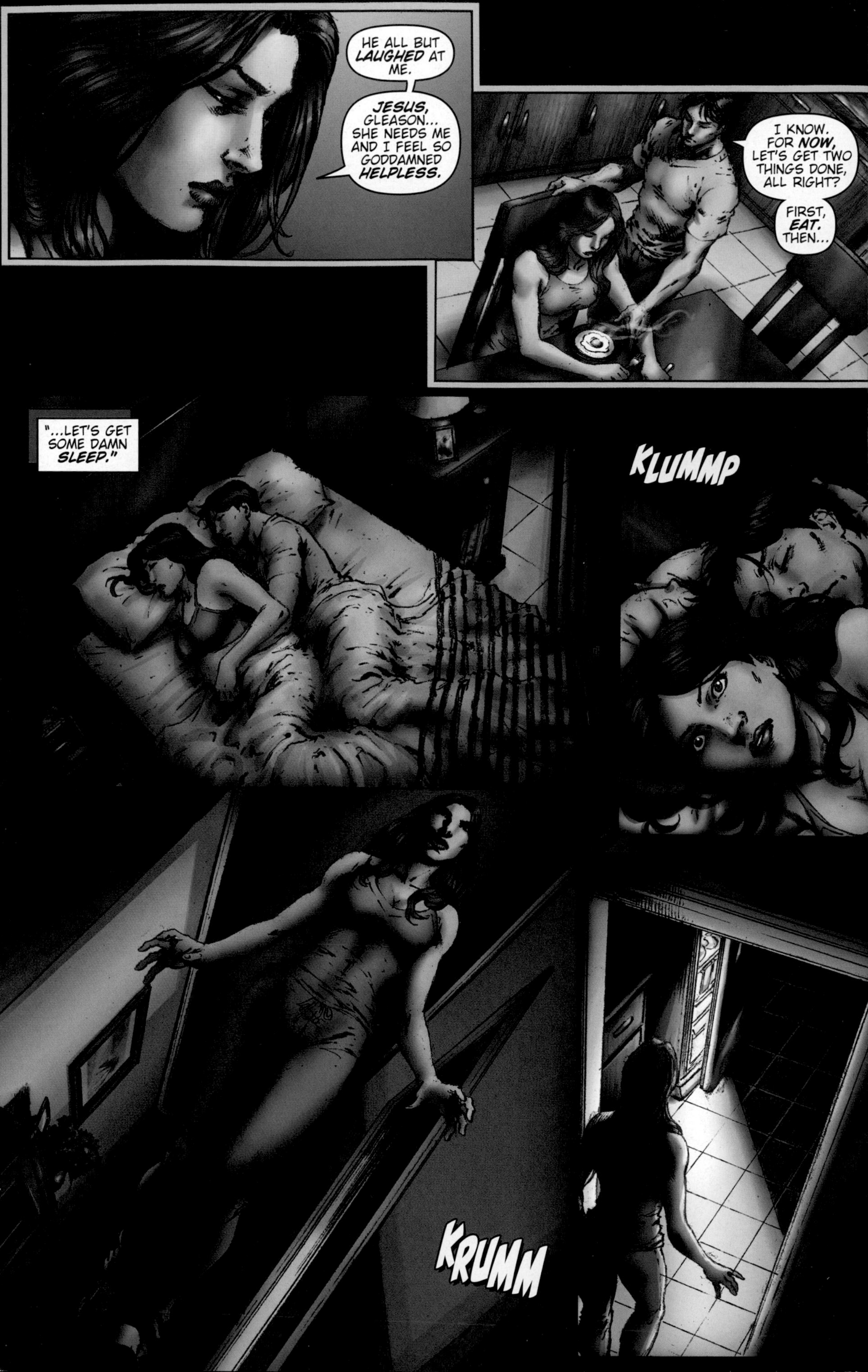

HE ALL BUT LAUGHED AT ME.
JESUS, GLEASON... SHE NEEDS ME AND I FEEL SO GODDAMNED HELPLESS.
I KNOW. FOR NOW, LET'S GET TWO THINGS DONE, ALL RIGHT?
FIRST, EAT. THEN...
"...LET'S GET SOME DAMN SLEEP."
KLUMMP
KRUMM

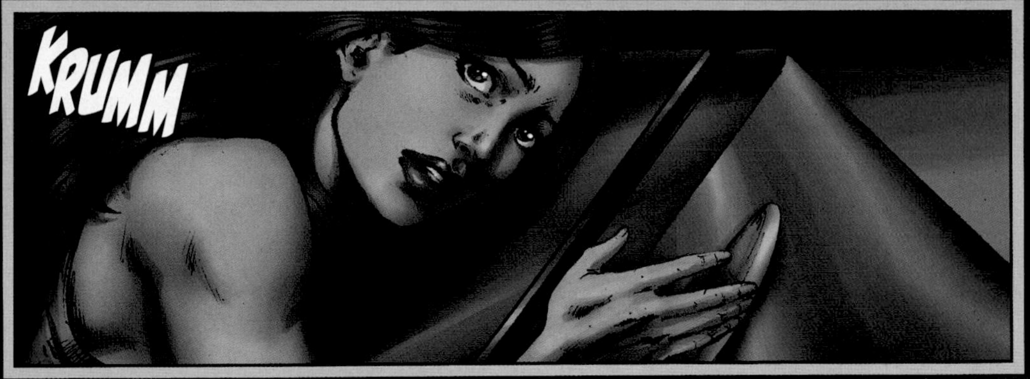
KRUMM

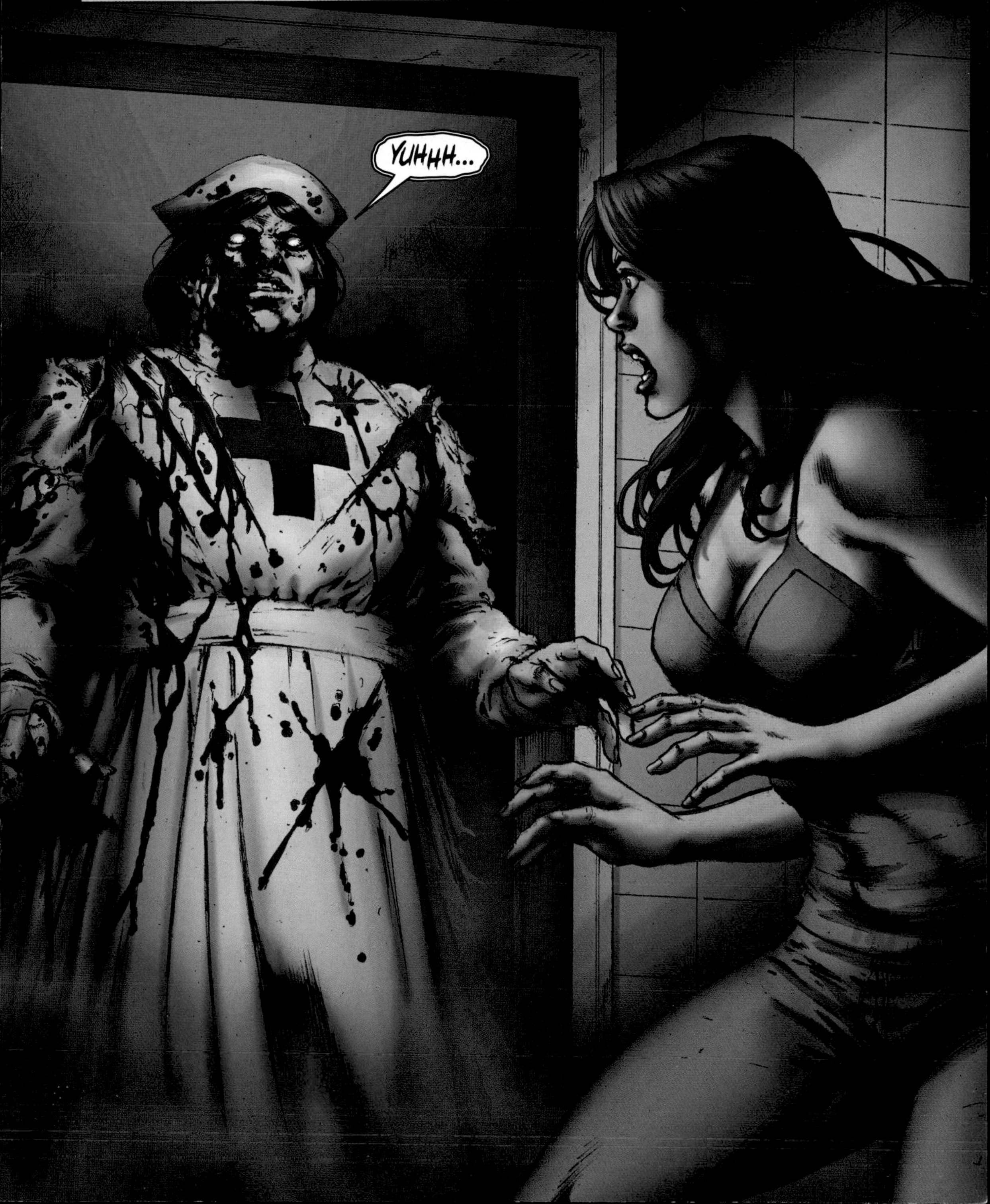
YUHHH...

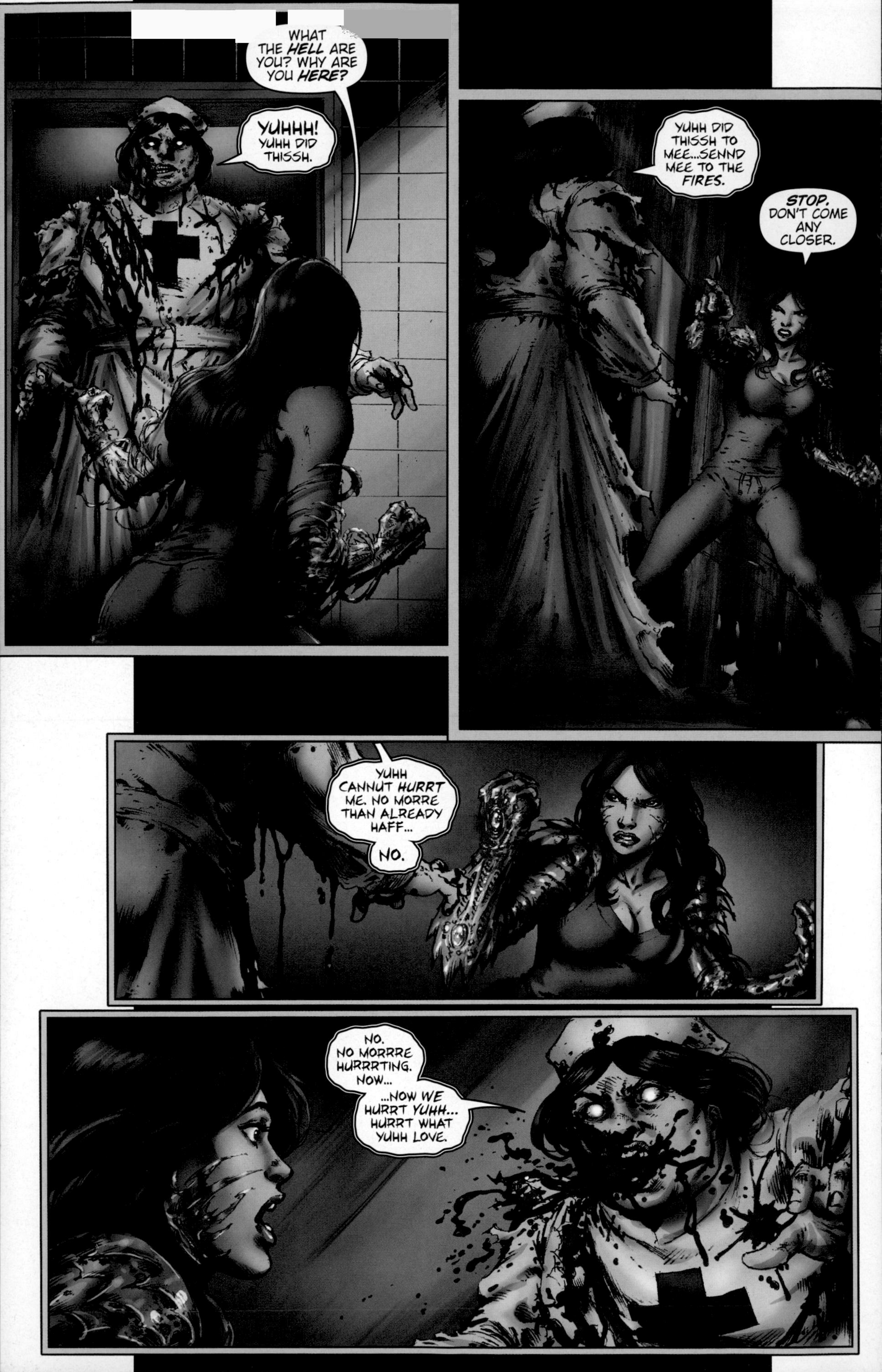
WHAT THE HELL ARE YOU? WHY ARE YOU HERE?
YUHHH! YUHH DID THISSH.
YUHH DID THISSH TO MEE...SENND MEE TO THE FIRES.
STOP. DON'T COME ANY CLOSER.
YUHH CANNUT HURRT ME. NO MORRE THAN ALREADY HAFF...
NO.
NO. NO MORRRE HURRRTING. NOW...
...NOW WE HURRT YUHH... HURRT WHAT YUHH LOVE.

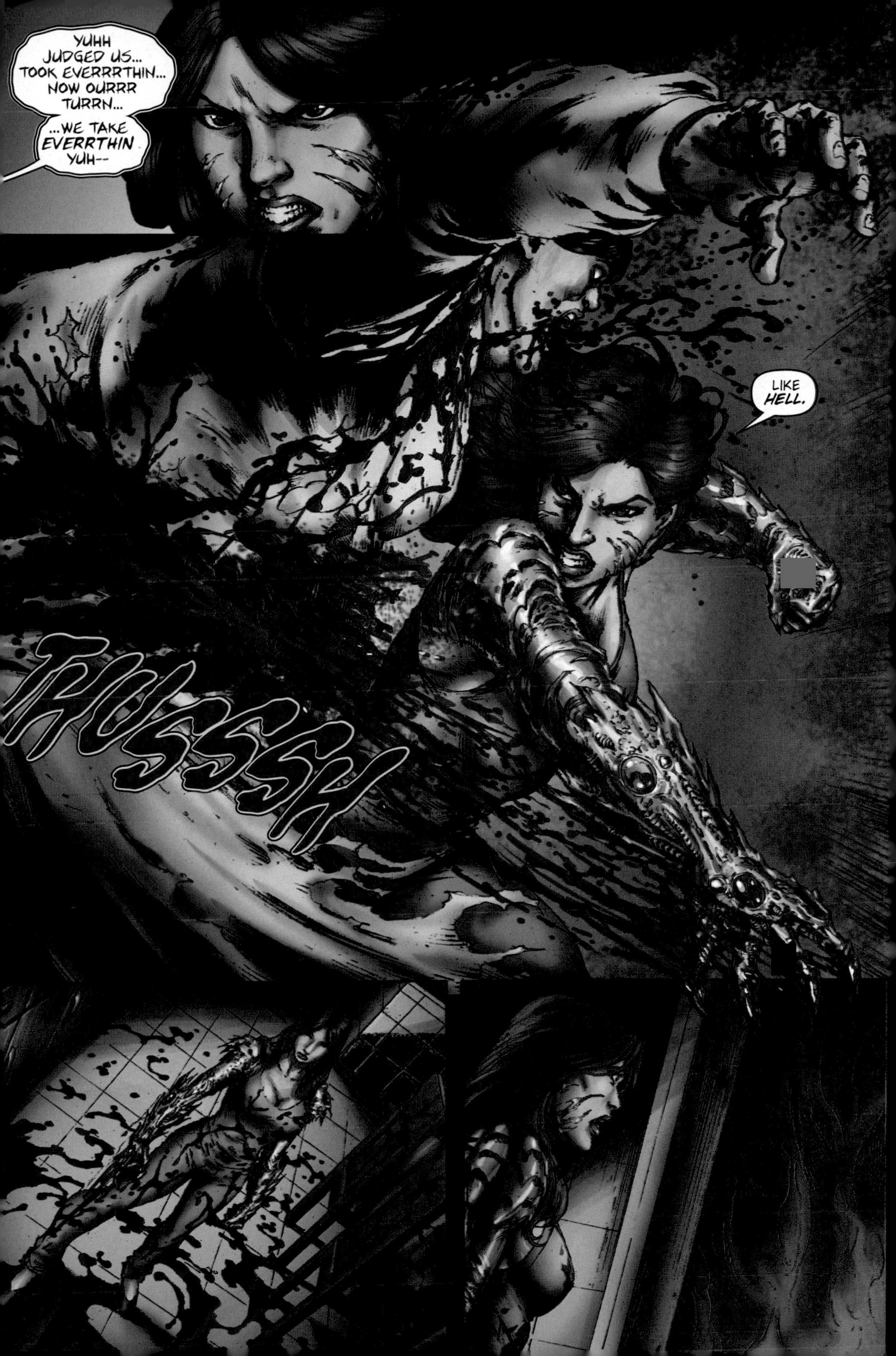
YUHH JUDGED US... TOOK EVERRRTHIN... NOW OURRR TURRN...
...WE TAKE EVERRTHIN YUH--
LIKE HELL.
THUSSSH

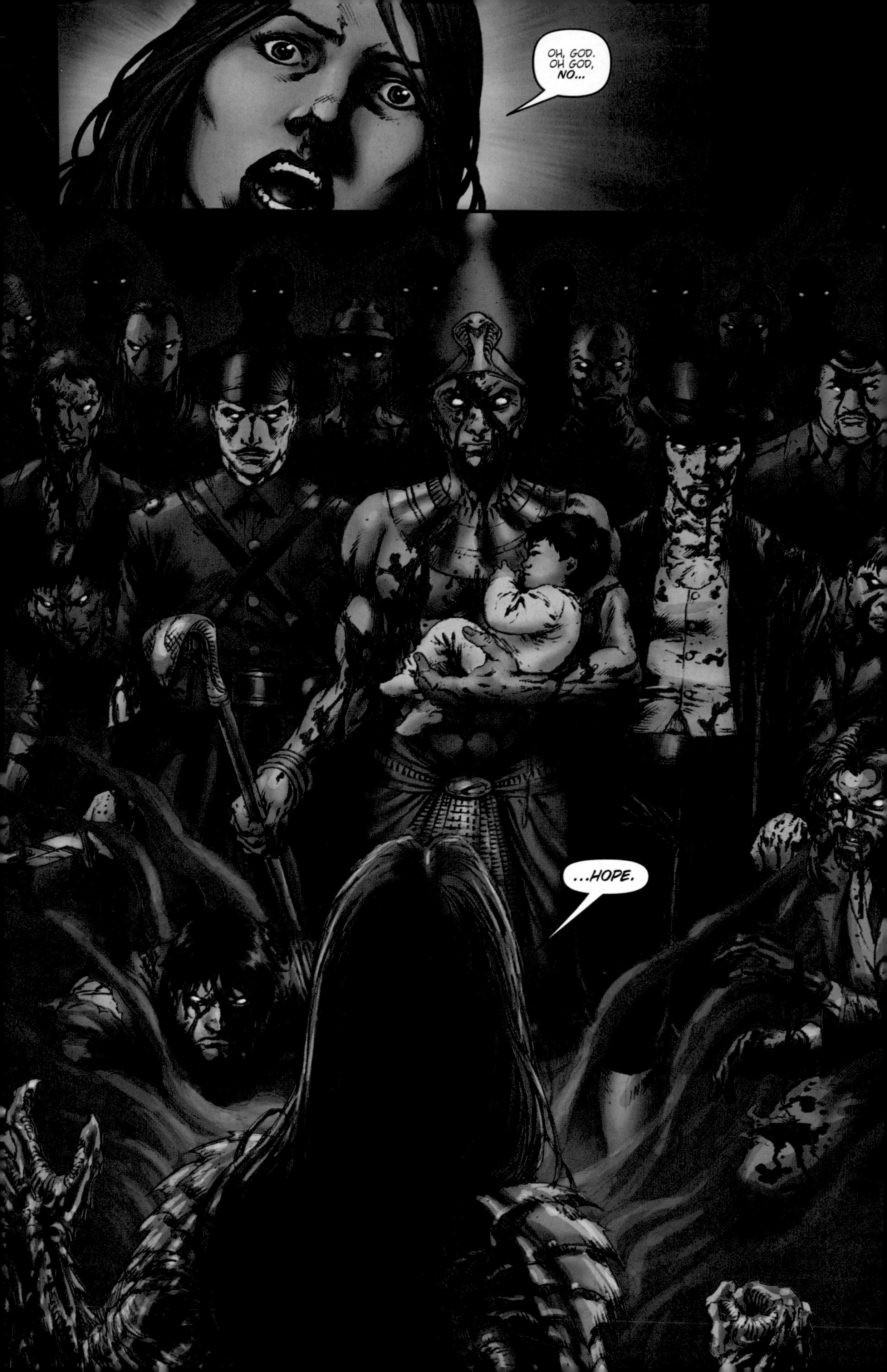
OH, GOD. OH GOD, NO...
...HOPE.

WITCHBLADE
DEMON REBORN

CHAPTER THREE

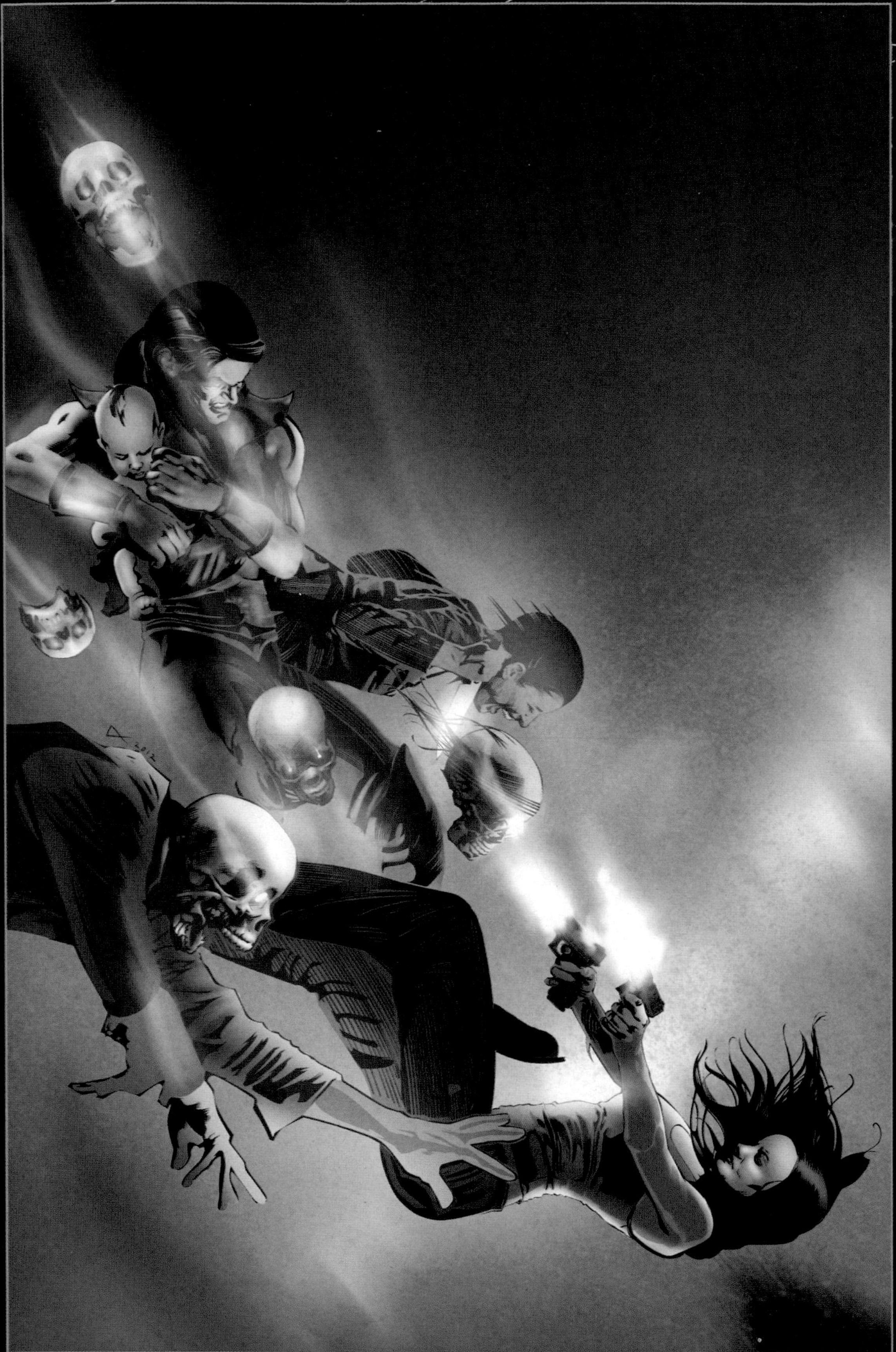

ISSUE #3 COVER BY DENNIS CALERO

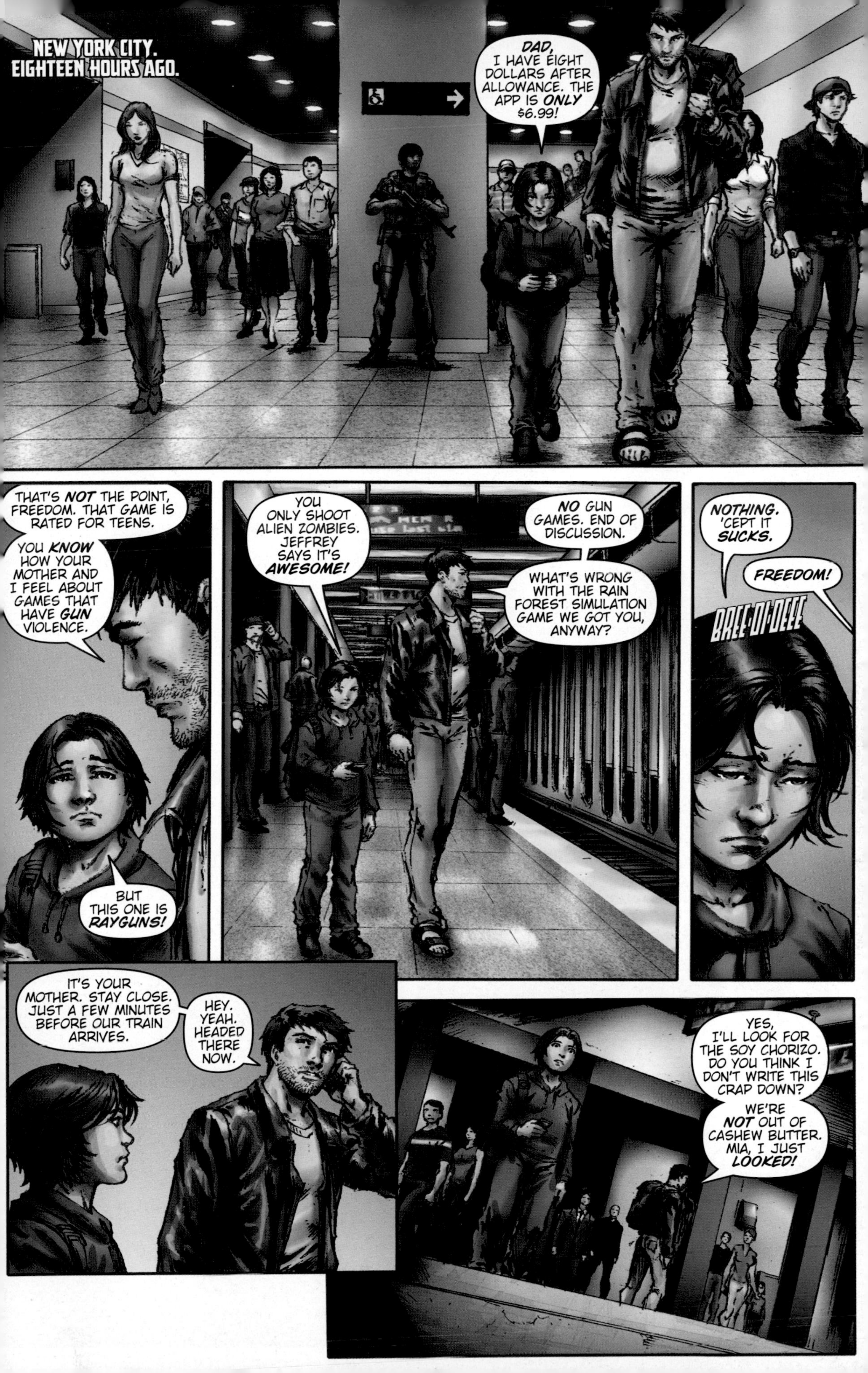
NEW YORK CITY. EIGHTEEN HOURS AGO.
DAD, I HAVE EIGHT DOLLARS AFTER ALLOWANCE. THE APP IS ONLY $6.99!
THAT'S NOT THE POINT, FREEDOM. THAT GAME IS RATED FOR TEENS.
YOU KNOW HOW YOUR MOTHER AND I FEEL ABOUT GAMES THAT HAVE GUN VIOLENCE.
BUT THIS ONE IS RAYGUNS!
YOU ONLY SHOOT ALIEN ZOMBIES. JEFFREY SAYS IT'S AWESOME!
NO GUN GAMES. END OF DISCUSSION.
WHAT'S WRONG WITH THE RAIN FOREST SIMULATION GAME WE GOT YOU, ANYWAY?
NOTHING. 'CEPT IT SUCKS.
FREEDOM!
BREE-DI-DEEE
IT'S YOUR MOTHER. STAY CLOSE. JUST A FEW MINUTES BEFORE OUR TRAIN ARRIVES.
HEY. YEAH. HEADED THERE NOW.
YES, I'LL LOOK FOR THE SOY CHORIZO. DO YOU THINK I DON'T WRITE THIS CRAP DOWN?
WE'RE NOT OUT OF CASHEW BUTTER. MIA, I JUST LOOKED!

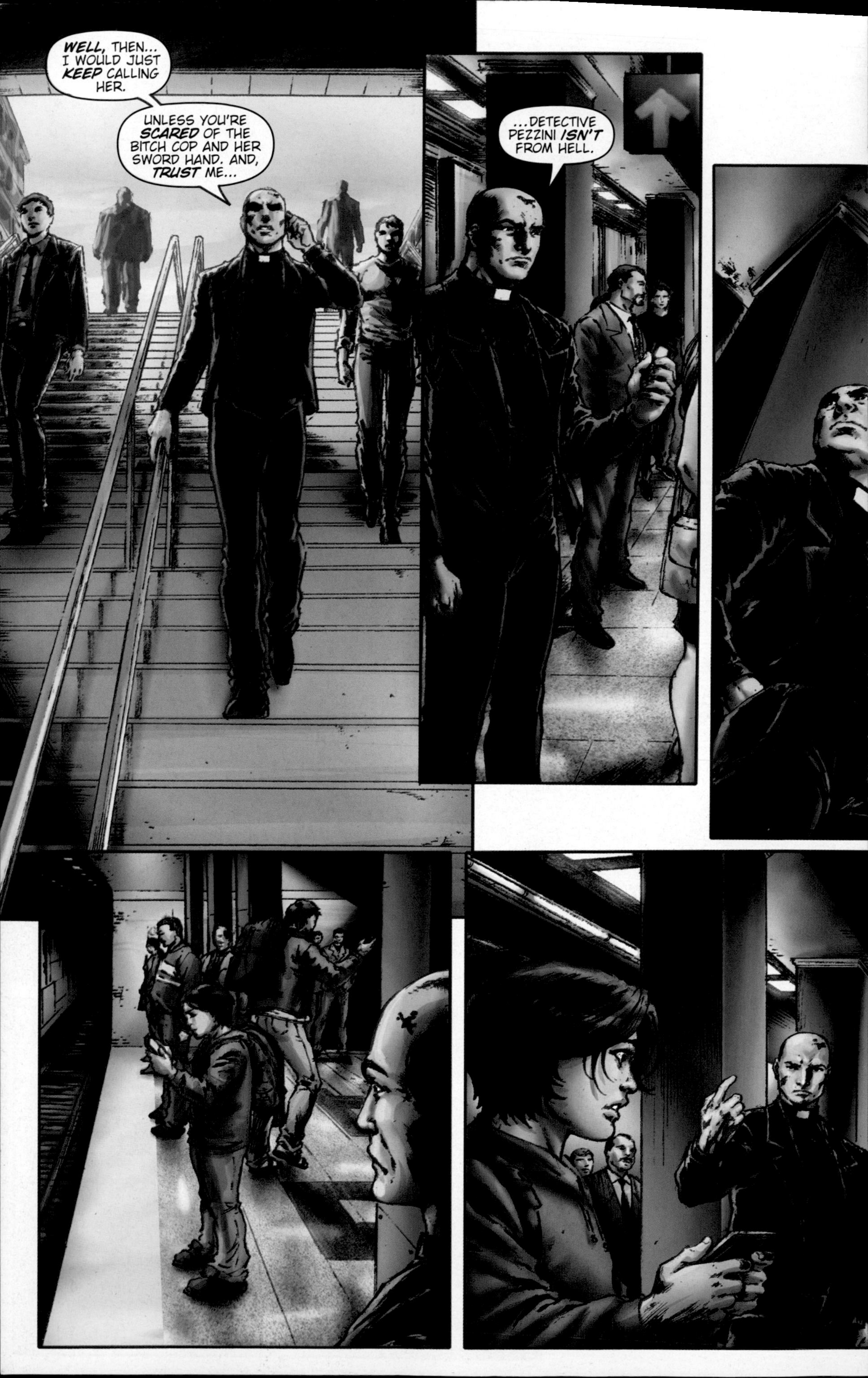
WELL, THEN... I WOULD JUST KEEP CALLING HER.
UNLESS YOU'RE SCARED OF THE BITCH COP AND HER SWORD HAND. AND, TRUST ME...
...DETECTIVE PEZZINI ISN'T FROM HELL.

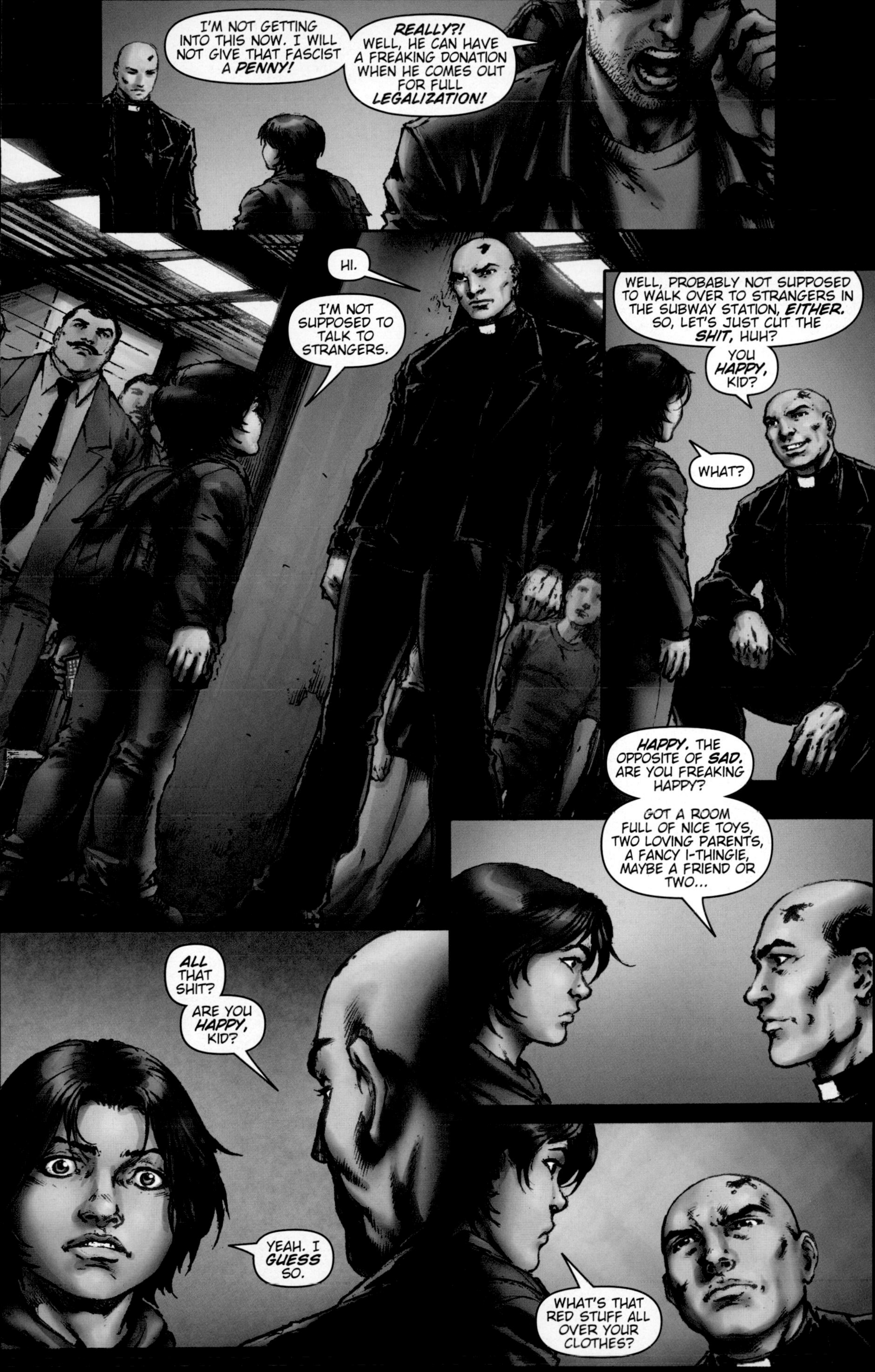
I'M NOT GETTING INTO THIS NOW. I WILL NOT GIVE THAT FASCIST A PENNY!
REALLY?! WELL, HE CAN HAVE A FREAKING DONATION WHEN HE COMES OUT FOR FULL LEGALIZATION!
HI.
I'M NOT SUPPOSED TO TALK TO STRANGERS.
WELL, PROBABLY NOT SUPPOSED TO WALK OVER TO STRANGERS IN THE SUBWAY STATION, EITHER. SO, LET'S JUST CUT THE SHIT, HUH?
YOU HAPPY, KID?
WHAT?
HAPPY. THE OPPOSITE OF SAD. ARE YOU FREAKING HAPPY?
GOT A ROOM FULL OF NICE TOYS, TWO LOVING PARENTS, A FANCY I-THINGIE, MAYBE A FRIEND OR TWO...
ALL THAT SHIT?
ARE YOU HAPPY, KID?
YEAH. I GUESS SO.
WHAT'S THAT RED STUFF ALL OVER YOUR CLOTHES?

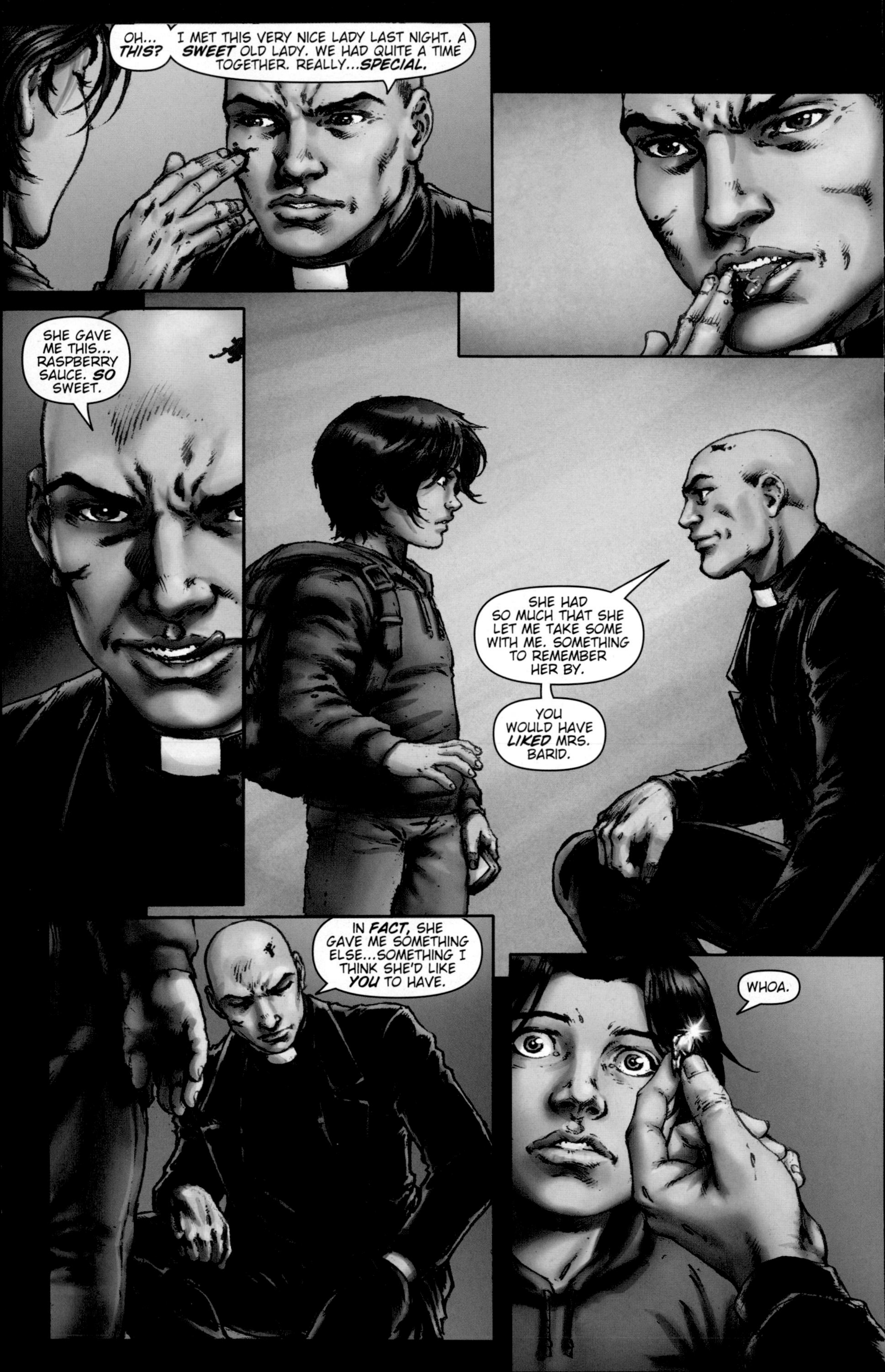
OH... THIS?
I MET THIS VERY NICE LADY LAST NIGHT. A SWEET OLD LADY. WE HAD QUITE A TIME TOGETHER. REALLY...SPECIAL.
SHE GAVE ME THIS... RASPBERRY SAUCE. SO SWEET.
SHE HAD SO MUCH THAT SHE LET ME TAKE SOME WITH ME. SOMETHING TO REMEMBER HER BY.
YOU WOULD HAVE LIKED MRS. BARID.
IN FACT, SHE GAVE ME SOMETHING ELSE...SOMETHING I THINK SHE'D LIKE YOU TO HAVE.
WHOA.

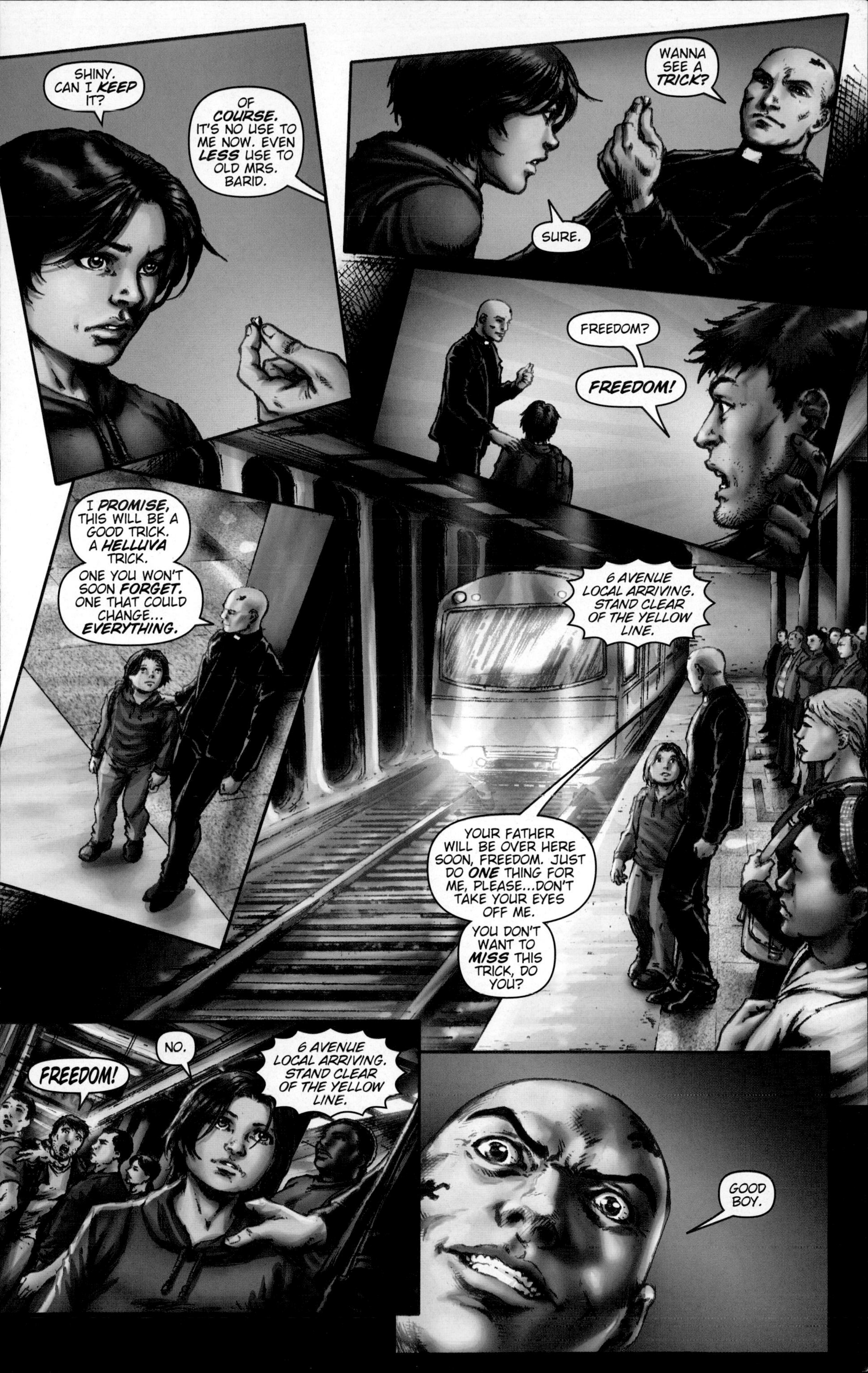
SHINY. CAN I KEEP IT?
OF COURSE. IT'S NO USE TO ME NOW. EVEN LESS USE TO OLD MRS. BARID.
WANNA SEE A TRICK?
SURE.
FREEDOM?
FREEDOM!
I PROMISE, THIS WILL BE A GOOD TRICK. A HELLUVA TRICK.
ONE YOU WON'T SOON FORGET. ONE THAT COULD CHANGE... EVERYTHING.
6 AVENUE LOCAL ARRIVING. STAND CLEAR OF THE YELLOW LINE.
YOUR FATHER WILL BE OVER HERE SOON, FREEDOM. JUST DO ONE THING FOR ME, PLEASE...DON'T TAKE YOUR EYES OFF ME.
YOU DON'T WANT TO MISS THIS TRICK, DO YOU?
FREEDOM!
NO.
6 AVENUE LOCAL ARRIVING. STAND CLEAR OF THE YELLOW LINE.
GOOD BOY.

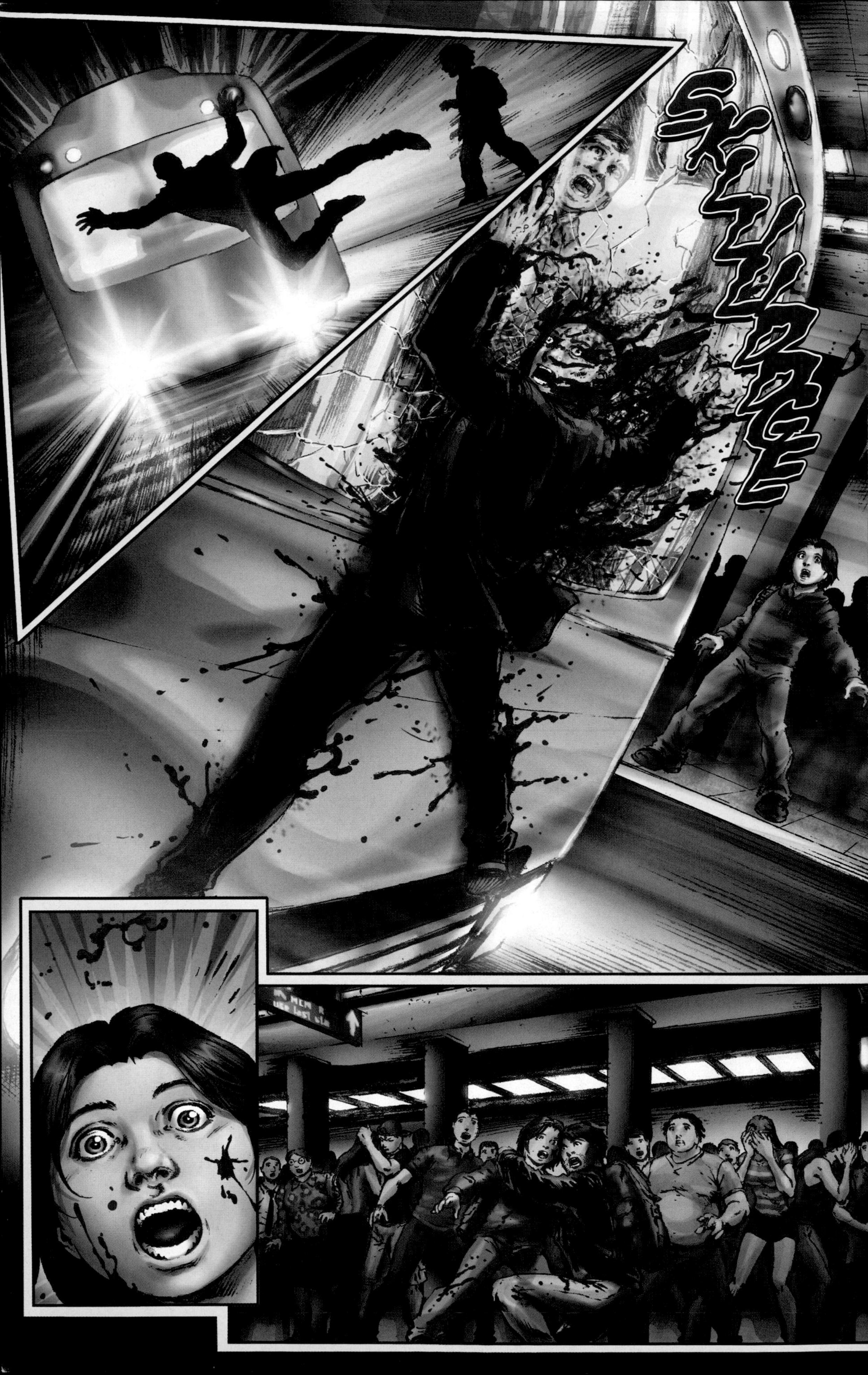
SKLUDGE

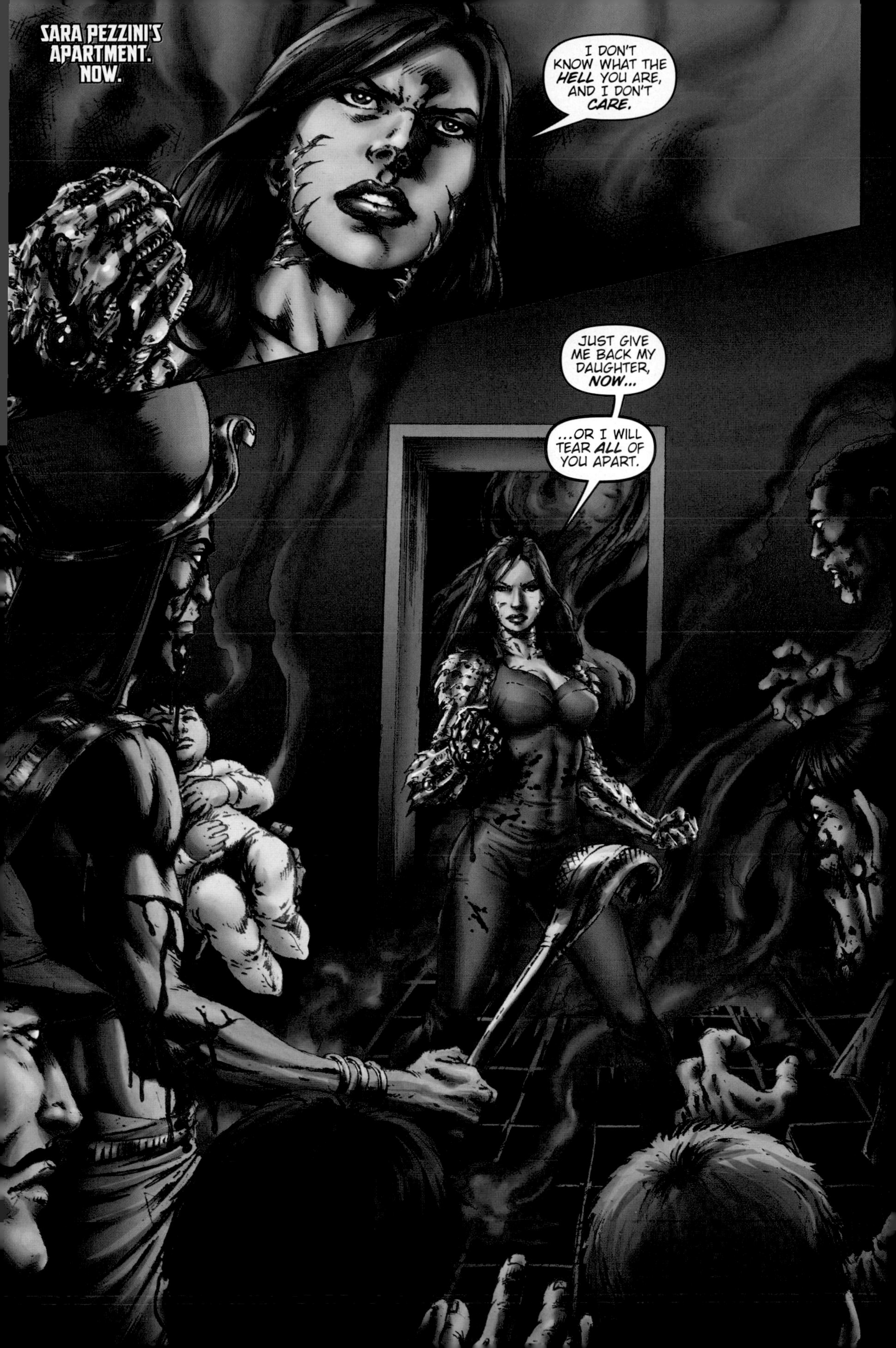
SARA PEZZINI'S APARTMENT. NOW.
I DON'T KNOW WHAT THE HELL YOU ARE, AND I DON'T CARE.
JUST GIVE ME BACK MY DAUGHTER, NOW...
...OR I WILL TEAR ALL OF YOU APART.

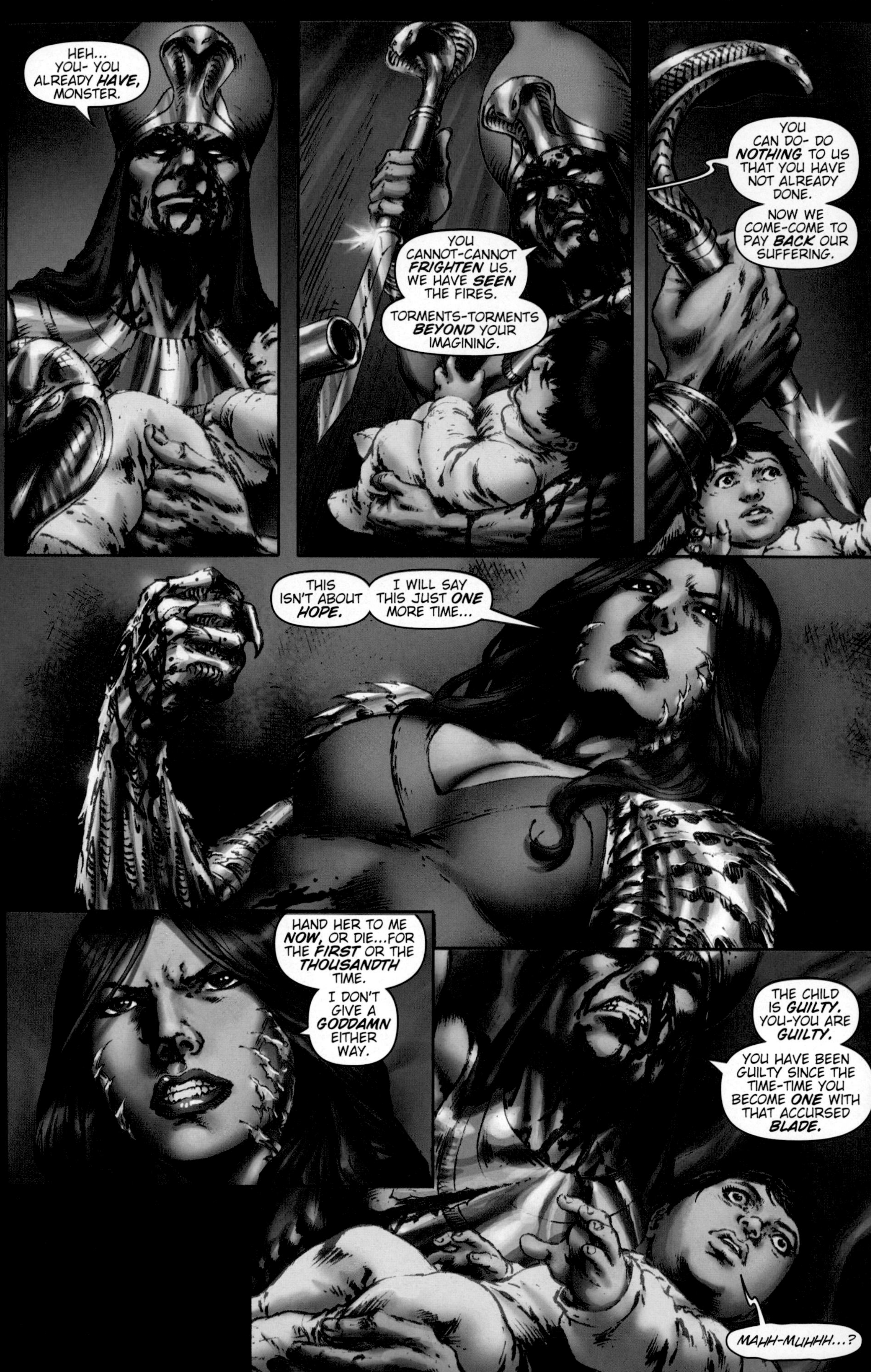
HEH... YOU- YOU ALREADY HAVE, MONSTER.
YOU CANNOT-CANNOT FRIGHTEN US. WE HAVE SEEN THE FIRES.
TORMENTS-TORMENTS BEYOND YOUR IMAGINING.
YOU CAN DO- DO NOTHING TO US THAT YOU HAVE NOT ALREADY DONE.
NOW WE COME-COME TO PAY BACK OUR SUFFERING.
I WILL SAY THIS JUST ONE MORE TIME...
THIS ISN'T ABOUT HOPE.
HAND HER TO ME NOW, OR DIE...FOR THE FIRST OR THE THOUSANDTH TIME.
I DON'T GIVE A GODDAMN EITHER WAY.
THE CHILD IS GUILTY. YOU-YOU ARE GUILTY.
YOU HAVE BEEN GUILTY SINCE THE TIME-TIME YOU BECOME ONE WITH THAT ACCURSED BLADE.
MAHH-MUHHH...?

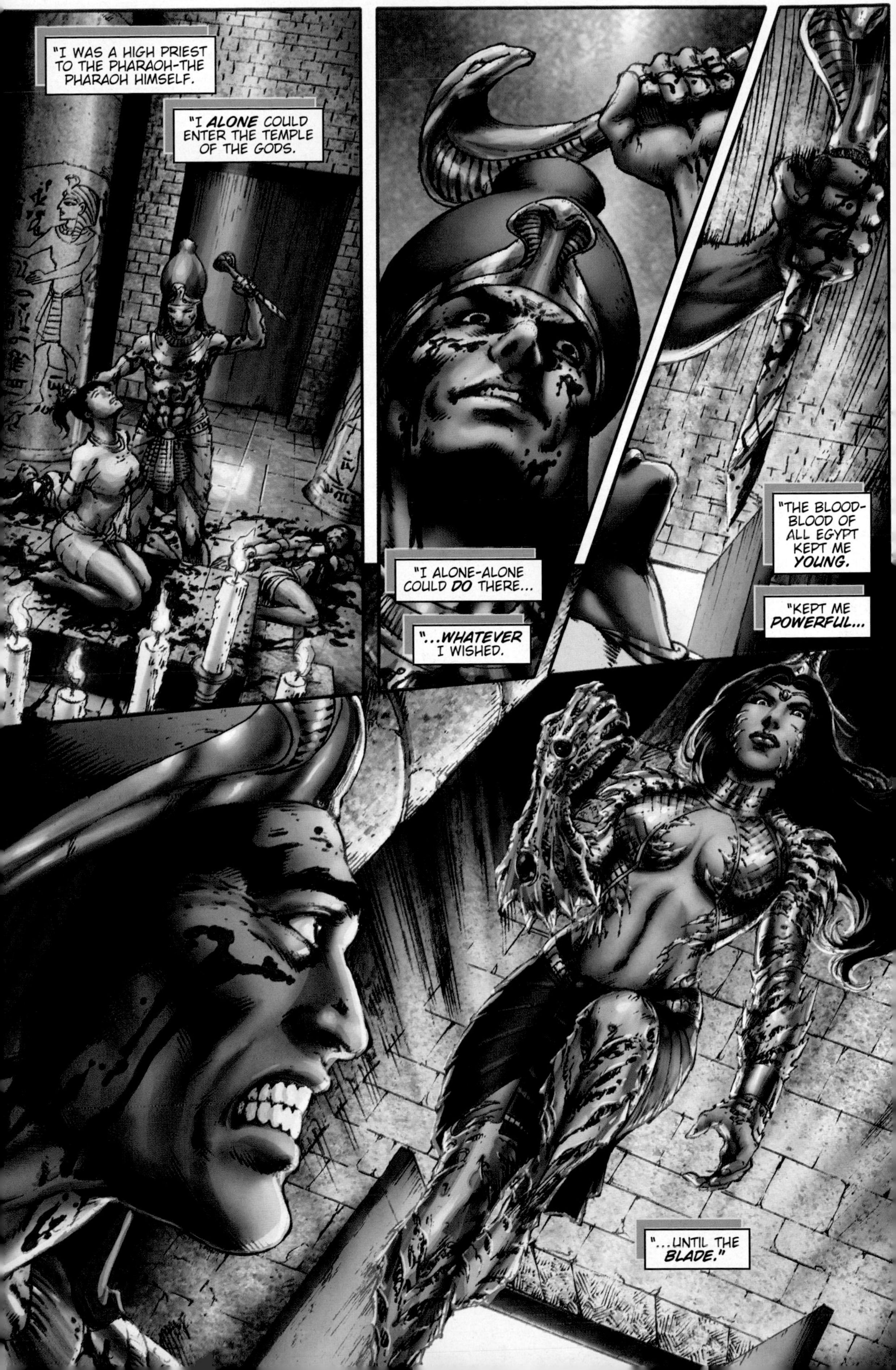
"I WAS A HIGH PRIEST TO THE PHARAOH-THE PHARAOH HIMSELF.
"I ALONE COULD ENTER THE TEMPLE OF THE GODS.
"I ALONE-ALONE COULD DO THERE...
"...WHATEVER I WISHED.
"THE BLOOD-BLOOD OF ALL EGYPT KEPT ME YOUNG.
"KEPT ME POWERFUL...
"...UNTIL THE BLADE."

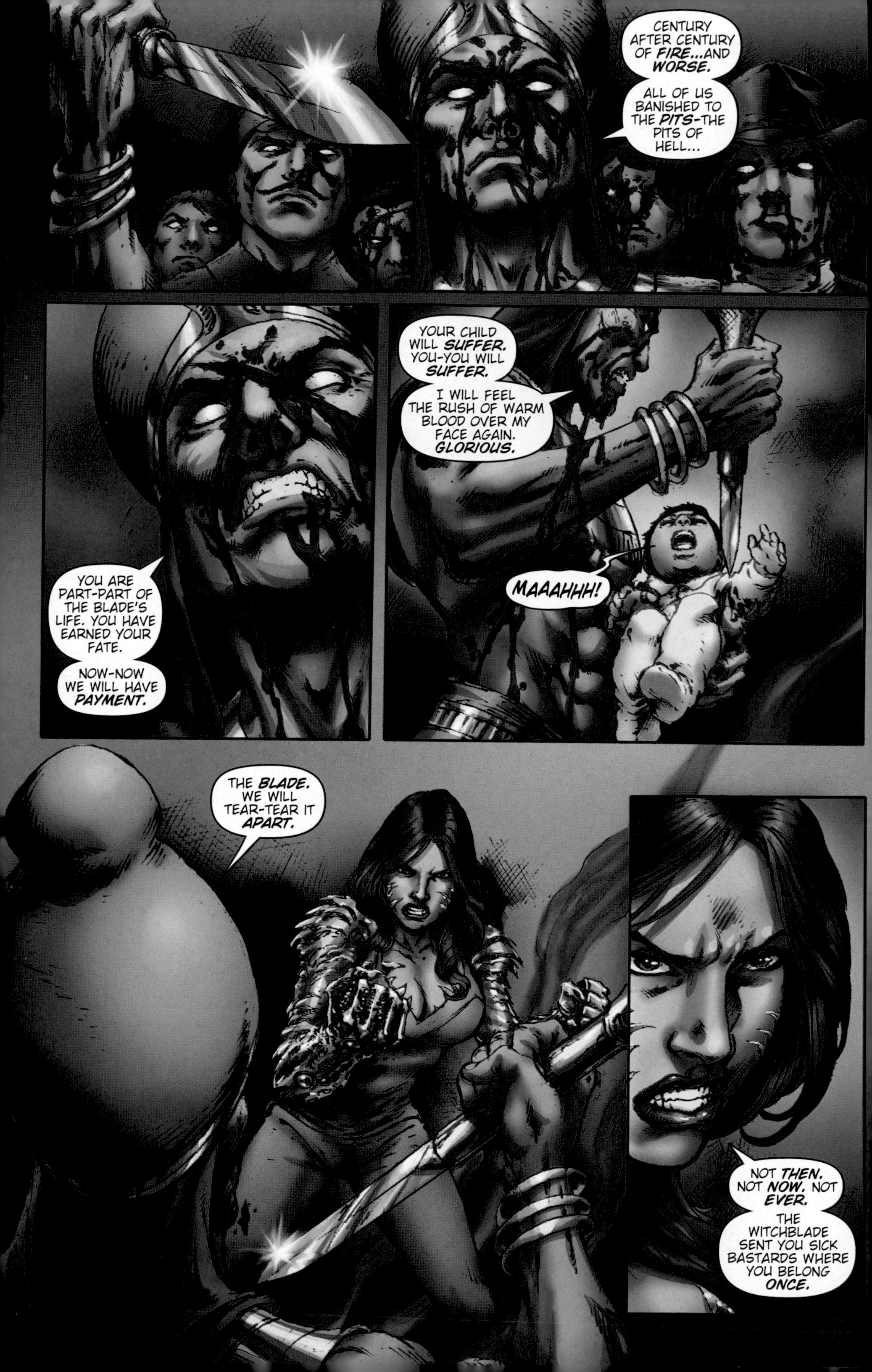
CENTURY AFTER CENTURY OF FIRE...AND WORSE.
ALL OF US BANISHED TO THE PITS-THE PITS OF HELL...
YOU ARE PART-PART OF THE BLADE'S LIFE. YOU HAVE EARNED YOUR FATE.
NOW-NOW WE WILL HAVE PAYMENT.
YOUR CHILD WILL SUFFER. YOU-YOU WILL SUFFER.
I WILL FEEL THE RUSH OF WARM BLOOD OVER MY FACE AGAIN. GLORIOUS.
MAAAHHH!
THE BLADE. WE WILL TEAR-TEAR IT APART.
NOT THEN. NOT NOW. NOT EVER.
THE WITCHBLADE SENT YOU SICK BASTARDS WHERE YOU BELONG ONCE.

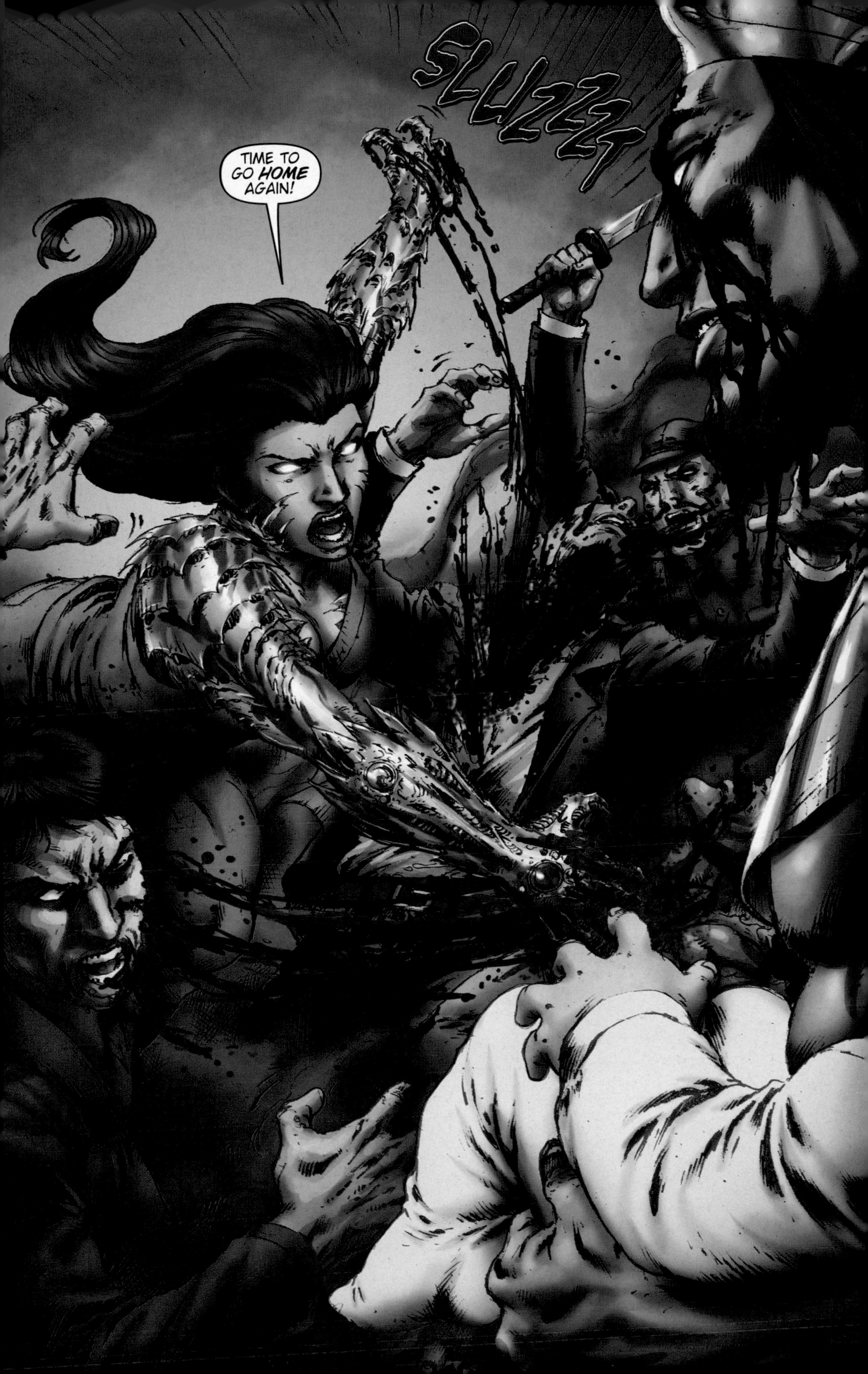
SLUZZZT
TIME TO GO HOME AGAIN!

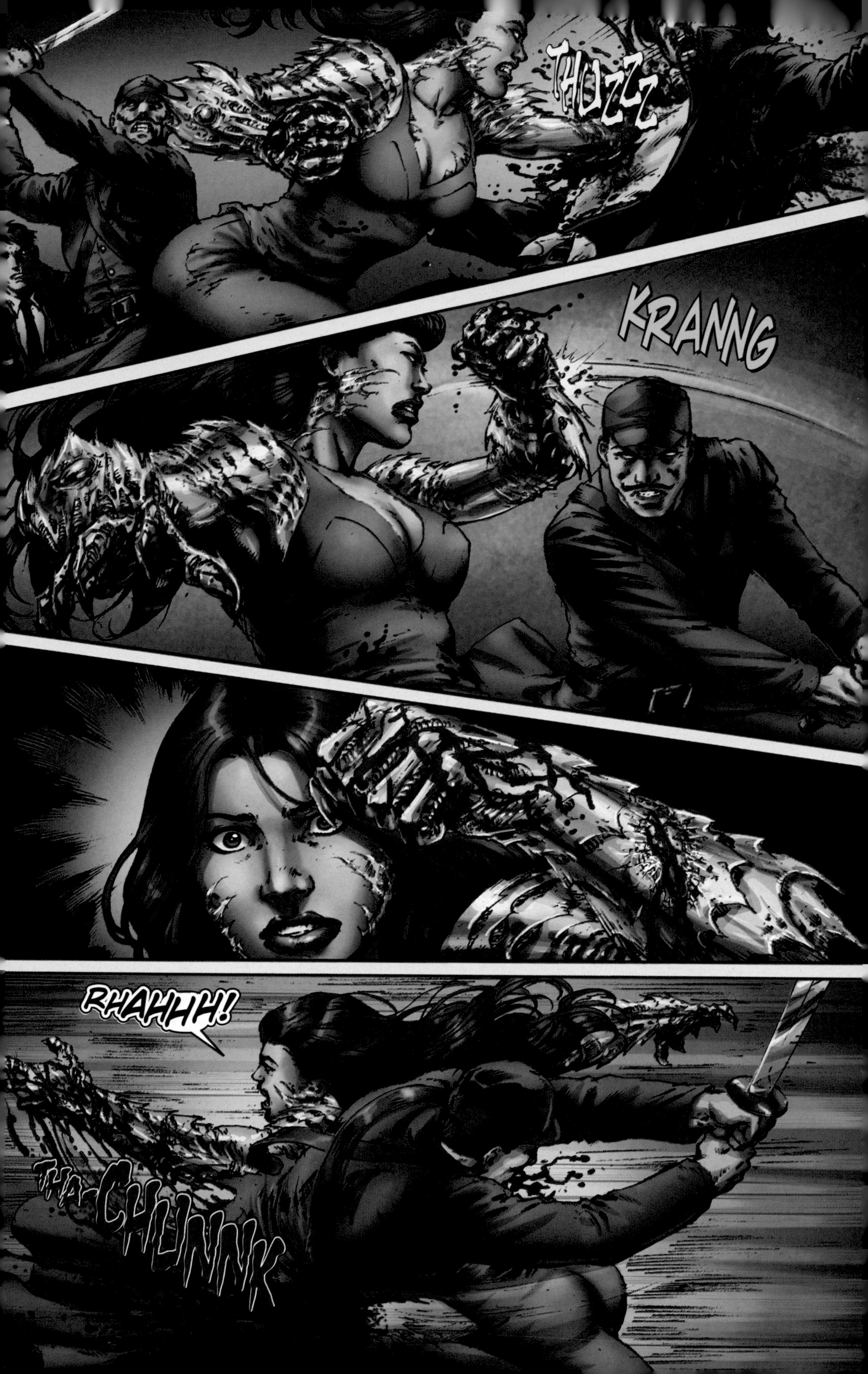
THUZZZ
KRANNG
RHAHHH!
THA-CHUNNK

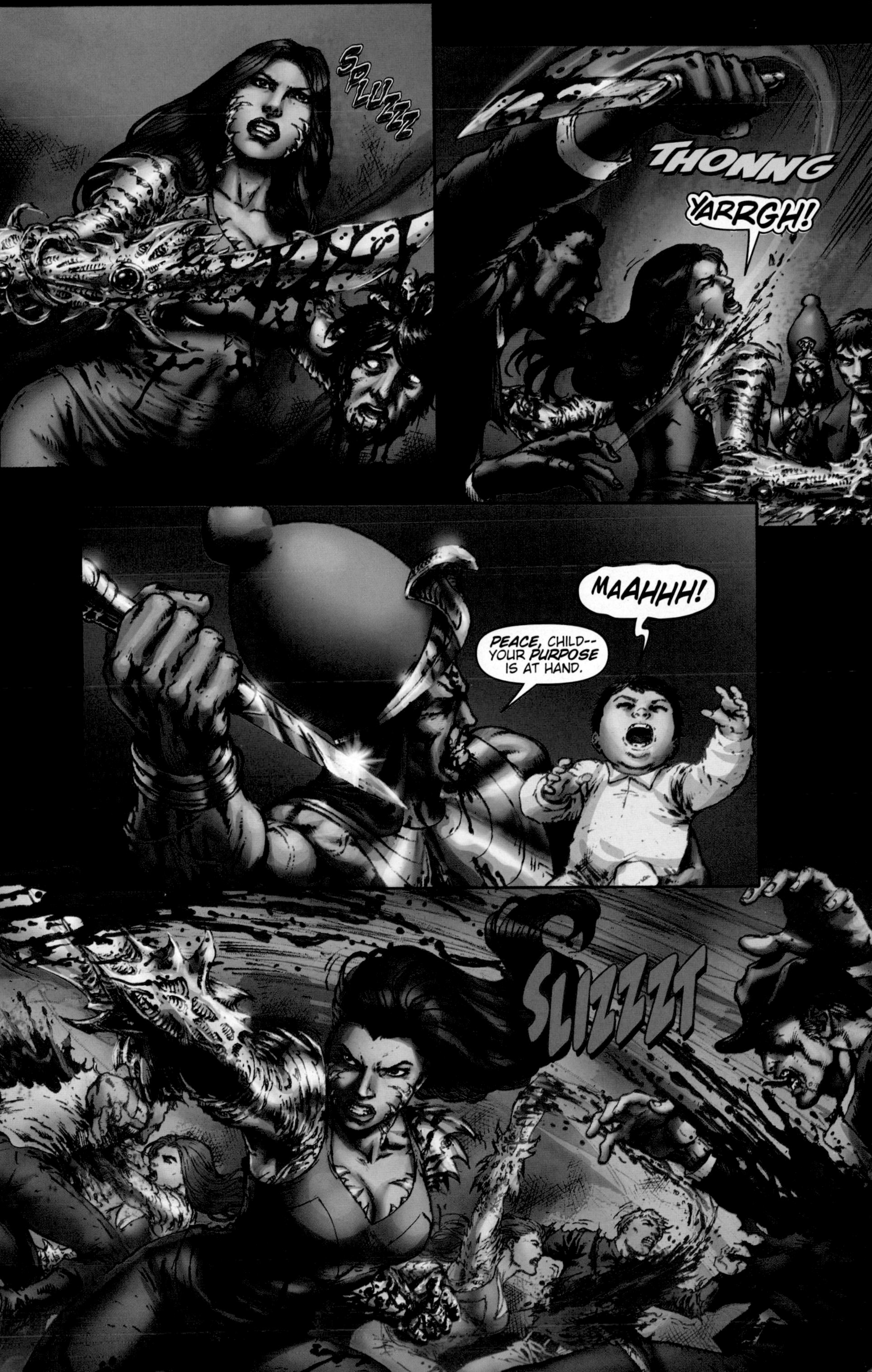
SPLUZZZ
THONNG
YARRGH!
MAAHHH!
PEACE, CHILD-- YOUR PURPOSE IS AT HAND.
SLIZZZT

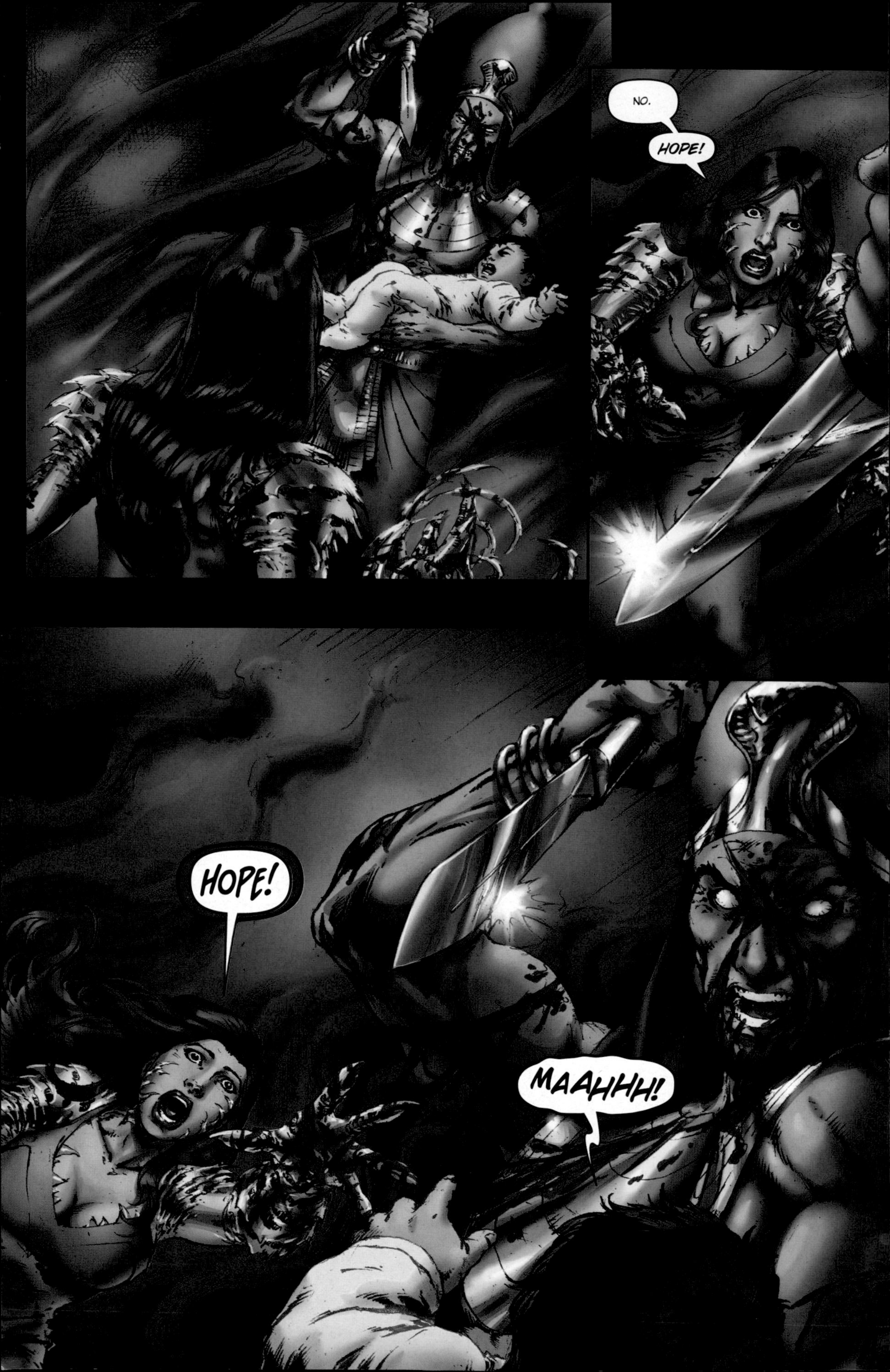
NO.
HOPE!
HOPE!
MAAHHH!

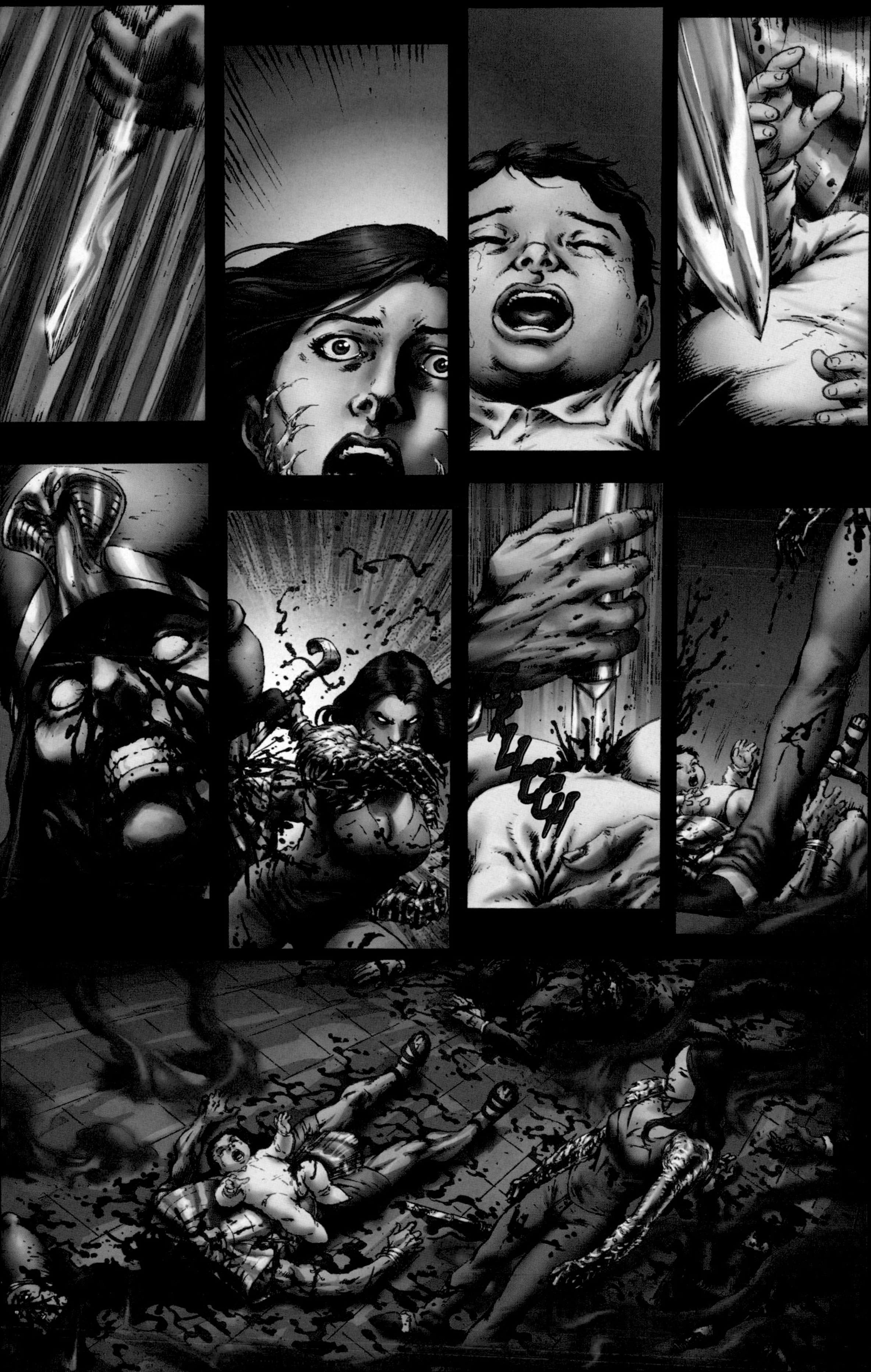

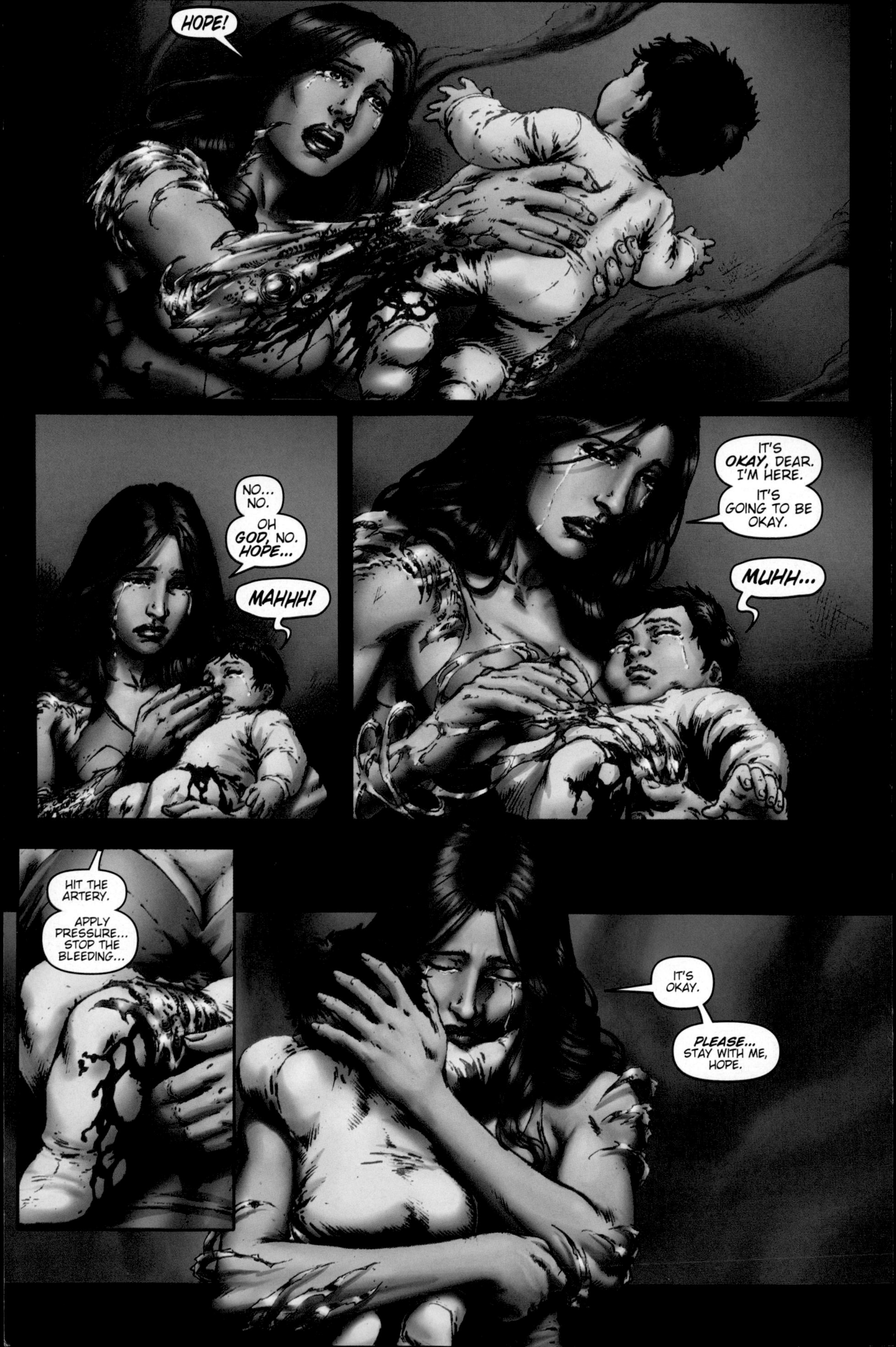
HOPE!
NO... NO. OH GOD, NO. HOPE...
MAHHH!
IT'S OKAY, DEAR. I'M HERE. IT'S GOING TO BE OKAY.
MUHH...
HIT THE ARTERY.
APPLY PRESSURE... STOP THE BLEEDING...
IT'S OKAY.
PLEASE... STAY WITH ME, HOPE.

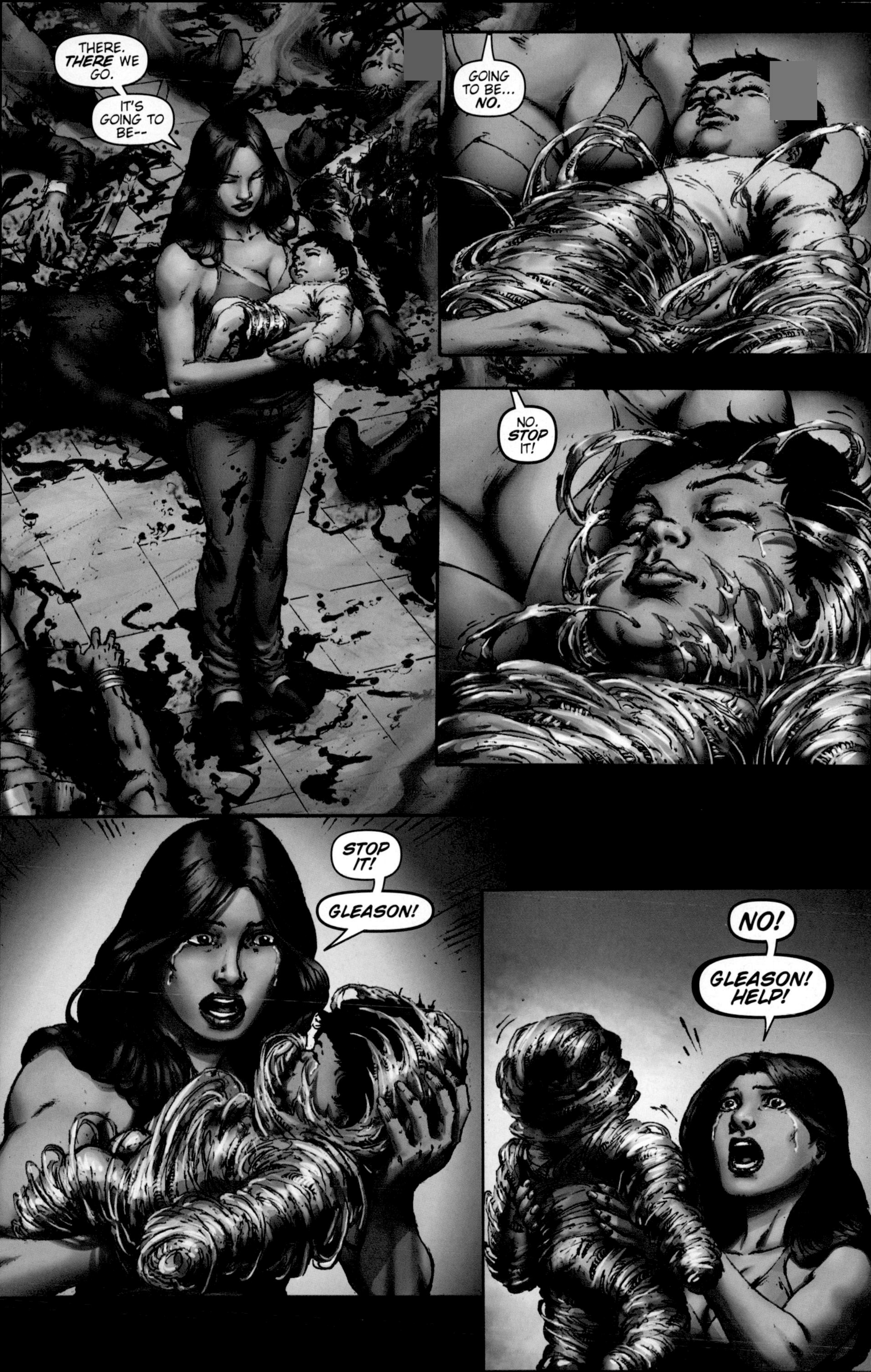
THERE. *THERE* WE GO.
IT'S GOING TO BE--
GOING TO BE... *NO.*
NO. *STOP* IT!
STOP IT!
GLEASON!
NO!
GLEASON! HELP!

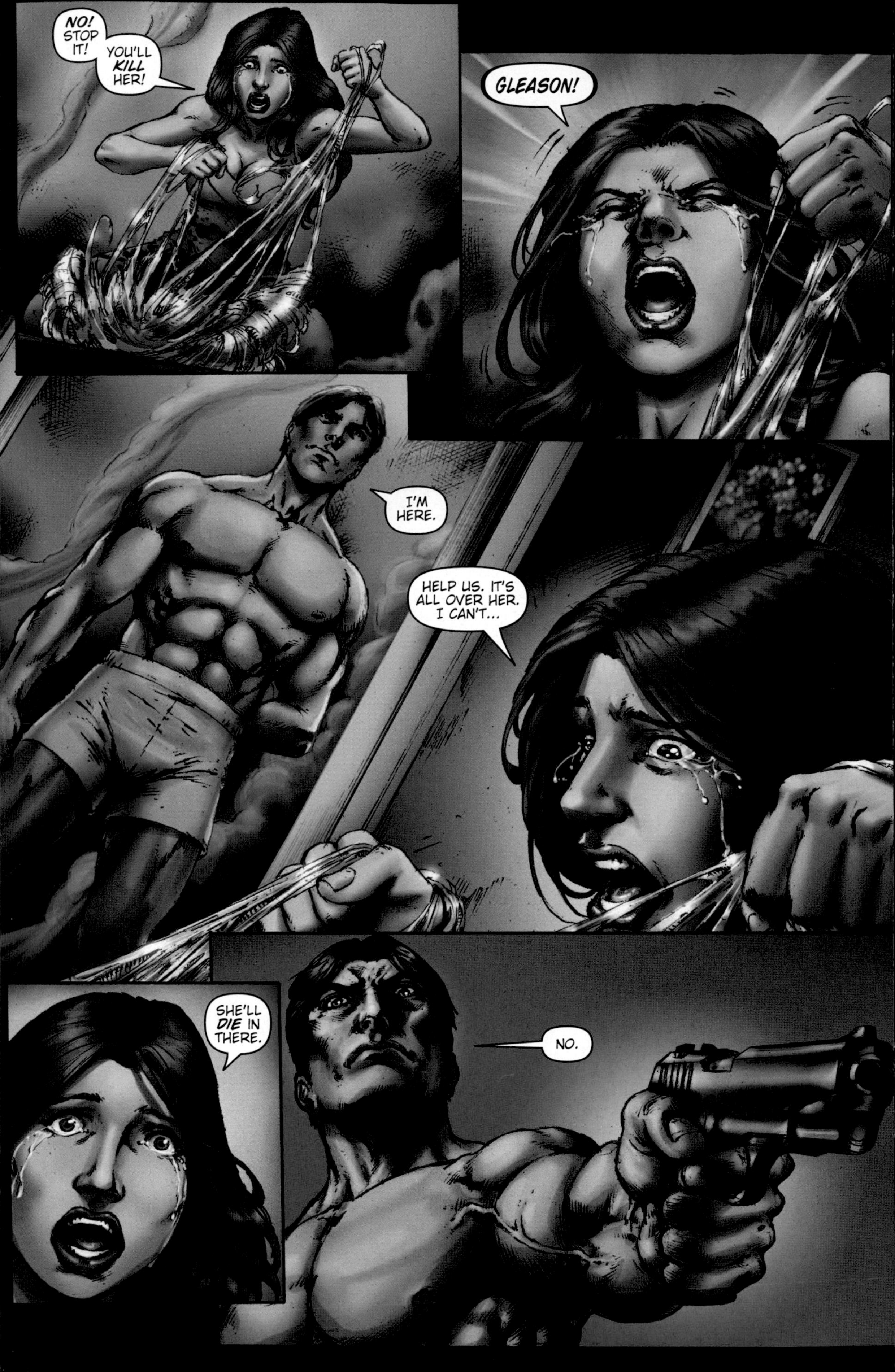
NO! STOP IT!
YOU'LL KILL HER!
GLEASON!
I'M HERE.
HELP US. IT'S ALL OVER HER. I CAN'T...
SHE'LL DIE IN THERE.
NO.

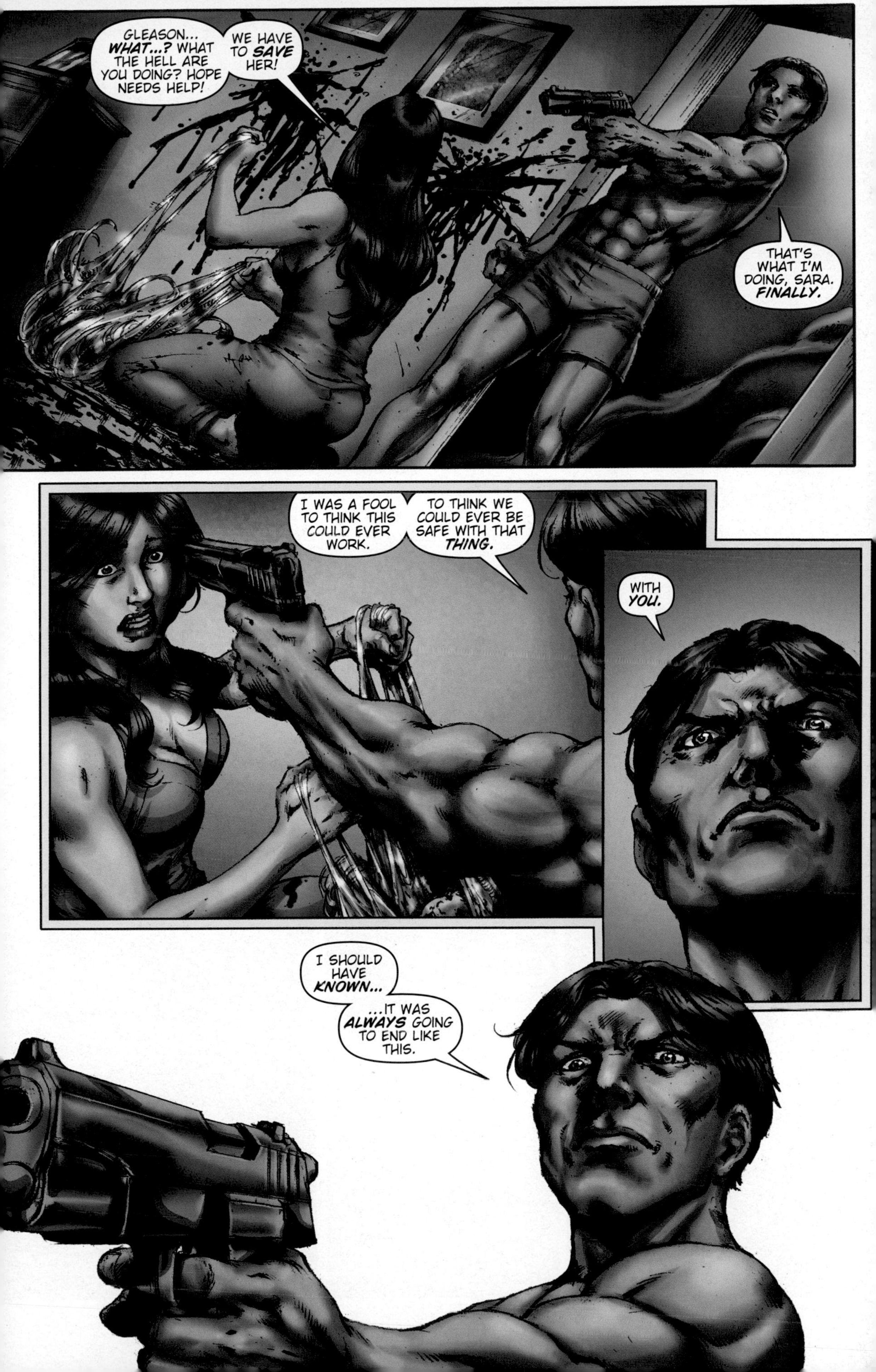
GLEASON... WHAT...? WHAT THE HELL ARE YOU DOING? HOPE NEEDS HELP!
WE HAVE TO SAVE HER!
THAT'S WHAT I'M DOING, SARA. FINALLY.
I WAS A FOOL TO THINK THIS COULD EVER WORK.
TO THINK WE COULD EVER BE SAFE WITH THAT THING.
WITH YOU.
I SHOULD HAVE KNOWN...
...IT WAS ALWAYS GOING TO END LIKE THIS.

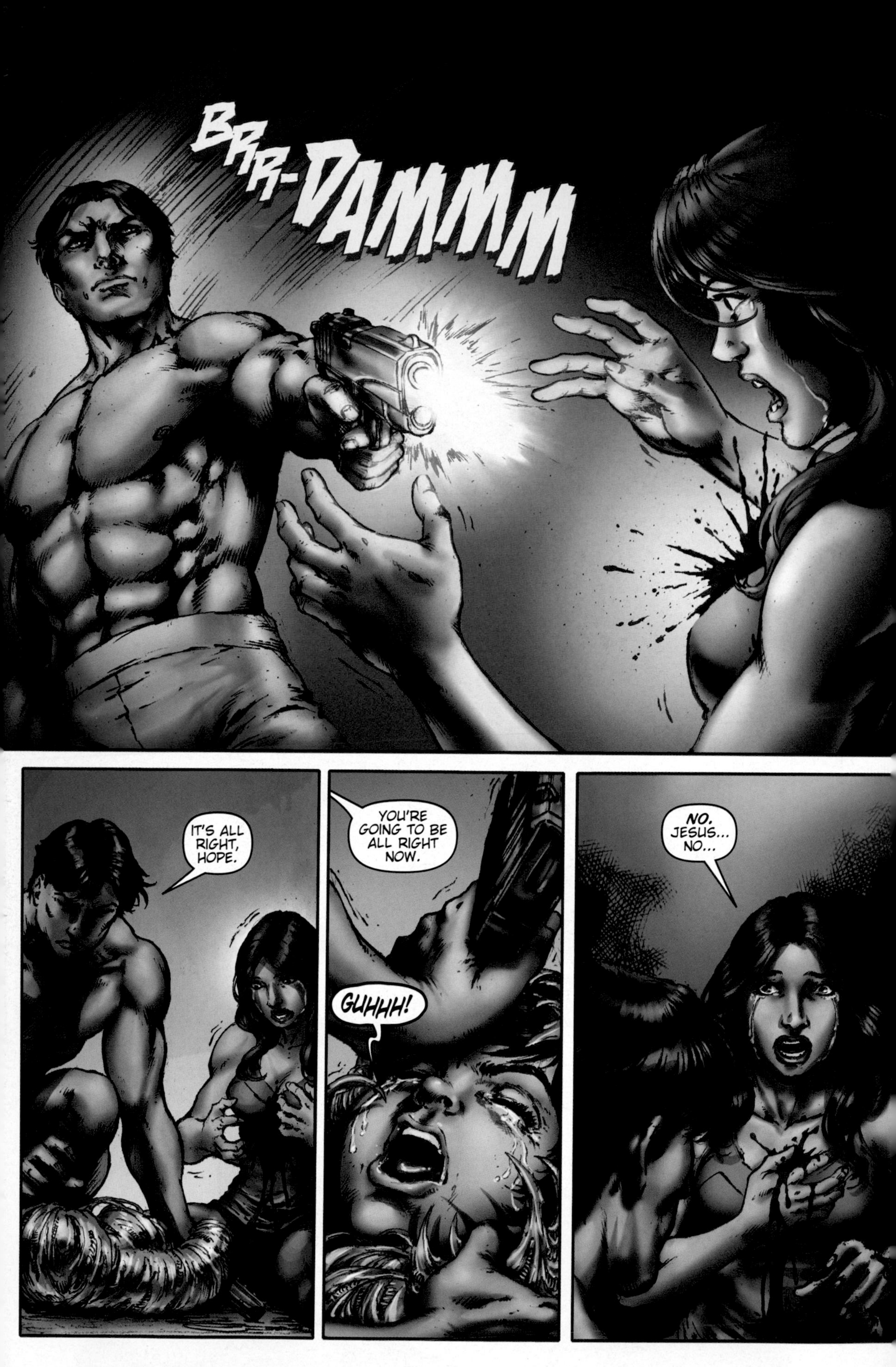
BRR-DAMMMM
IT'S ALL RIGHT, HOPE.
YOU'RE GOING TO BE ALL RIGHT NOW.
GUHHH!
NO. JESUS... NO...

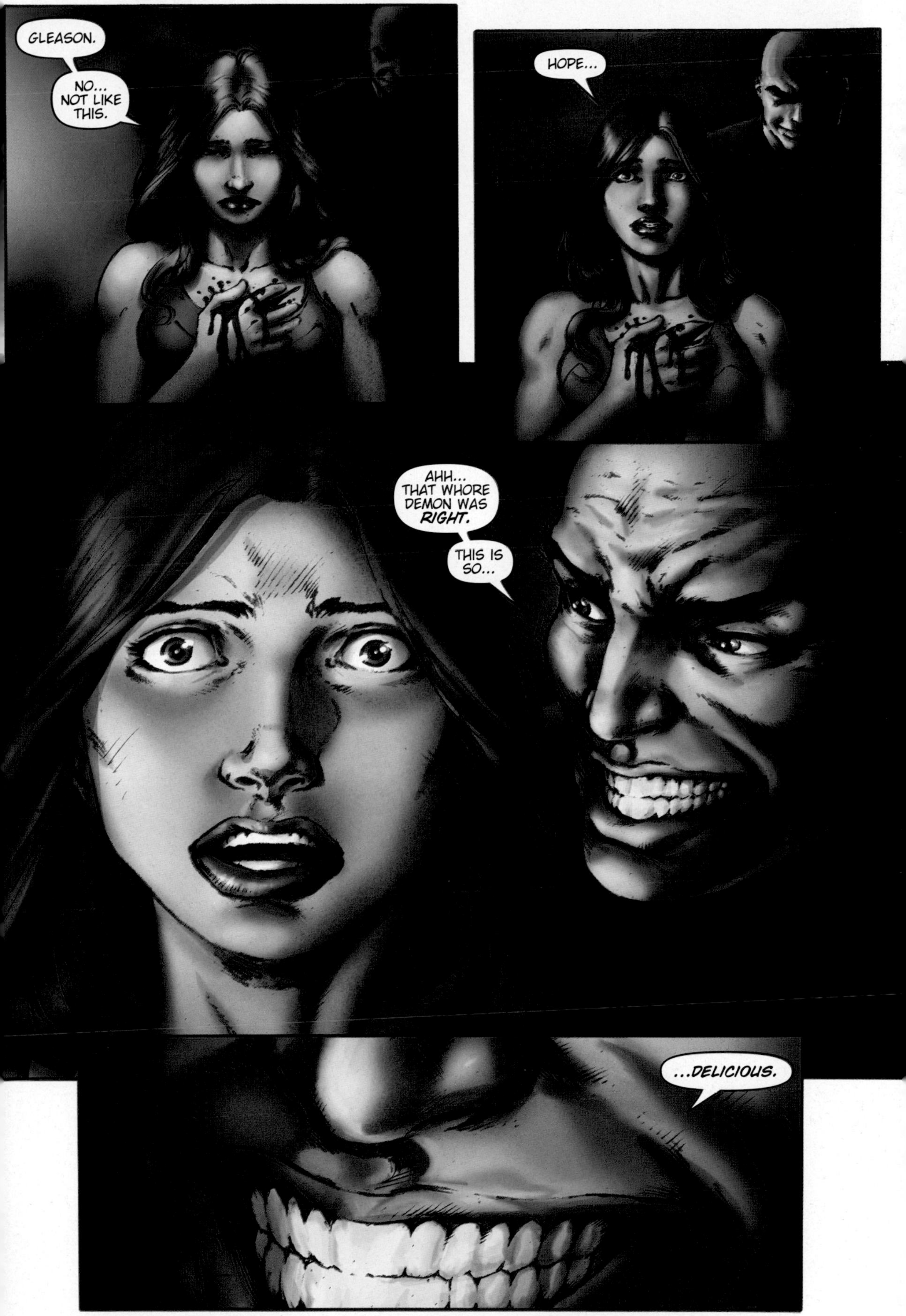
GLEASON.
NO... NOT LIKE THIS.
HOPE...
AHH... THAT WHORE DEMON WAS *RIGHT.*
THIS IS SO...
...DELICIOUS.

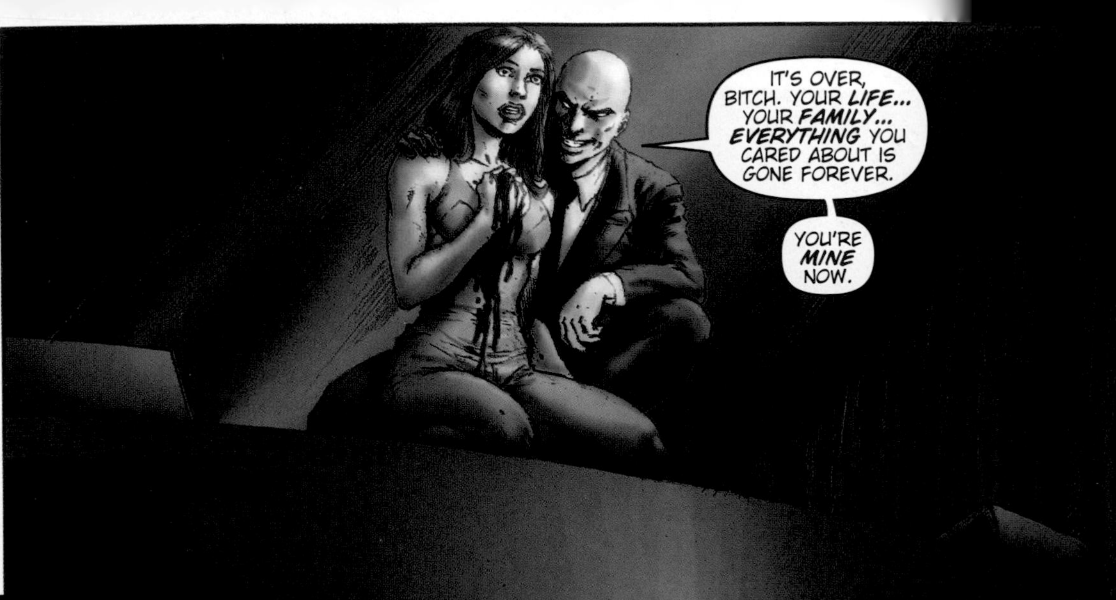
IT'S OVER, BITCH. YOUR LIFE... YOUR FAMILY... EVERYTHING YOU CARED ABOUT IS GONE FOREVER.
YOU'RE MINE NOW.

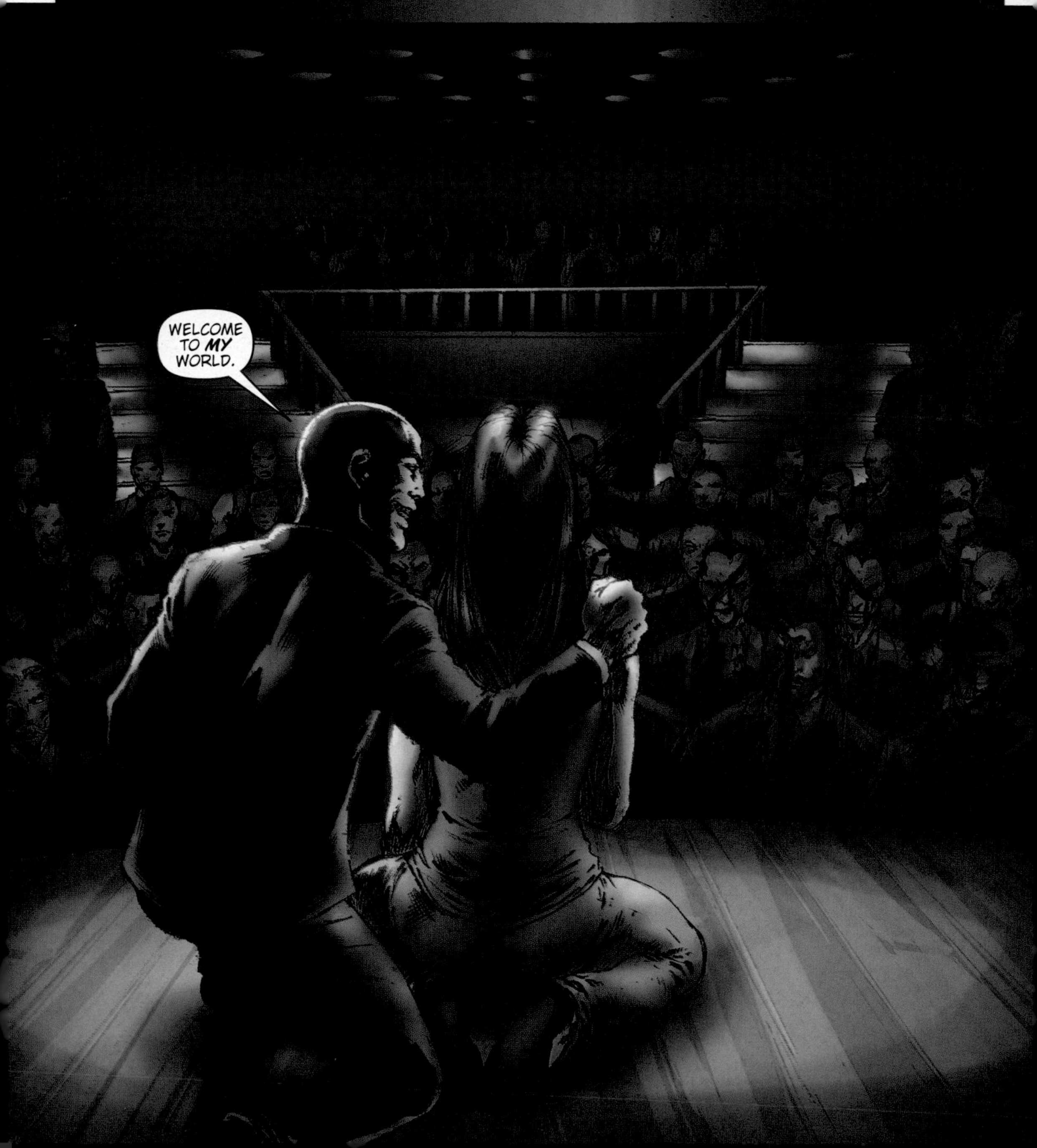
WELCOME TO MY WORLD.

WITCHBLADE
DEMON REBORN

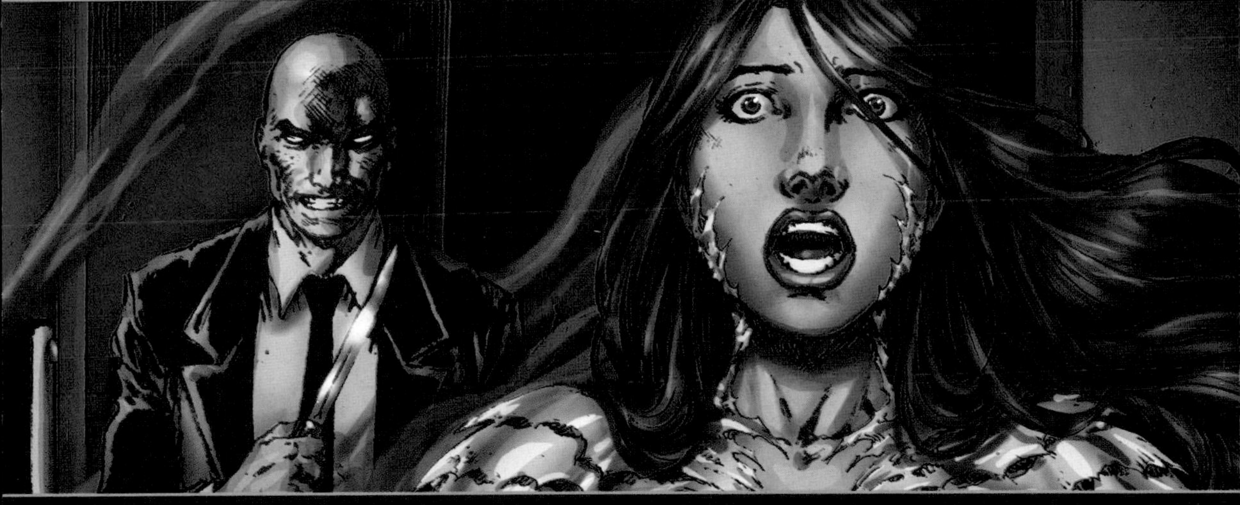

CHAPTER FOUR

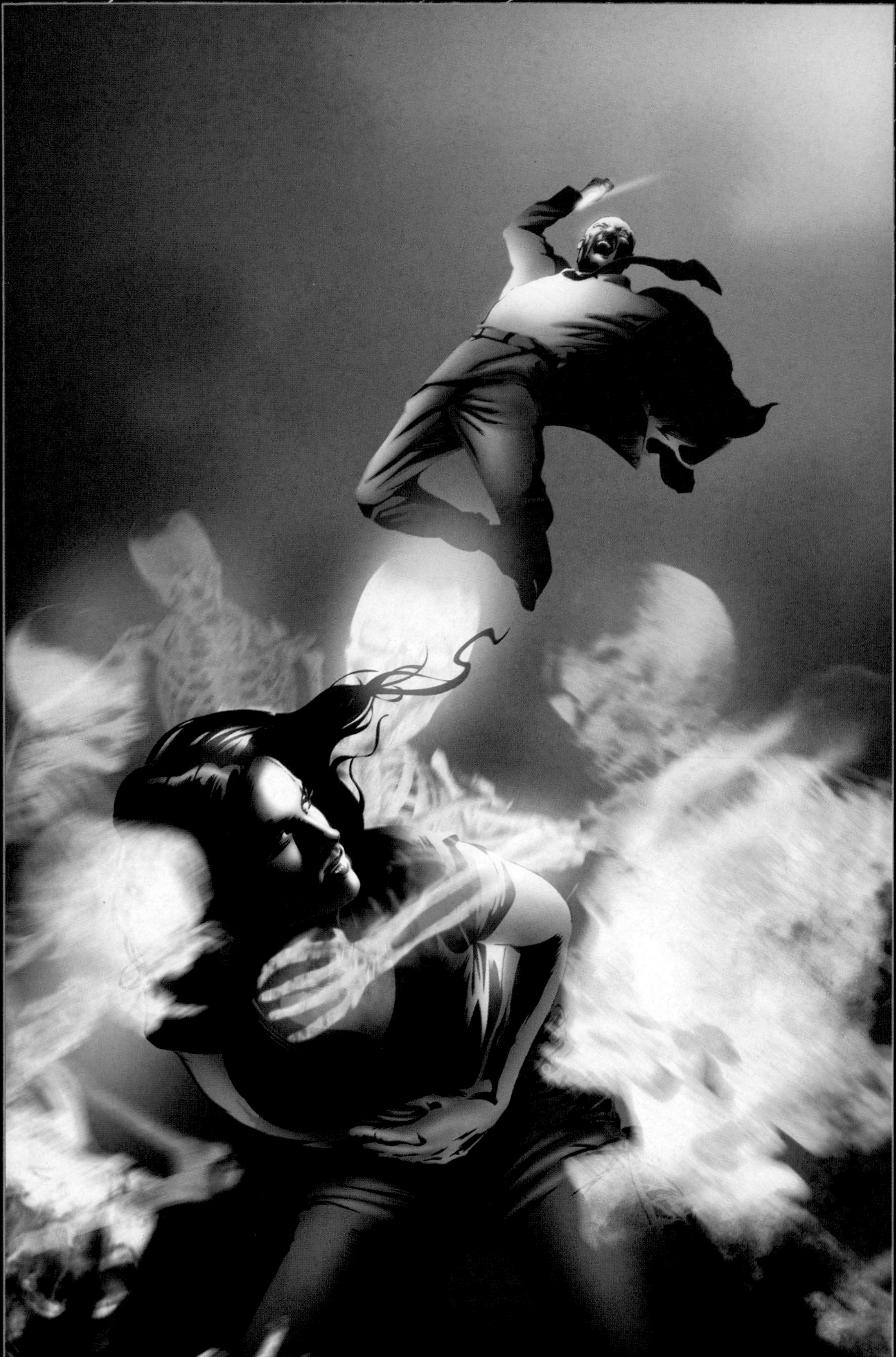

ISSUE #4 COVER BY DENNIS CALERO

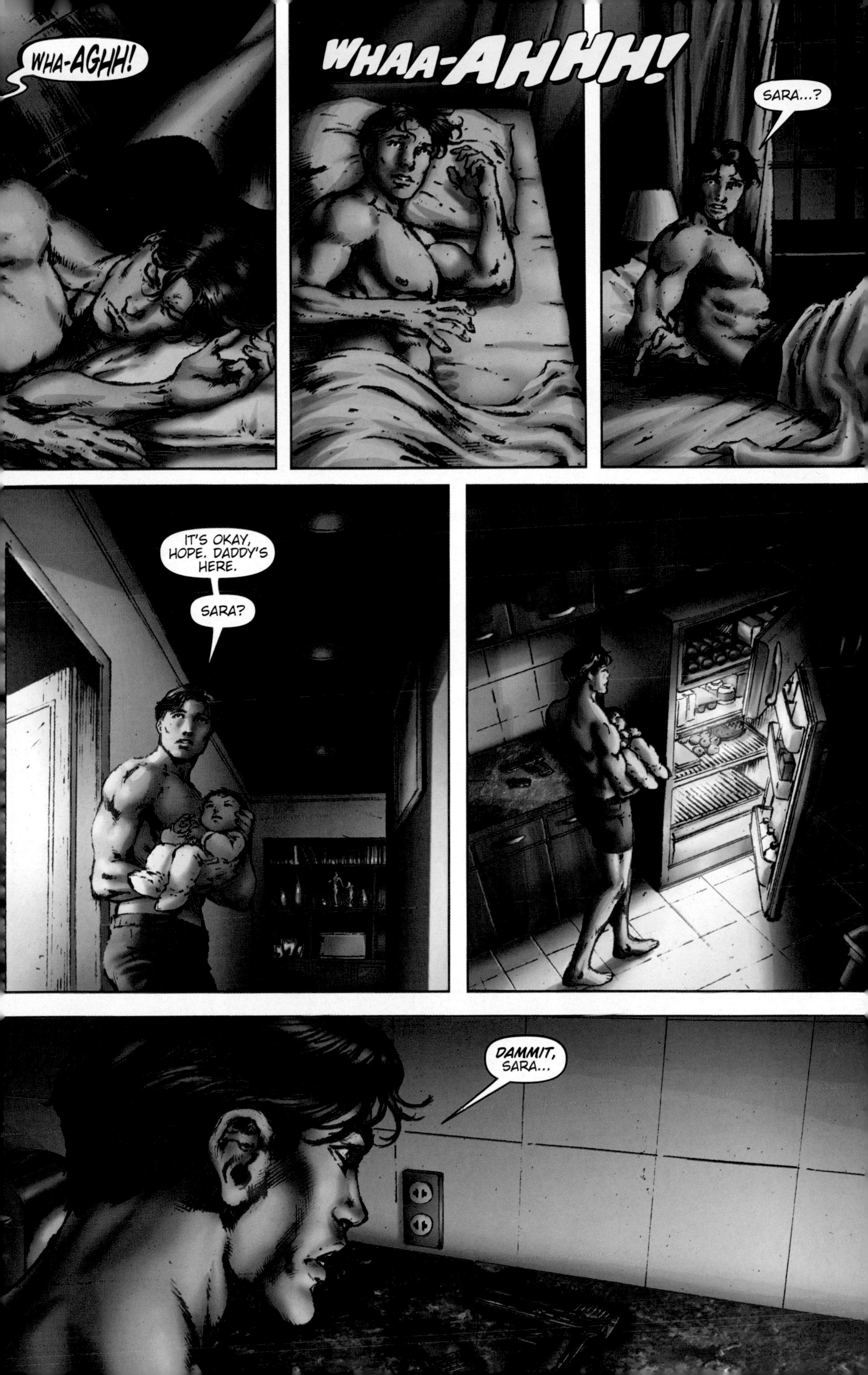

WHA-AGHH!
WHAA-AHHH!
SARA...?
IT'S OKAY, HOPE. DADDY'S HERE.
SARA?
DAMMIT, SARA...

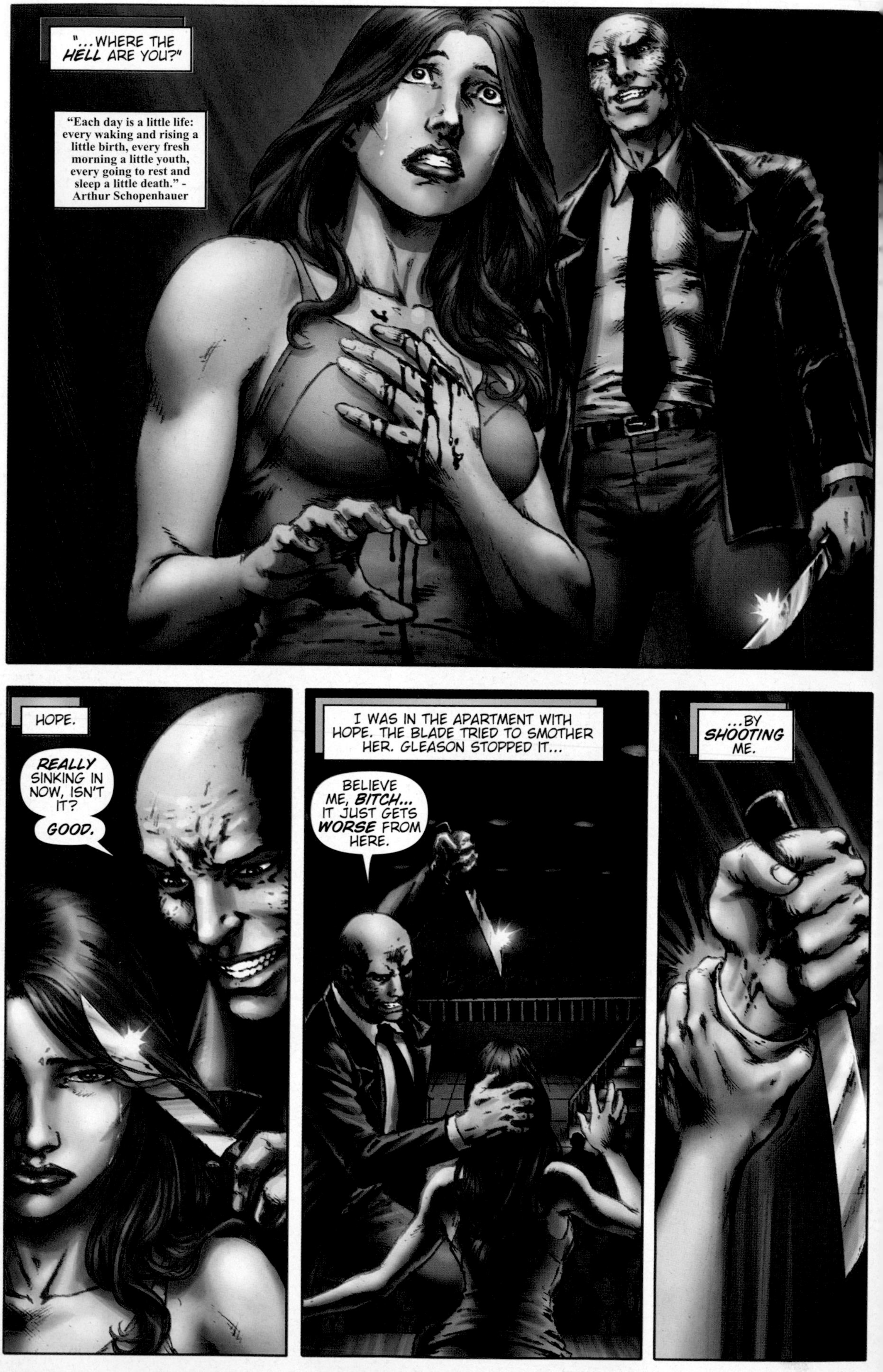
"...WHERE THE HELL ARE YOU?"
"Each day is a little life: every waking and rising a little birth, every fresh morning a little youth, every going to rest and sleep a little death." - Arthur Schopenhauer
HOPE.
REALLY SINKING IN NOW, ISN'T IT? GOOD.
I WAS IN THE APARTMENT WITH HOPE. THE BLADE TRIED TO SMOTHER HER. GLEASON STOPPED IT...
BELIEVE ME, BITCH... IT JUST GETS WORSE FROM HERE.
...BY SHOOTING ME.

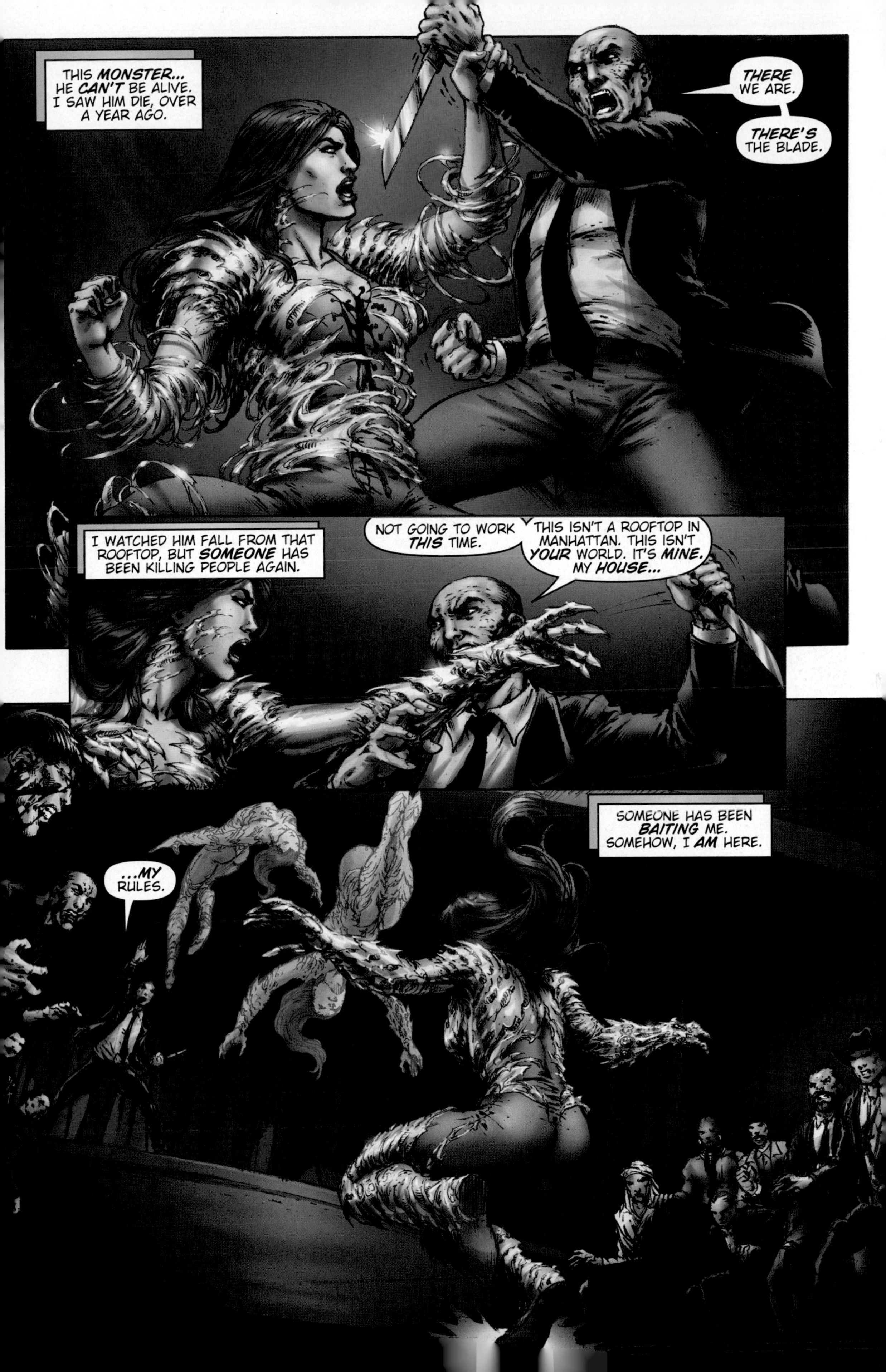

THIS MONSTER... HE CAN'T BE ALIVE. I SAW HIM DIE, OVER A YEAR AGO.
THERE WE ARE.
THERE'S THE BLADE.
I WATCHED HIM FALL FROM THAT ROOFTOP, BUT SOMEONE HAS BEEN KILLING PEOPLE AGAIN.
NOT GOING TO WORK THIS TIME.
THIS ISN'T A ROOFTOP IN MANHATTAN. THIS ISN'T YOUR WORLD. IT'S MINE. MY HOUSE...
...MY RULES.
SOMEONE HAS BEEN BAITING ME. SOMEHOW, I AM HERE.

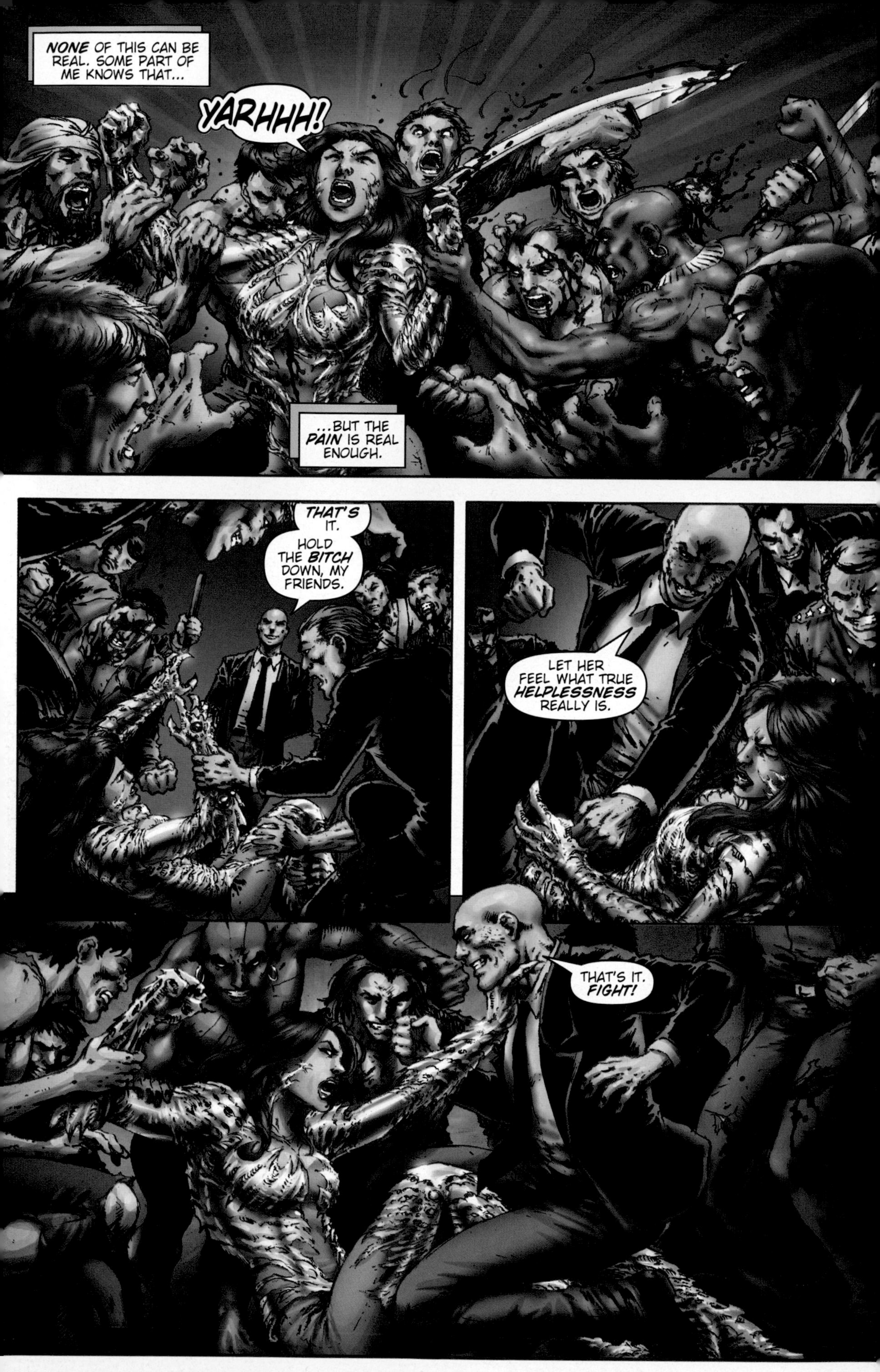
NONE OF THIS CAN BE REAL. SOME PART OF ME KNOWS THAT...
YARHHH!
...BUT THE PAIN IS REAL ENOUGH.
THAT'S IT.
HOLD THE BITCH DOWN, MY FRIENDS.
LET HER FEEL WHAT TRUE HELPLESSNESS REALLY IS.
THAT'S IT. FIGHT!

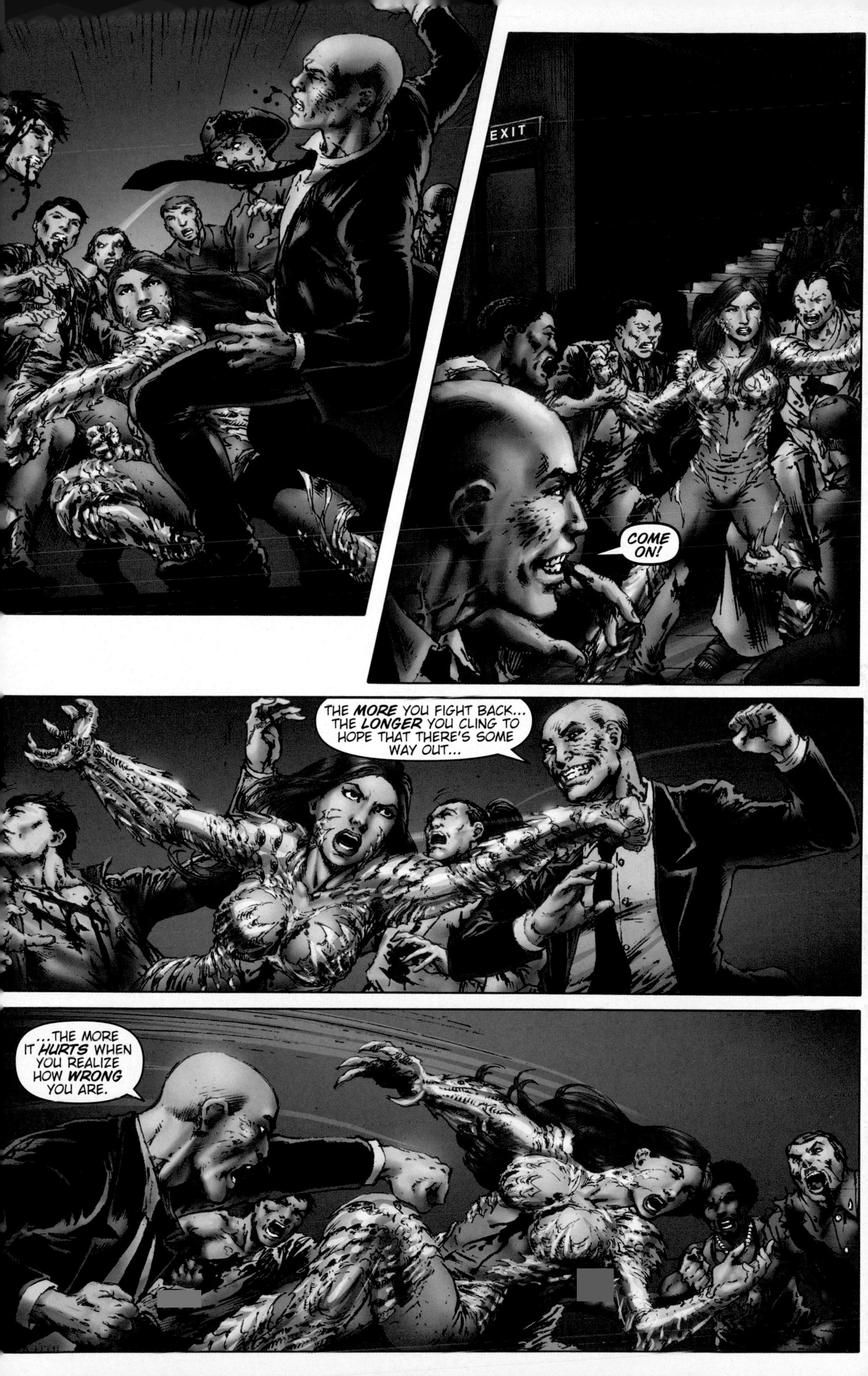
EXIT
COME ON!
THE MORE YOU FIGHT BACK... THE LONGER YOU CLING TO HOPE THAT THERE'S SOME WAY OUT...
...THE MORE IT HURTS WHEN YOU REALIZE HOW WRONG YOU ARE.

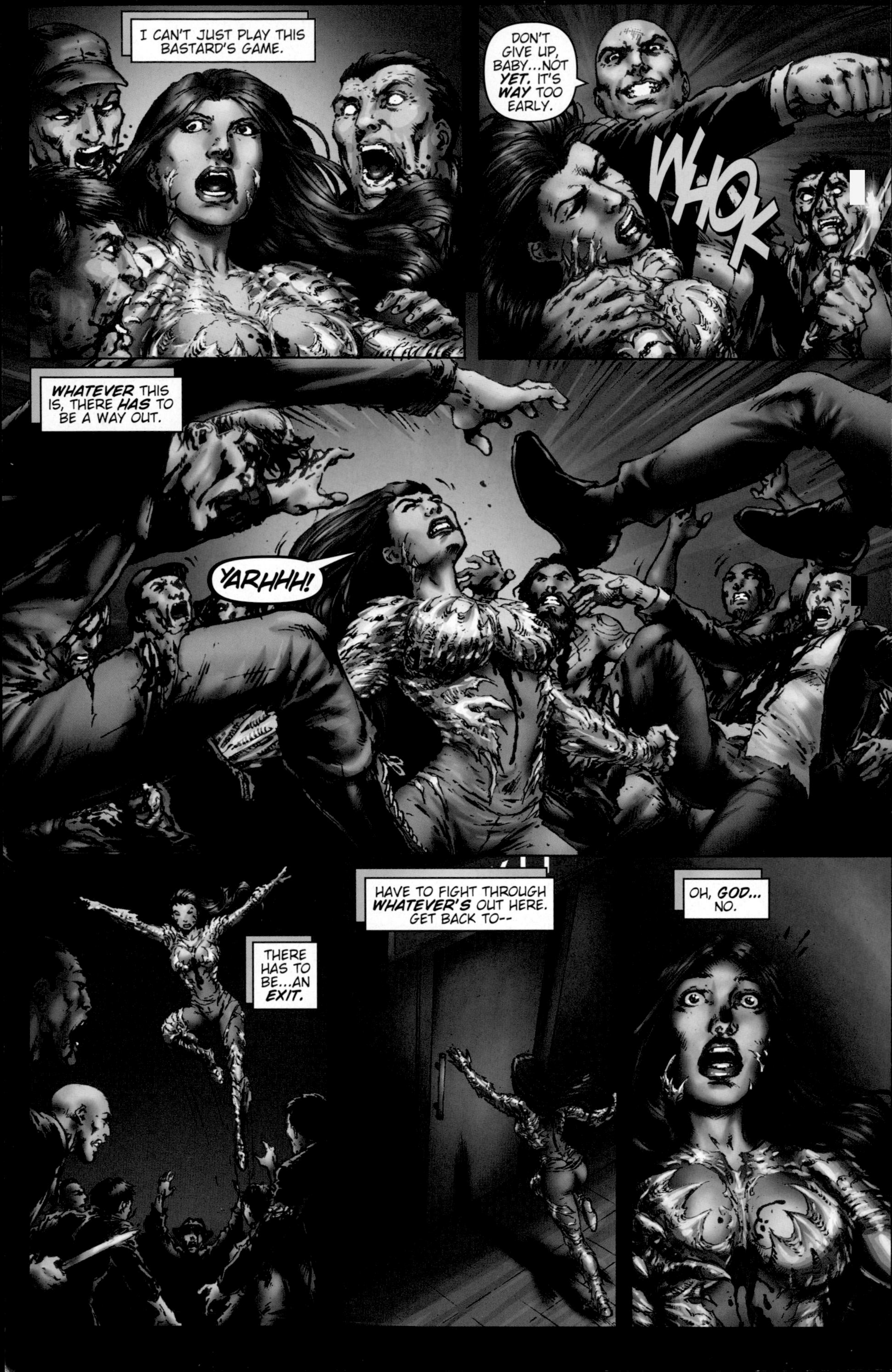
I CAN'T JUST PLAY THIS BASTARD'S GAME.
DON'T GIVE UP, BABY...NOT YET. IT'S WAY TOO EARLY.
WHOK
WHATEVER THIS IS, THERE HAS TO BE A WAY OUT.
YARHHH!
THERE HAS TO BE...AN EXIT.
HAVE TO FIGHT THROUGH WHATEVER'S OUT HERE. GET BACK TO--
OH, GOD... NO.

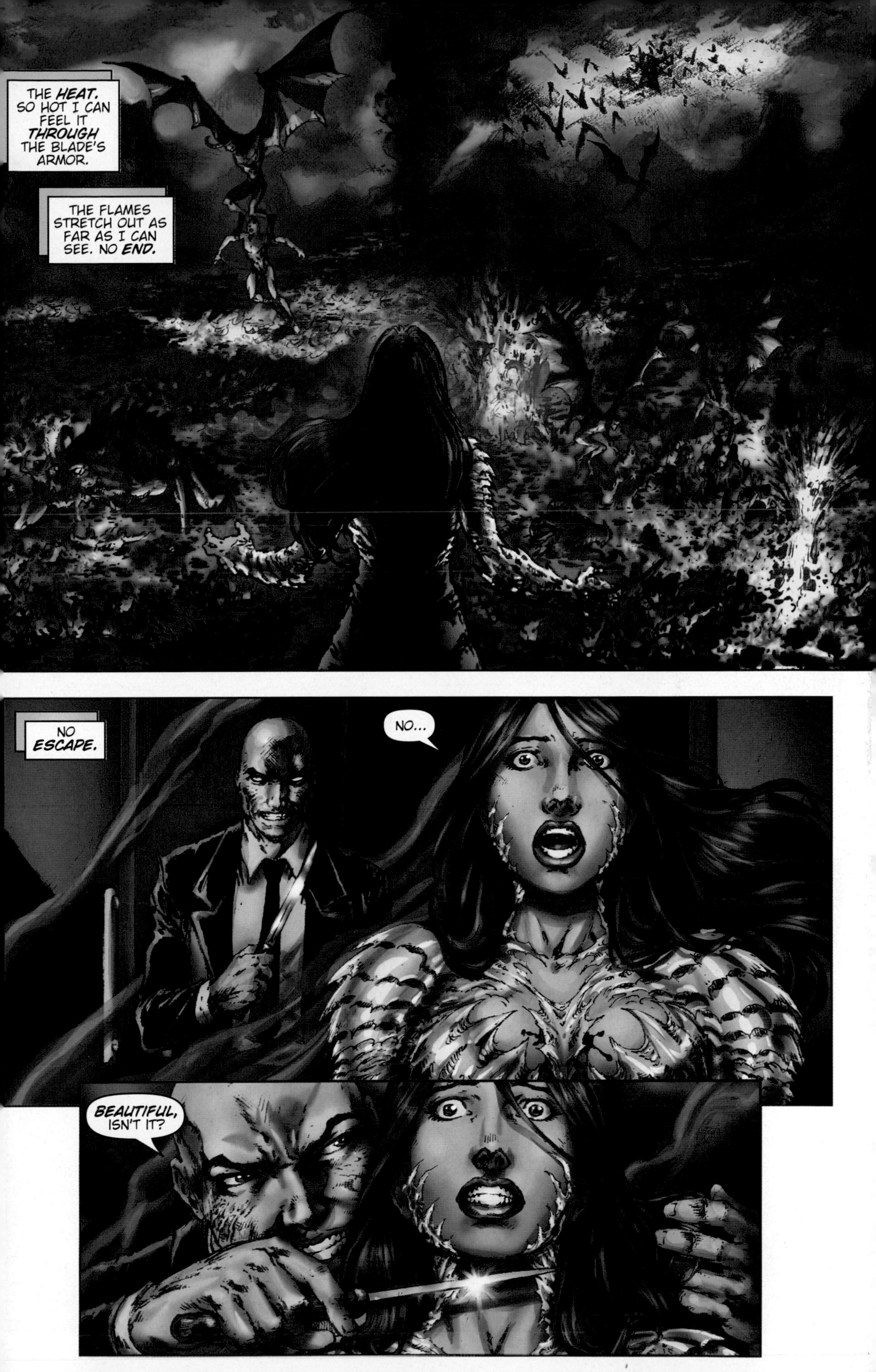
THE **HEAT.** SO HOT I CAN FEEL IT ***THROUGH*** THE BLADE'S ARMOR.
THE FLAMES STRETCH OUT AS FAR AS I CAN SEE. NO ***END.***
NO ***ESCAPE.***
NO...
BEAUTIFUL, ISN'T IT?

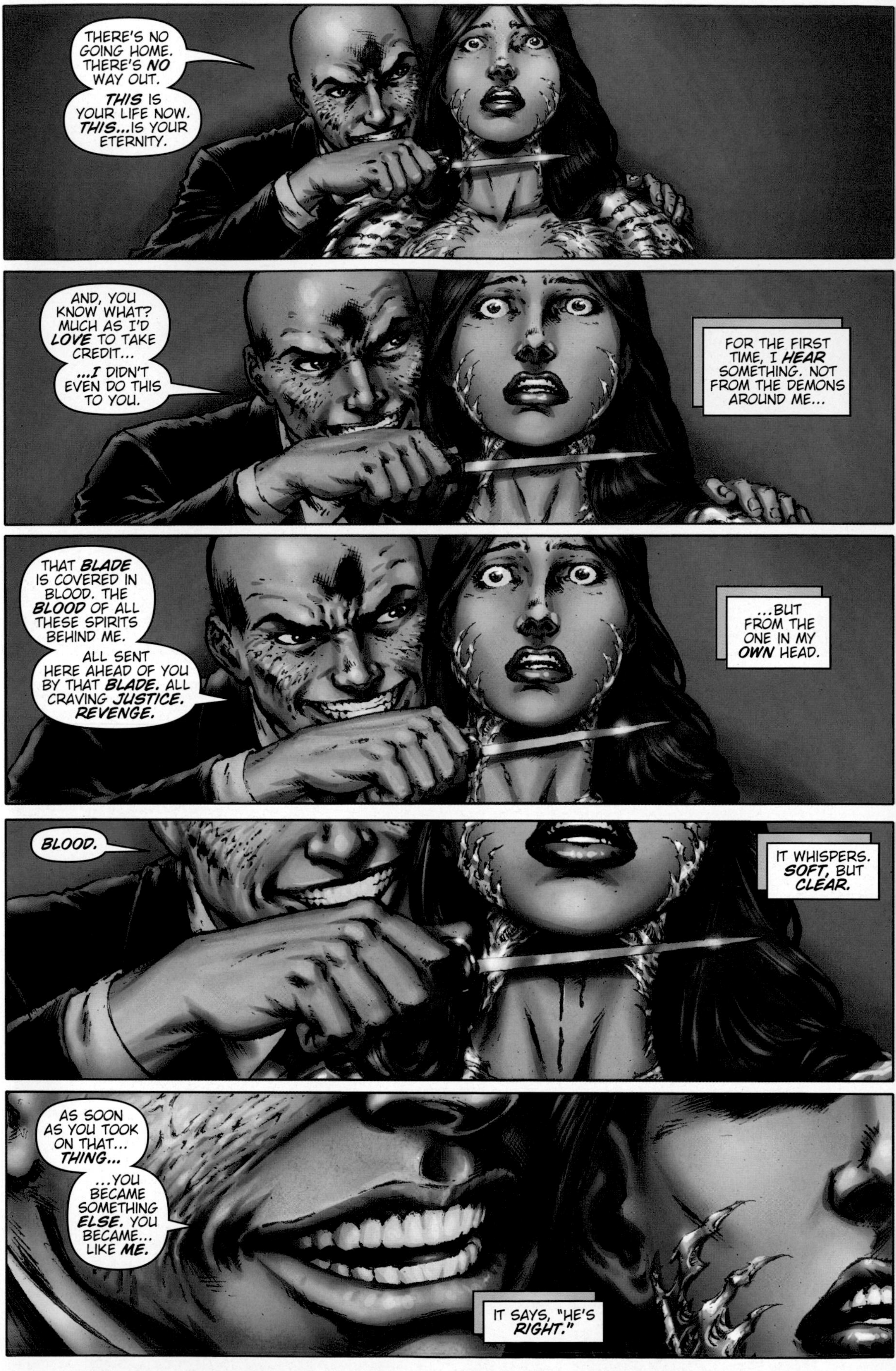
THERE'S NO GOING HOME. THERE'S NO WAY OUT.
THIS IS YOUR LIFE NOW. THIS...IS YOUR ETERNITY.
AND, YOU KNOW WHAT? MUCH AS I'D LOVE TO TAKE CREDIT...
...I DIDN'T EVEN DO THIS TO YOU.
FOR THE FIRST TIME, I HEAR SOMETHING. NOT FROM THE DEMONS AROUND ME...
THAT BLADE IS COVERED IN BLOOD. THE BLOOD OF ALL THESE SPIRITS BEHIND ME.
ALL SENT HERE AHEAD OF YOU BY THAT BLADE. ALL CRAVING JUSTICE. REVENGE.
...BUT FROM THE ONE IN MY OWN HEAD.
BLOOD.
IT WHISPERS. SOFT, BUT CLEAR.
AS SOON AS YOU TOOK ON THAT... THING...
...YOU BECAME SOMETHING ELSE. YOU BECAME... LIKE ME.
IT SAYS, "HE'S RIGHT."

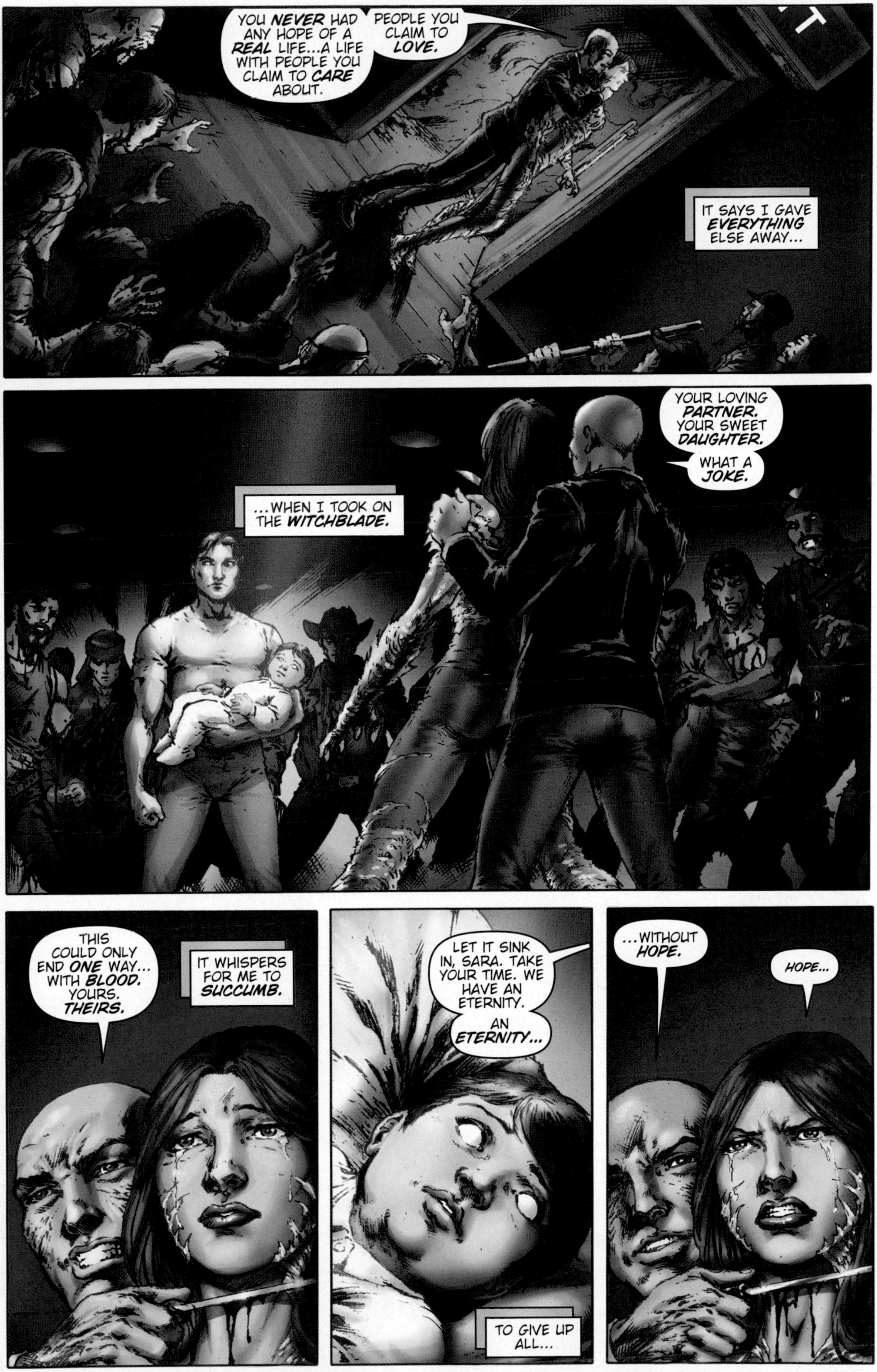

YOU NEVER HAD ANY HOPE OF A REAL LIFE...A LIFE WITH PEOPLE YOU CLAIM TO CARE ABOUT.
PEOPLE YOU CLAIM TO LOVE.
IT SAYS I GAVE EVERYTHING ELSE AWAY...
...WHEN I TOOK ON THE WITCHBLADE.
YOUR LOVING PARTNER. YOUR SWEET DAUGHTER.
WHAT A JOKE.
THIS COULD ONLY END ONE WAY... WITH BLOOD. YOURS. THEIRS.
IT WHISPERS FOR ME TO SUCCUMB.
LET IT SINK IN, SARA. TAKE YOUR TIME. WE HAVE AN ETERNITY.
AN ETERNITY...
TO GIVE UP ALL...
...WITHOUT HOPE.
HOPE...

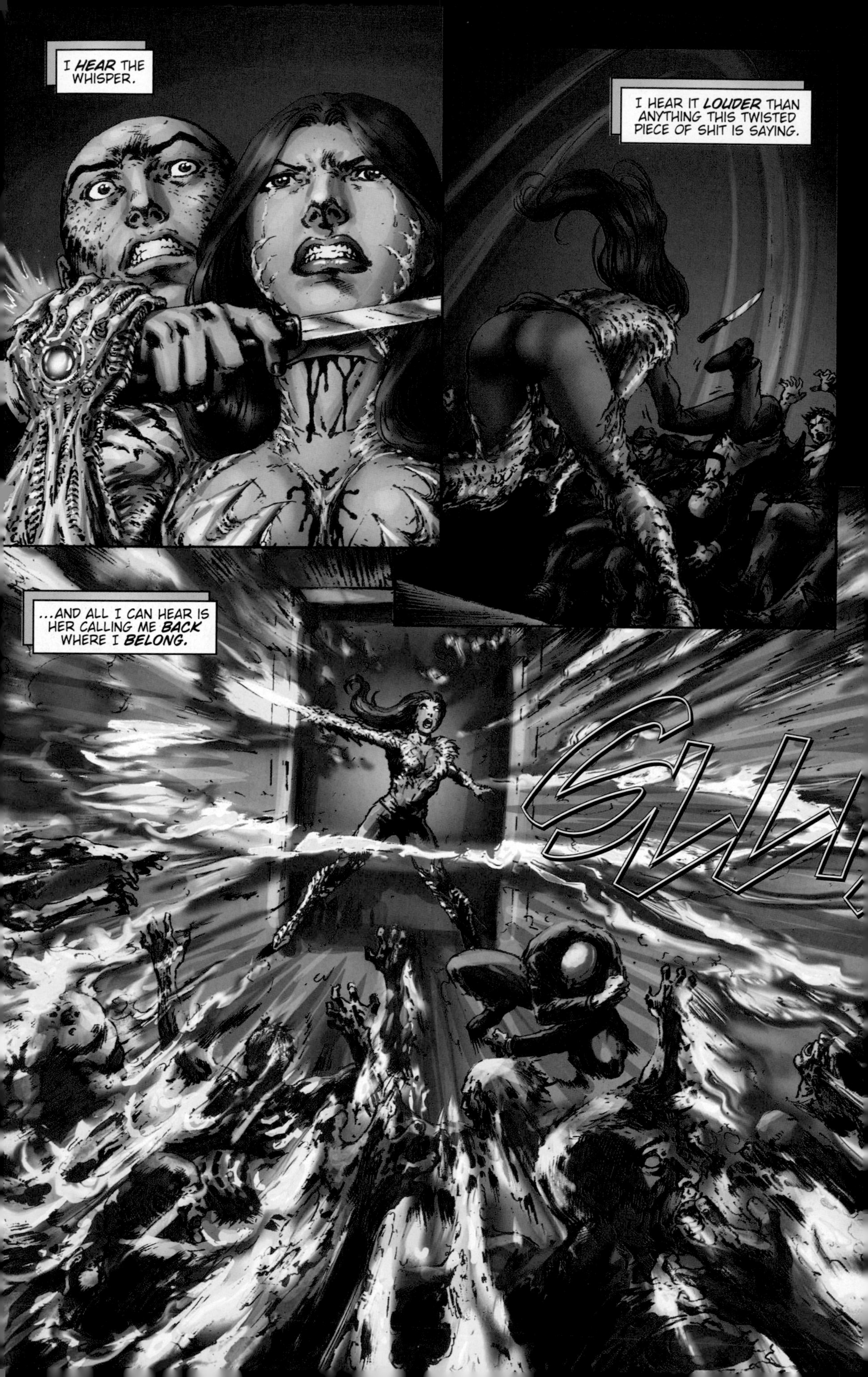
I HEAR THE WHISPER.
I HEAR IT LOUDER THAN ANYTHING THIS TWISTED PIECE OF SHIT IS SAYING.
...AND ALL I CAN HEAR IS HER CALLING ME BACK WHERE I BELONG.

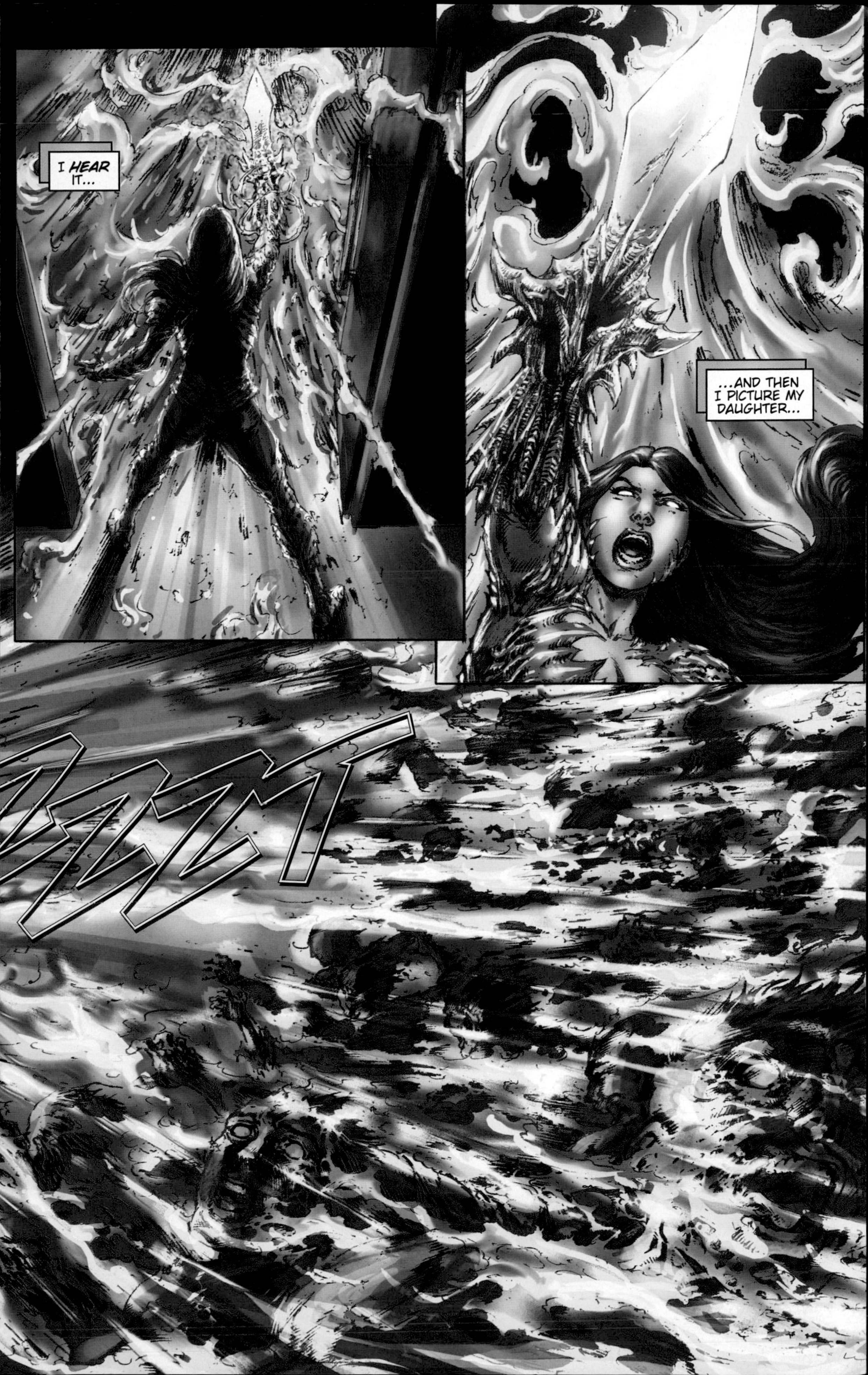
I HEAR IT...
...AND THEN I PICTURE MY DAUGHTER...

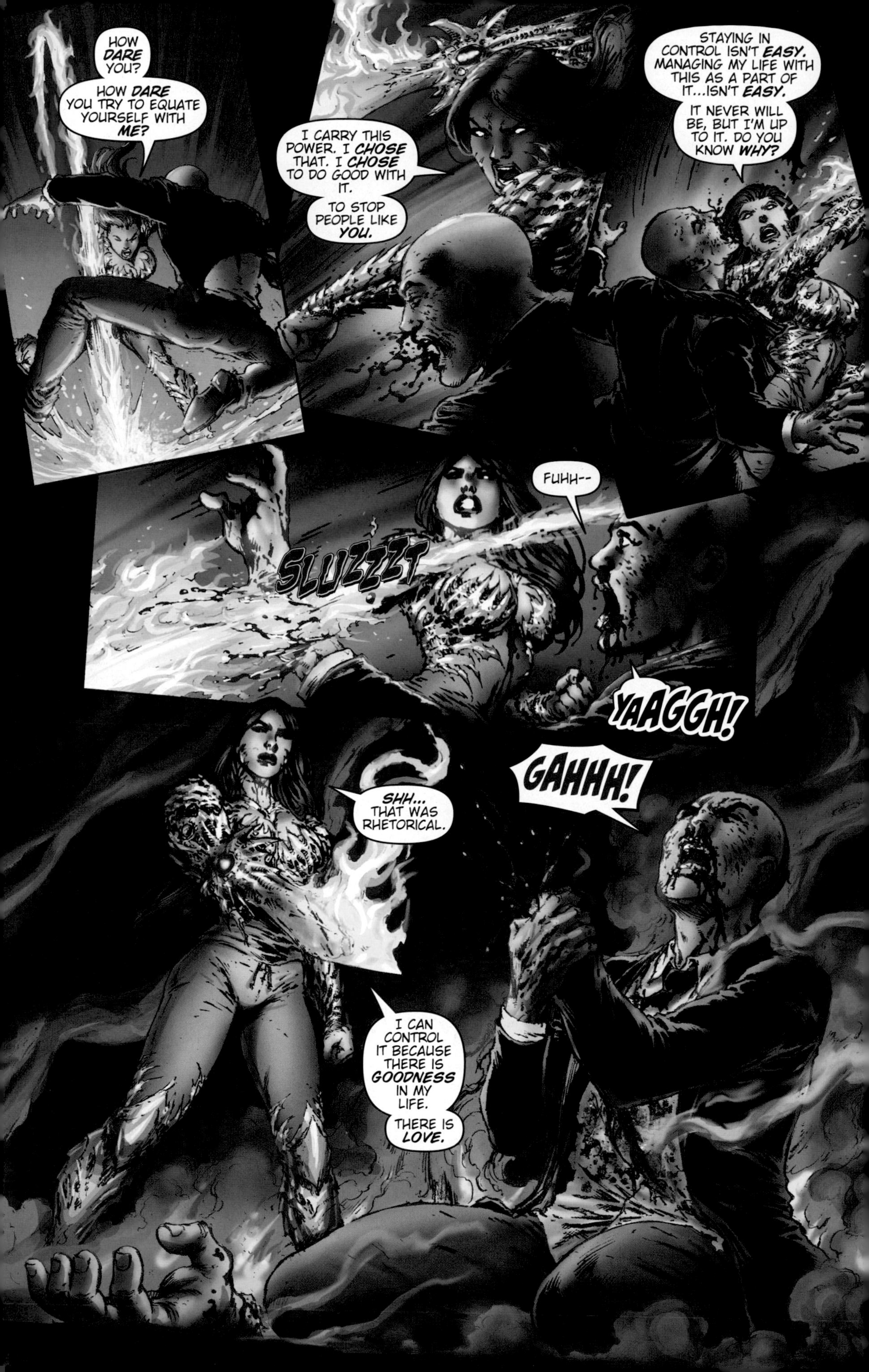
HOW DARE YOU?
HOW DARE YOU TRY TO EQUATE YOURSELF WITH ME?
I CARRY THIS POWER. I CHOSE THAT. I CHOSE TO DO GOOD WITH IT.
TO STOP PEOPLE LIKE YOU.
STAYING IN CONTROL ISN'T EASY. MANAGING MY LIFE WITH THIS AS A PART OF IT...ISN'T EASY.
IT NEVER WILL BE, BUT I'M UP TO IT. DO YOU KNOW WHY?
FUHH--
SLUZZZT
YAAGGH!
GAHHH!
SHH... THAT WAS RHETORICAL.
I CAN CONTROL IT BECAUSE THERE IS GOODNESS IN MY LIFE.
THERE IS LOVE.

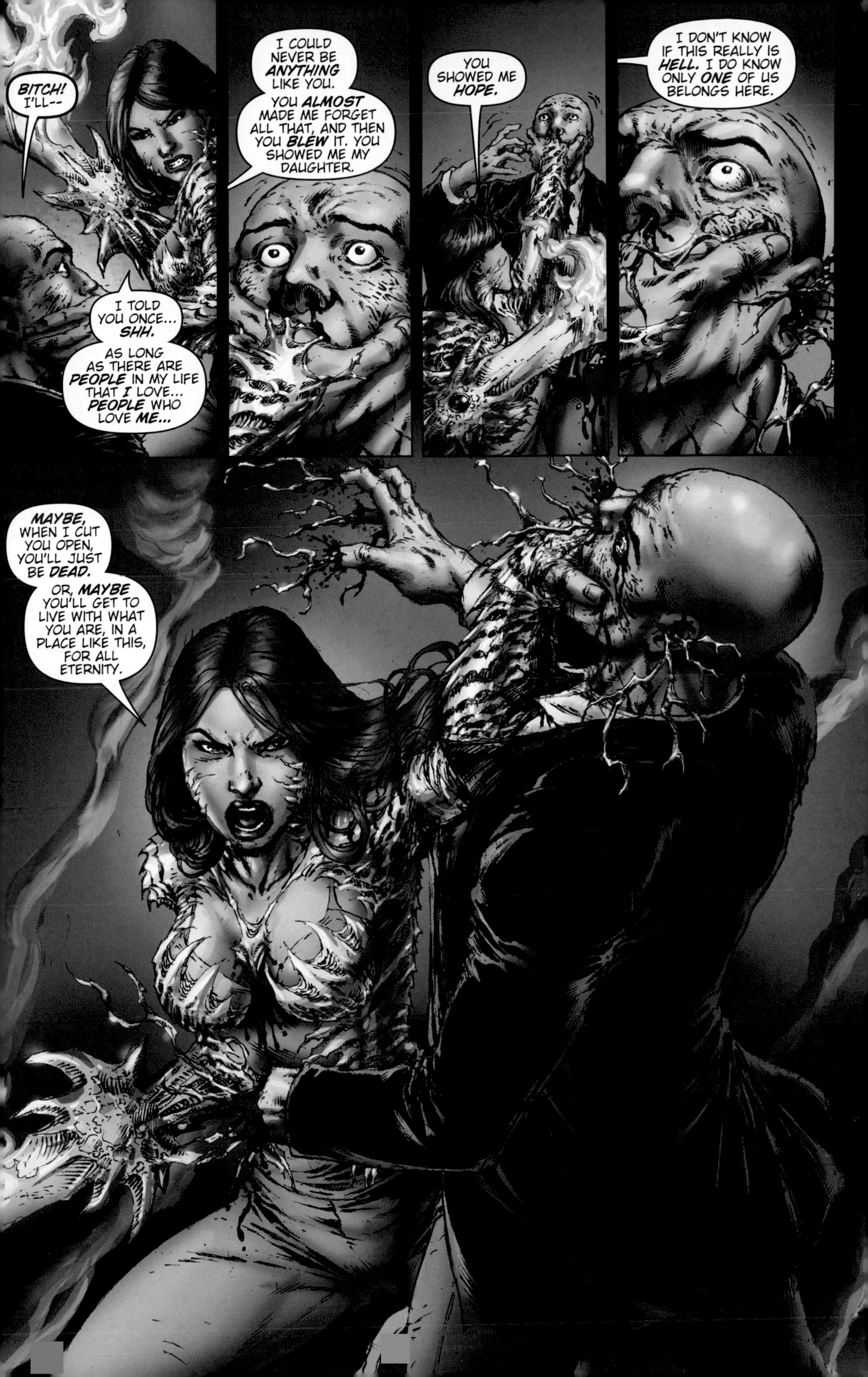
BITCH! I'LL--
I TOLD YOU ONCE... SHH.
AS LONG AS THERE ARE PEOPLE IN MY LIFE THAT I LOVE... PEOPLE WHO LOVE ME...
I COULD NEVER BE ANYTHING LIKE YOU.
YOU ALMOST MADE ME FORGET ALL THAT, AND THEN YOU BLEW IT. YOU SHOWED ME MY DAUGHTER.
YOU SHOWED ME HOPE.
I DON'T KNOW IF THIS REALLY IS HELL. I DO KNOW ONLY ONE OF US BELONGS HERE.
MAYBE, WHEN I CUT YOU OPEN, YOU'LL JUST BE DEAD.
OR, MAYBE YOU'LL GET TO LIVE WITH WHAT YOU ARE, IN A PLACE LIKE THIS, FOR ALL ETERNITY.

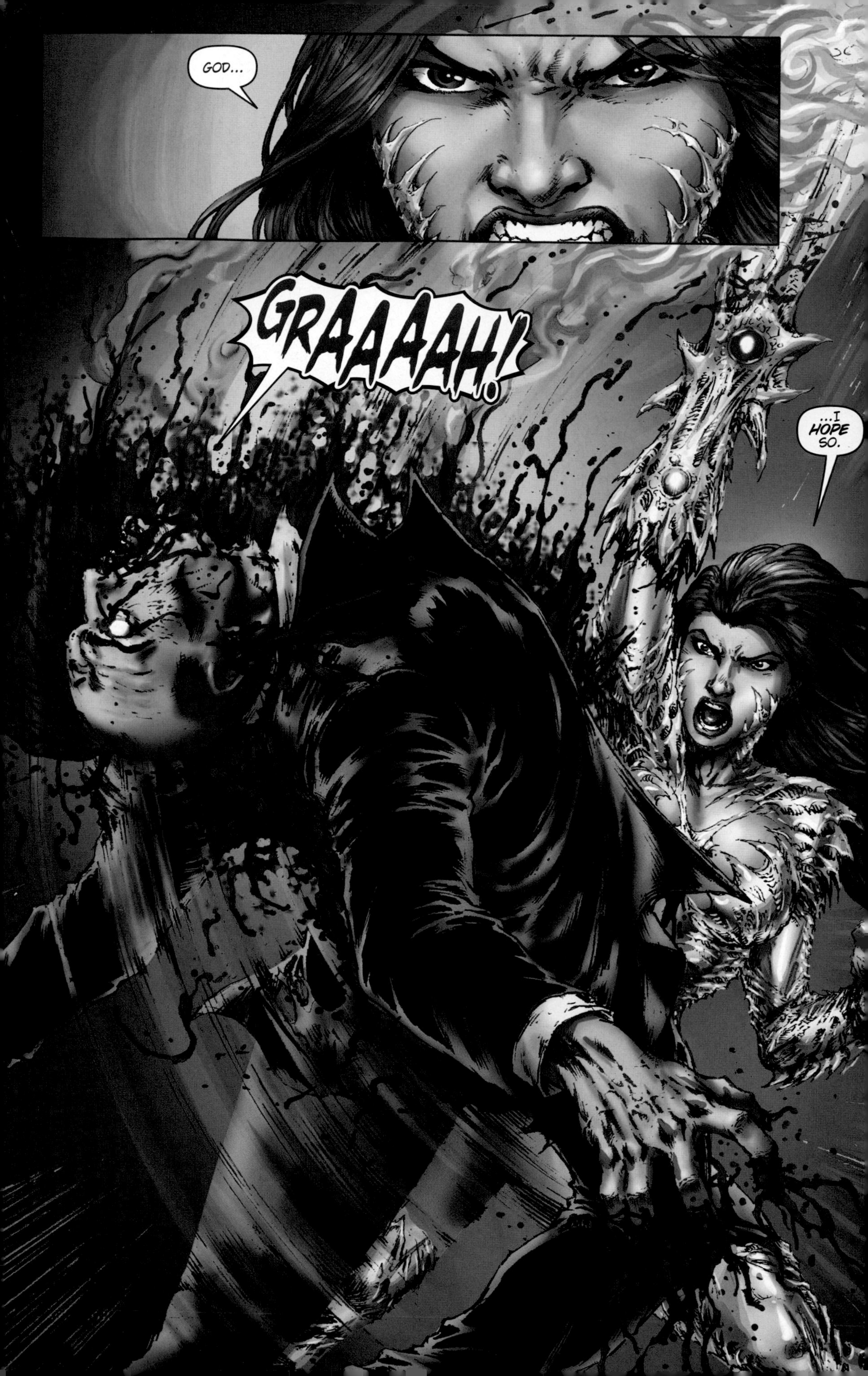
GOD...
GRAAAAH!
...I HOPE SO.

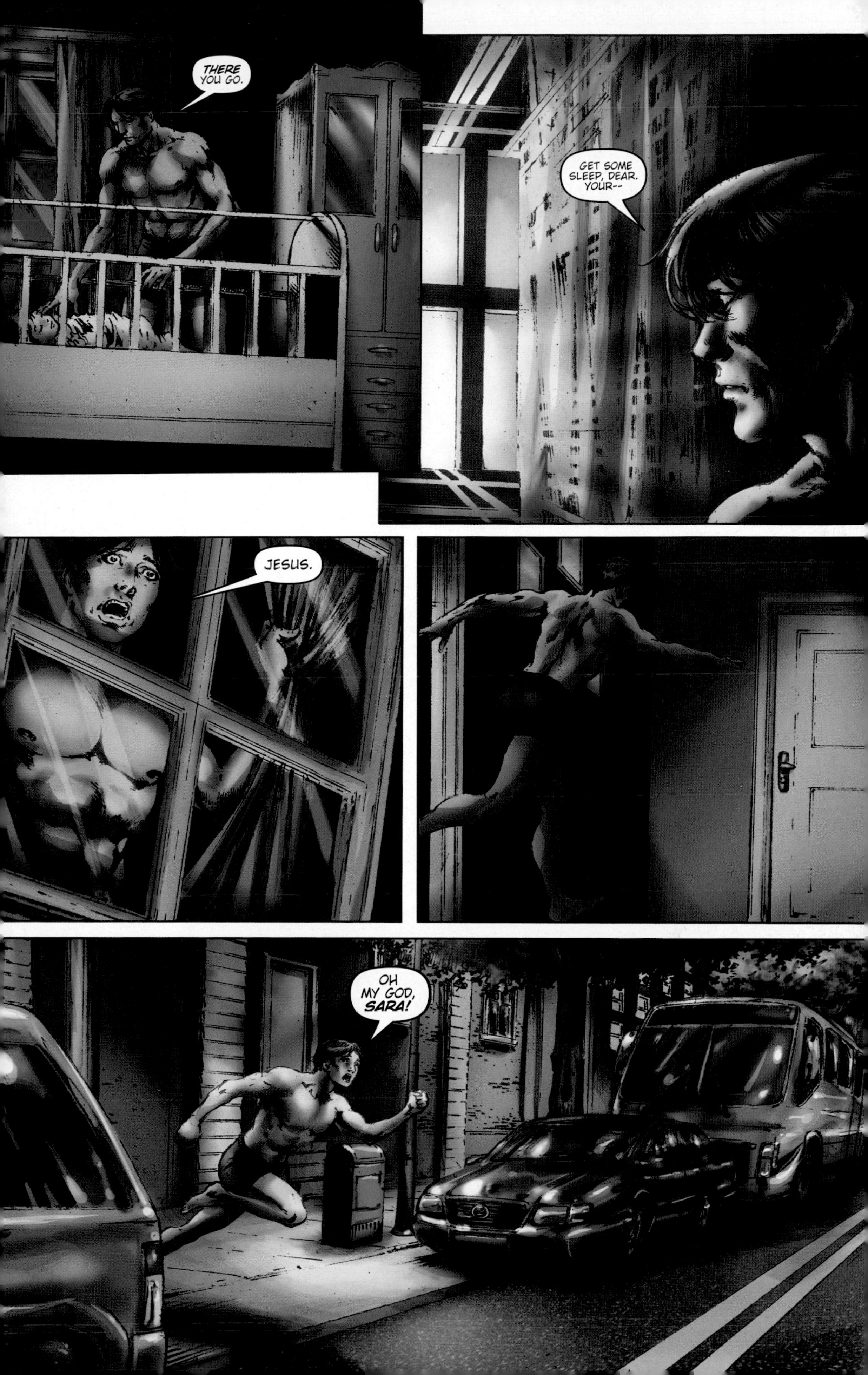
THERE YOU GO.
GET SOME SLEEP, DEAR. YOUR--
JESUS.
OH MY GOD, SARA!

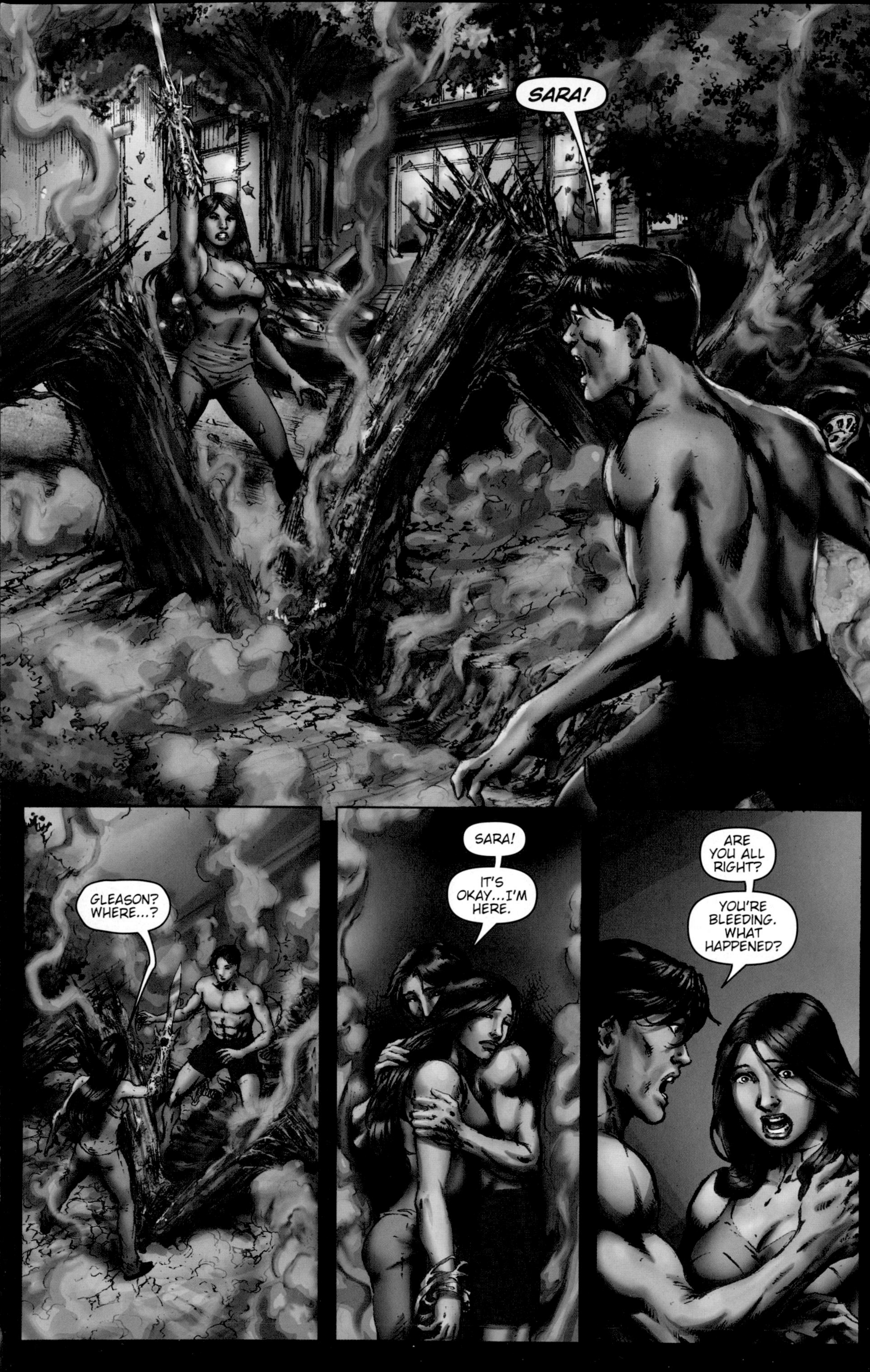
SARA!
GLEASON? WHERE...?
SARA!
IT'S OKAY...I'M HERE.
ARE YOU ALL RIGHT?
YOU'RE BLEEDING. WHAT HAPPENED?

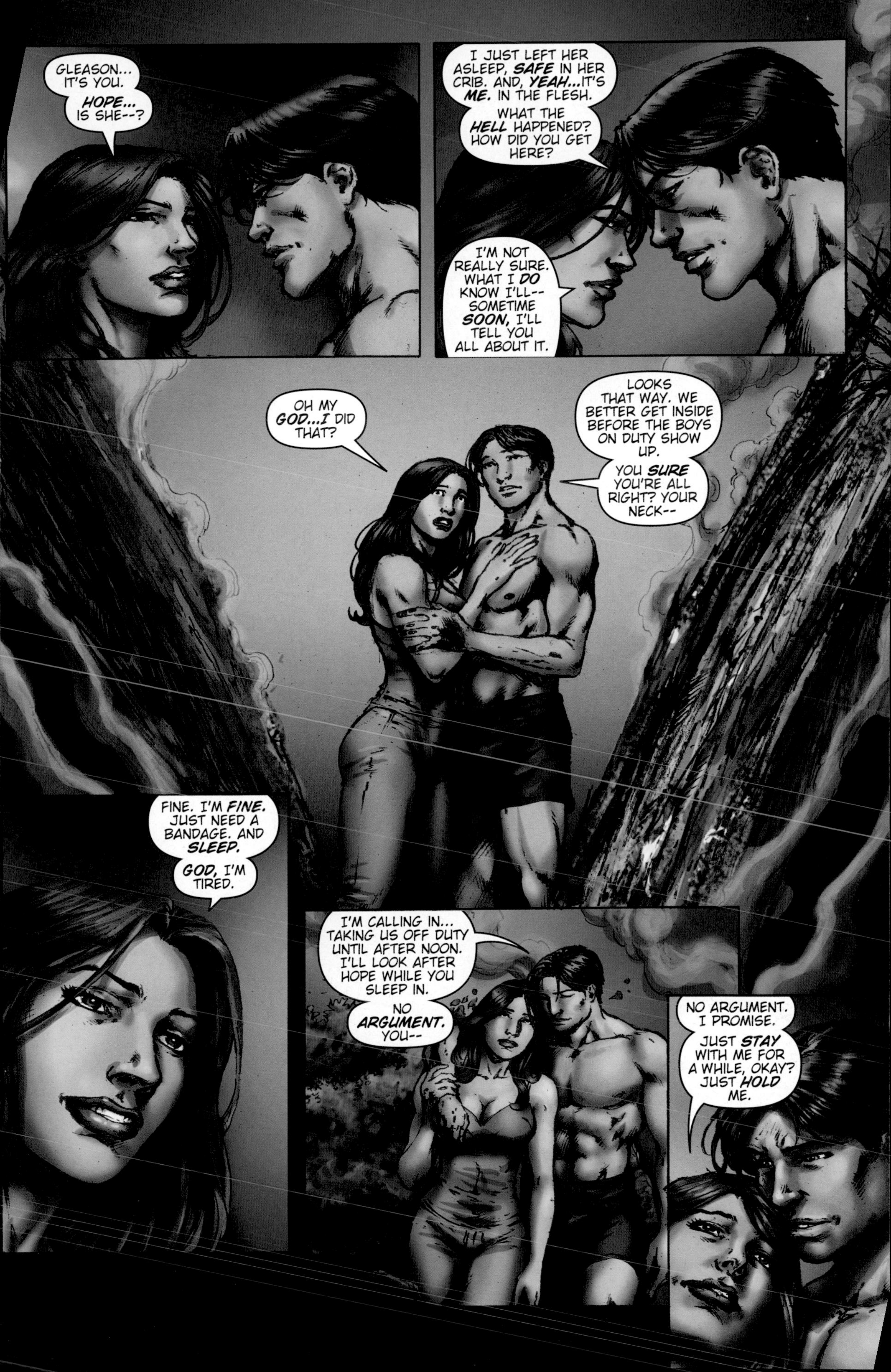
GLEASON... IT'S YOU. HOPE... IS SHE--?
I JUST LEFT HER ASLEEP, SAFE IN HER CRIB. AND, YEAH...IT'S ME. IN THE FLESH.
WHAT THE HELL HAPPENED? HOW DID YOU GET HERE?
I'M NOT REALLY SURE. WHAT I DO KNOW I'LL-- SOMETIME SOON, I'LL TELL YOU ALL ABOUT IT.
OH MY GOD...I DID THAT?
LOOKS THAT WAY. WE BETTER GET INSIDE BEFORE THE BOYS ON DUTY SHOW UP.
YOU SURE YOU'RE ALL RIGHT? YOUR NECK--
FINE. I'M FINE. JUST NEED A BANDAGE. AND SLEEP.
GOD, I'M TIRED.
I'M CALLING IN... TAKING US OFF DUTY UNTIL AFTER NOON. I'LL LOOK AFTER HOPE WHILE YOU SLEEP IN.
NO ARGUMENT. YOU--
NO ARGUMENT. I PROMISE.
JUST STAY WITH ME FOR A WHILE, OKAY? JUST HOLD ME.

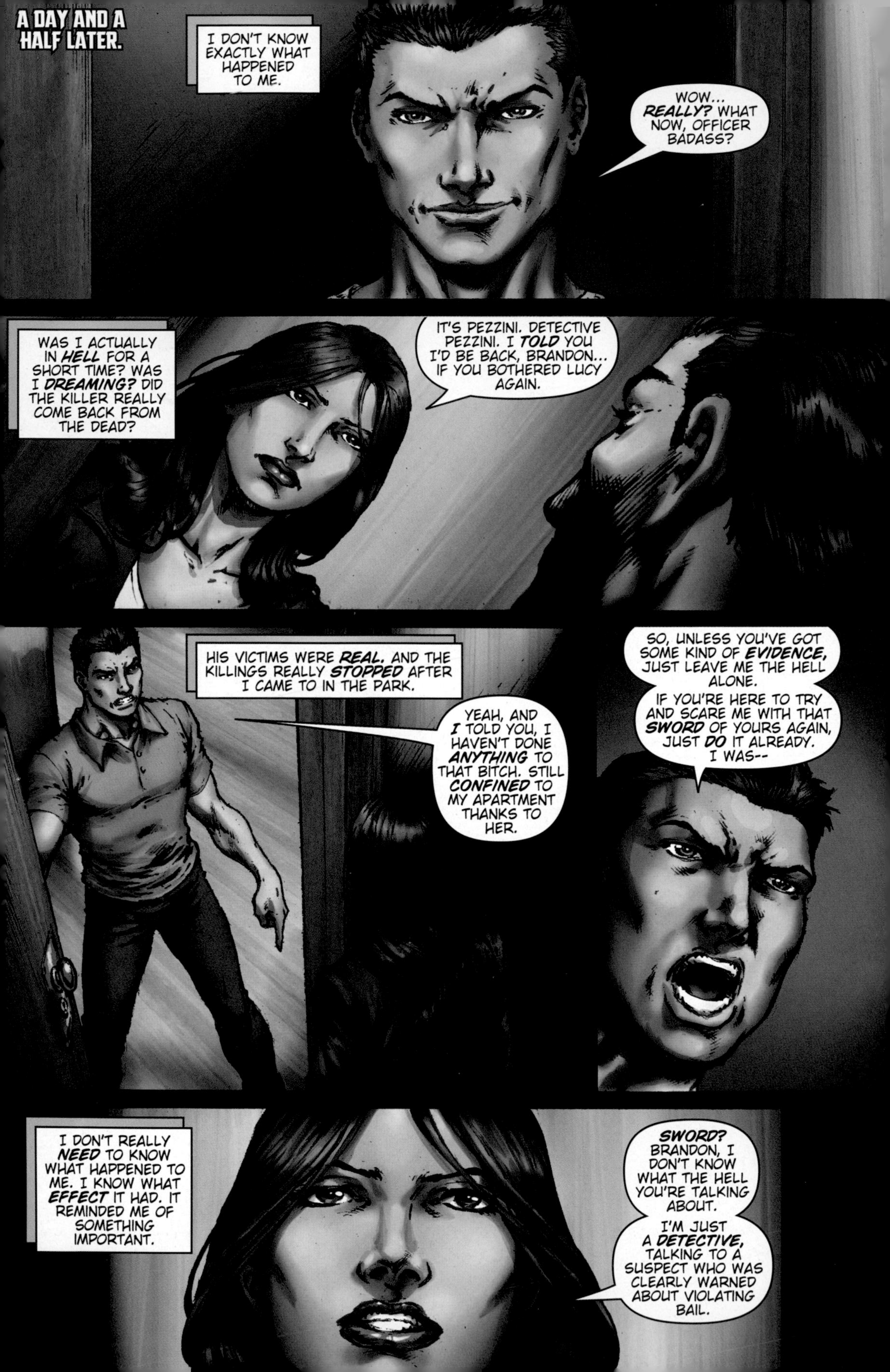
A DAY AND A HALF LATER.
I DON'T KNOW EXACTLY WHAT HAPPENED TO ME.
WOW... REALLY? WHAT NOW, OFFICER BADASS?
WAS I ACTUALLY IN HELL FOR A SHORT TIME? WAS I DREAMING? DID THE KILLER REALLY COME BACK FROM THE DEAD?
IT'S PEZZINI. DETECTIVE PEZZINI. I TOLD YOU I'D BE BACK, BRANDON... IF YOU BOTHERED LUCY AGAIN.
HIS VICTIMS WERE REAL. AND THE KILLINGS REALLY STOPPED AFTER I CAME TO IN THE PARK.
YEAH, AND I TOLD YOU, I HAVEN'T DONE ANYTHING TO THAT BITCH. STILL CONFINED TO MY APARTMENT THANKS TO HER.
SO, UNLESS YOU'VE GOT SOME KIND OF EVIDENCE, JUST LEAVE ME THE HELL ALONE.
IF YOU'RE HERE TO TRY AND SCARE ME WITH THAT SWORD OF YOURS AGAIN, JUST DO IT ALREADY. I WAS--
I DON'T REALLY NEED TO KNOW WHAT HAPPENED TO ME. I KNOW WHAT EFFECT IT HAD. IT REMINDED ME OF SOMETHING IMPORTANT.
SWORD? BRANDON, I DON'T KNOW WHAT THE HELL YOU'RE TALKING ABOUT.
I'M JUST A DETECTIVE, TALKING TO A SUSPECT WHO WAS CLEARLY WARNED ABOUT VIOLATING BAIL.

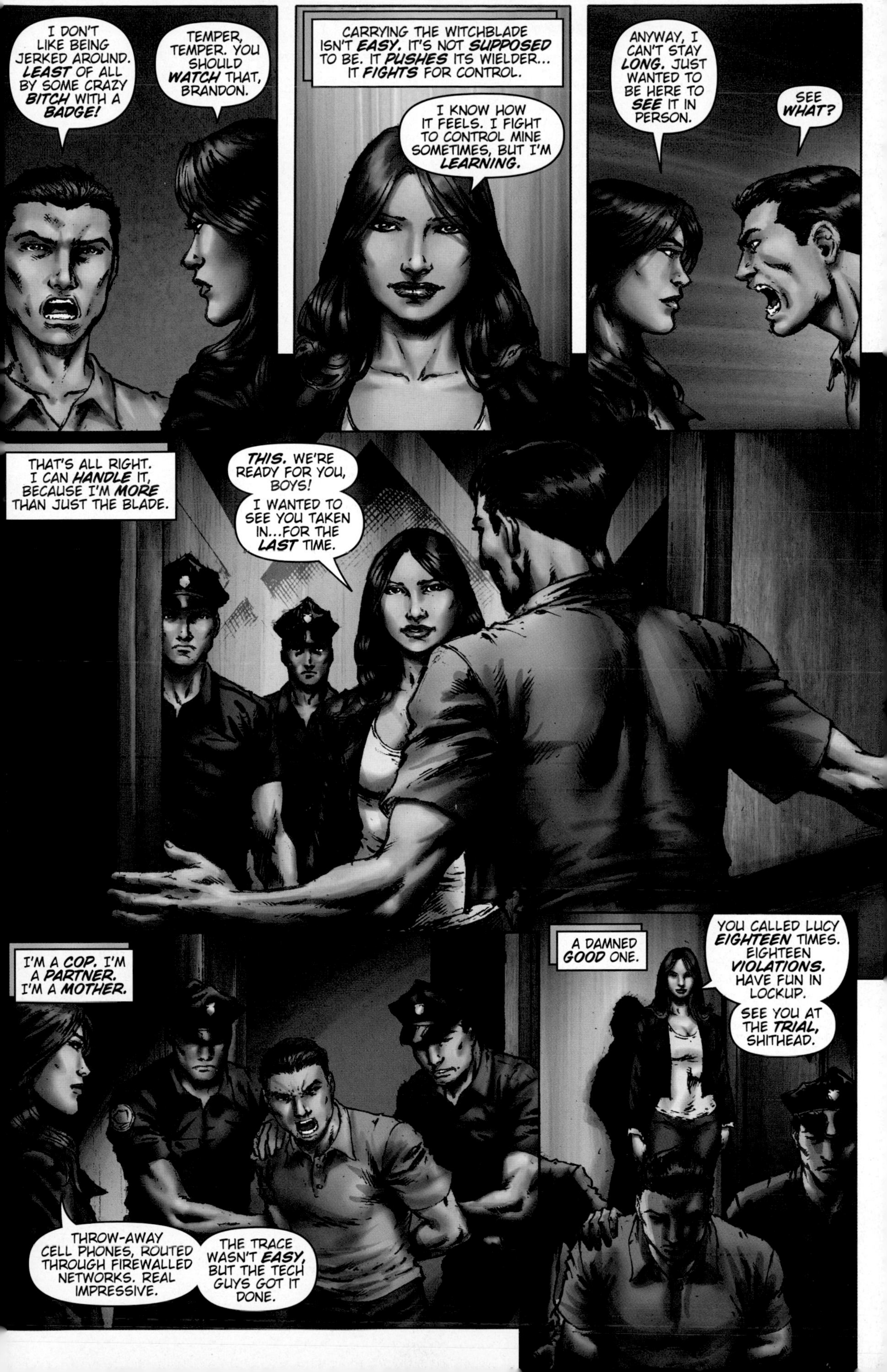
I DON'T LIKE BEING JERKED AROUND. LEAST OF ALL BY SOME CRAZY BITCH WITH A BADGE!
TEMPER, TEMPER. YOU SHOULD WATCH THAT, BRANDON.
CARRYING THE WITCHBLADE ISN'T EASY. IT'S NOT SUPPOSED TO BE. IT PUSHES ITS WIELDER... IT FIGHTS FOR CONTROL.
I KNOW HOW IT FEELS. I FIGHT TO CONTROL MINE SOMETIMES, BUT I'M LEARNING.
ANYWAY, I CAN'T STAY LONG. JUST WANTED TO BE HERE TO SEE IT IN PERSON.
SEE WHAT?
THAT'S ALL RIGHT. I CAN HANDLE IT, BECAUSE I'M MORE THAN JUST THE BLADE.
THIS. WE'RE READY FOR YOU, BOYS!
I WANTED TO SEE YOU TAKEN IN...FOR THE LAST TIME.
I'M A COP. I'M A PARTNER. I'M A MOTHER.
THROW-AWAY CELL PHONES, ROUTED THROUGH FIREWALLED NETWORKS. REAL IMPRESSIVE.
THE TRACE WASN'T EASY, BUT THE TECH GUYS GOT IT DONE.
A DAMNED GOOD ONE.
YOU CALLED LUCY EIGHTEEN TIMES. EIGHTEEN VIOLATIONS. HAVE FUN IN LOCKUP.
SEE YOU AT THE TRIAL, SHITHEAD.

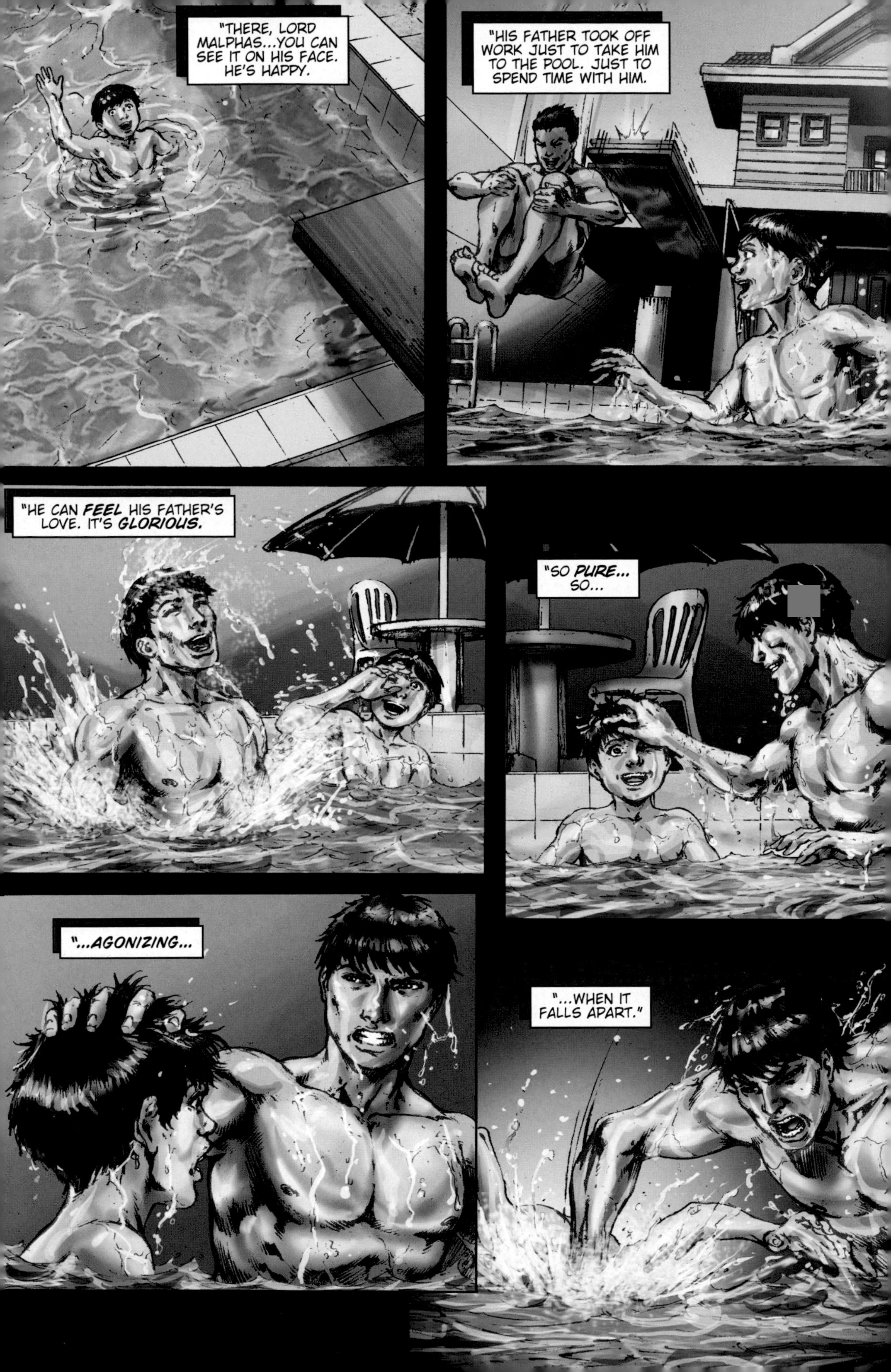
"THERE, LORD MALPHAS...YOU CAN SEE IT ON HIS FACE. HE'S HAPPY.
"HIS FATHER TOOK OFF WORK JUST TO TAKE HIM TO THE POOL. JUST TO SPEND TIME WITH HIM.
"HE CAN FEEL HIS FATHER'S LOVE. IT'S GLORIOUS.
"SO PURE... SO...
"...AGONIZING...
"...WHEN IT FALLS APART."

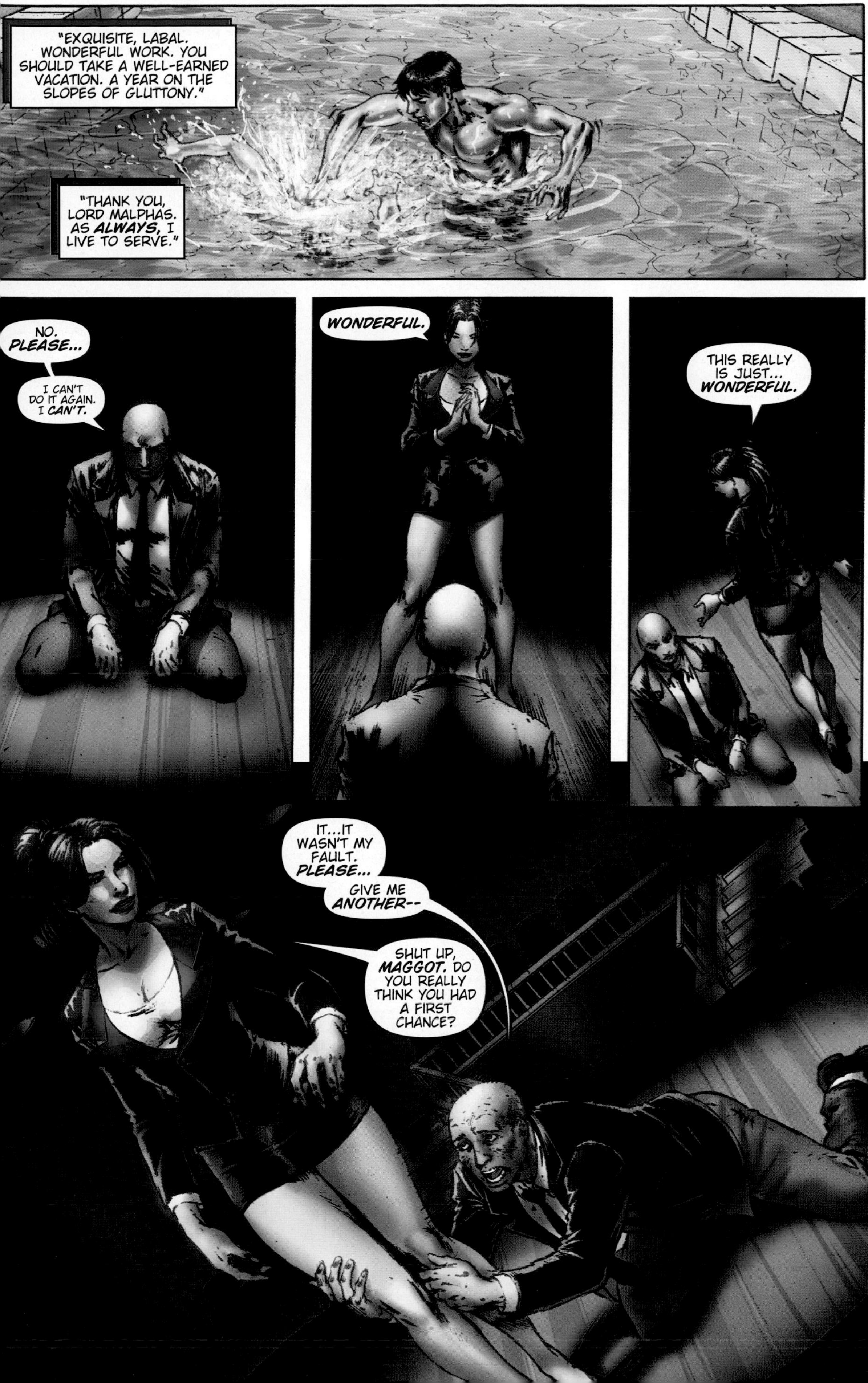
"EXQUISITE, LABAL. WONDERFUL WORK. YOU SHOULD TAKE A WELL-EARNED VACATION. A YEAR ON THE SLOPES OF GLUTTONY."
"THANK YOU, LORD MALPHAS. AS ALWAYS, I LIVE TO SERVE."
NO. PLEASE...
I CAN'T DO IT AGAIN. I CAN'T.
WONDERFUL.
THIS REALLY IS JUST... WONDERFUL.
IT...IT WASN'T MY FAULT. PLEASE...
GIVE ME ANOTHER--
SHUT UP, MAGGOT. DO YOU REALLY THINK YOU HAD A FIRST CHANCE?

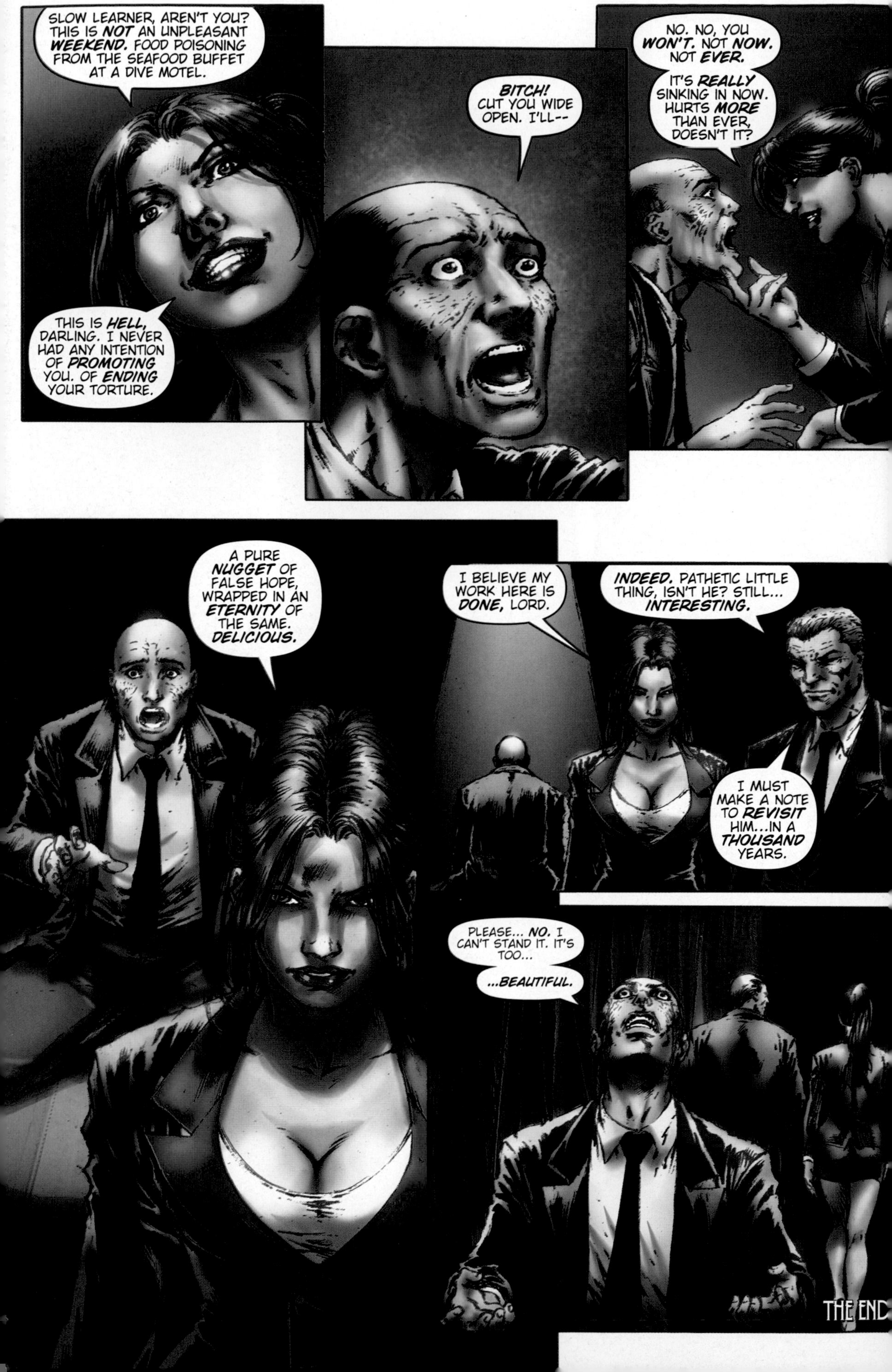
SLOW LEARNER, AREN'T YOU? THIS IS NOT AN UNPLEASANT WEEKEND. FOOD POISONING FROM THE SEAFOOD BUFFET AT A DIVE MOTEL.
THIS IS HELL, DARLING. I NEVER HAD ANY INTENTION OF PROMOTING YOU. OF ENDING YOUR TORTURE.
BITCH! CUT YOU WIDE OPEN. I'LL--
NO. NO, YOU WON'T. NOT NOW. NOT EVER.
IT'S REALLY SINKING IN NOW. HURTS MORE THAN EVER, DOESN'T IT?
A PURE NUGGET OF FALSE HOPE, WRAPPED IN AN ETERNITY OF THE SAME. DELICIOUS.
I BELIEVE MY WORK HERE IS DONE, LORD.
INDEED. PATHETIC LITTLE THING, ISN'T HE? STILL... INTERESTING.
I MUST MAKE A NOTE TO REVISIT HIM...IN A THOUSAND YEARS.
PLEASE... NO. I CAN'T STAND IT. IT'S TOO...
...BEAUTIFUL.
THE END

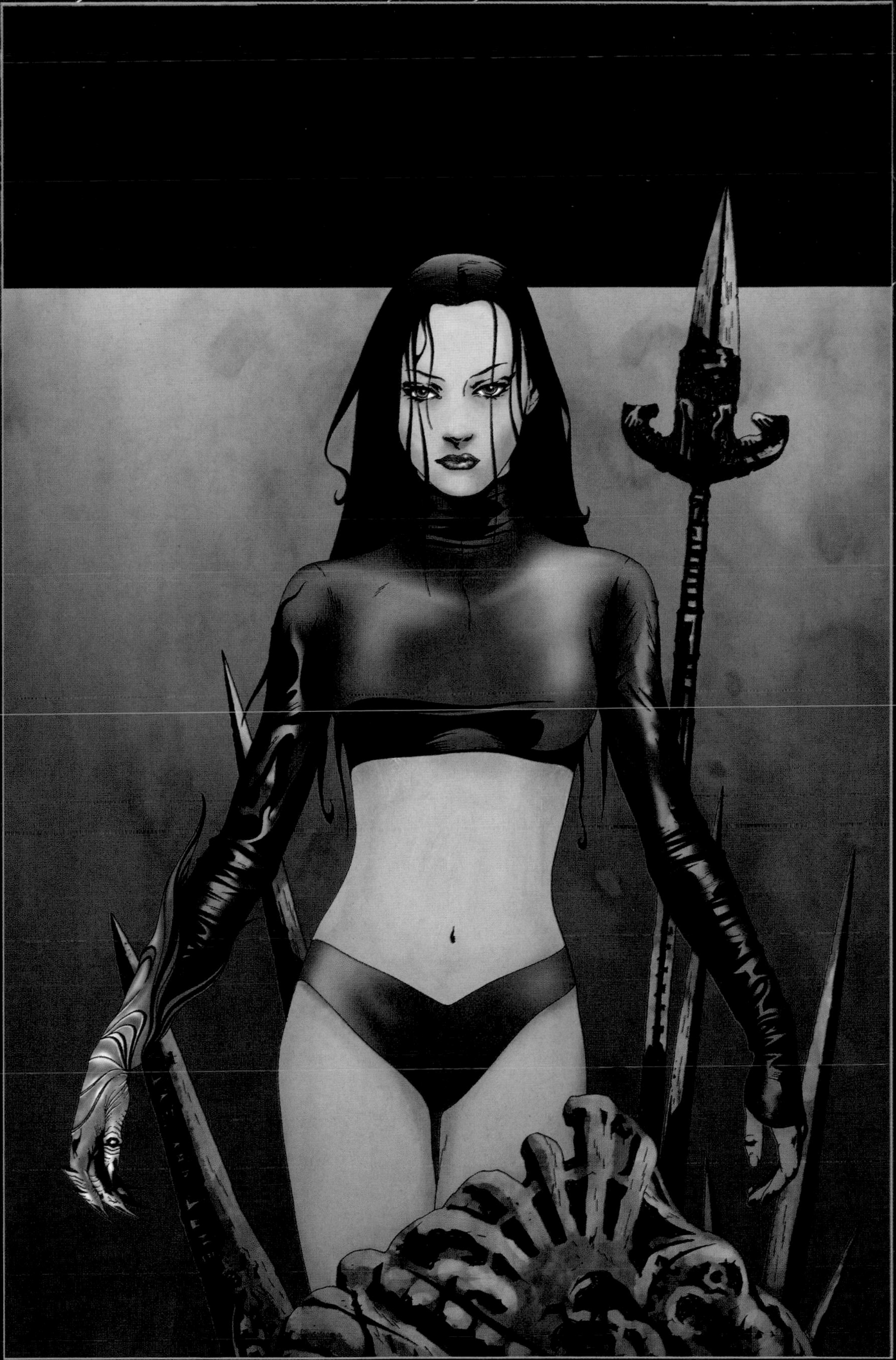

ISSUE #1 COVER BY JAE LEE

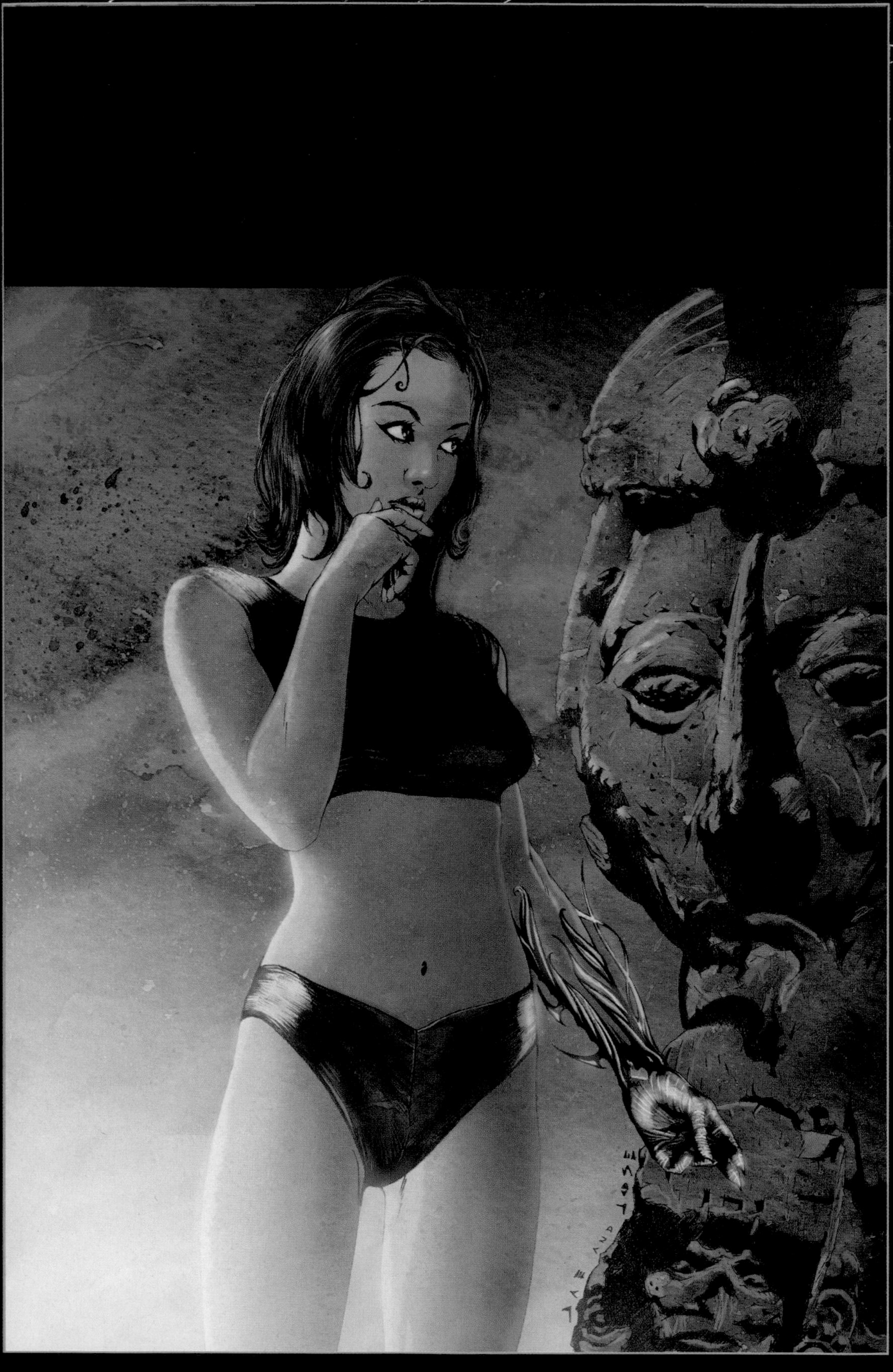

ISSUE #2 COVER BY JAE LEE

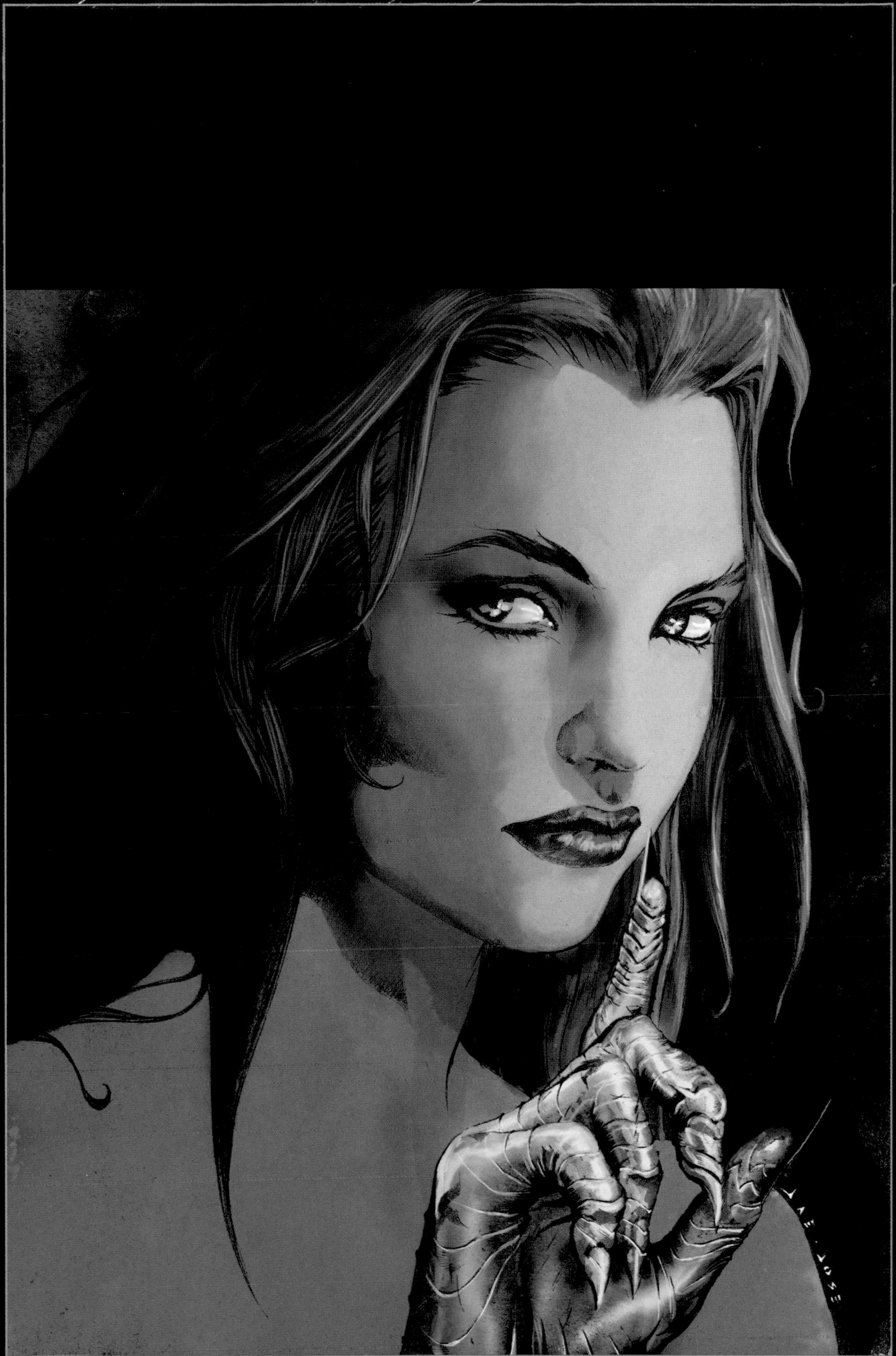

ISSUE #3 COVER BY JAE LEE

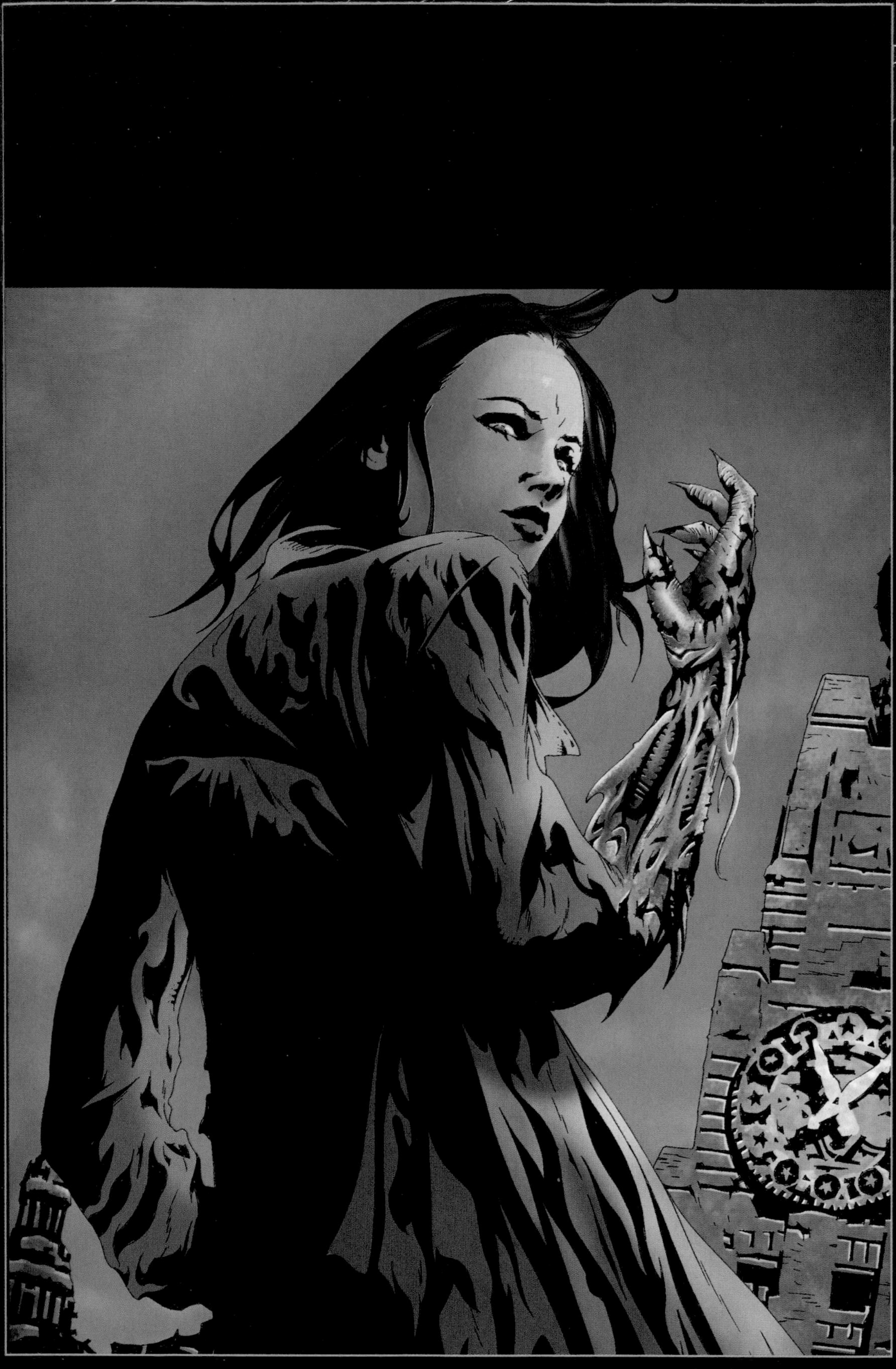

ISSUE #4 COVER BY JAE LEE

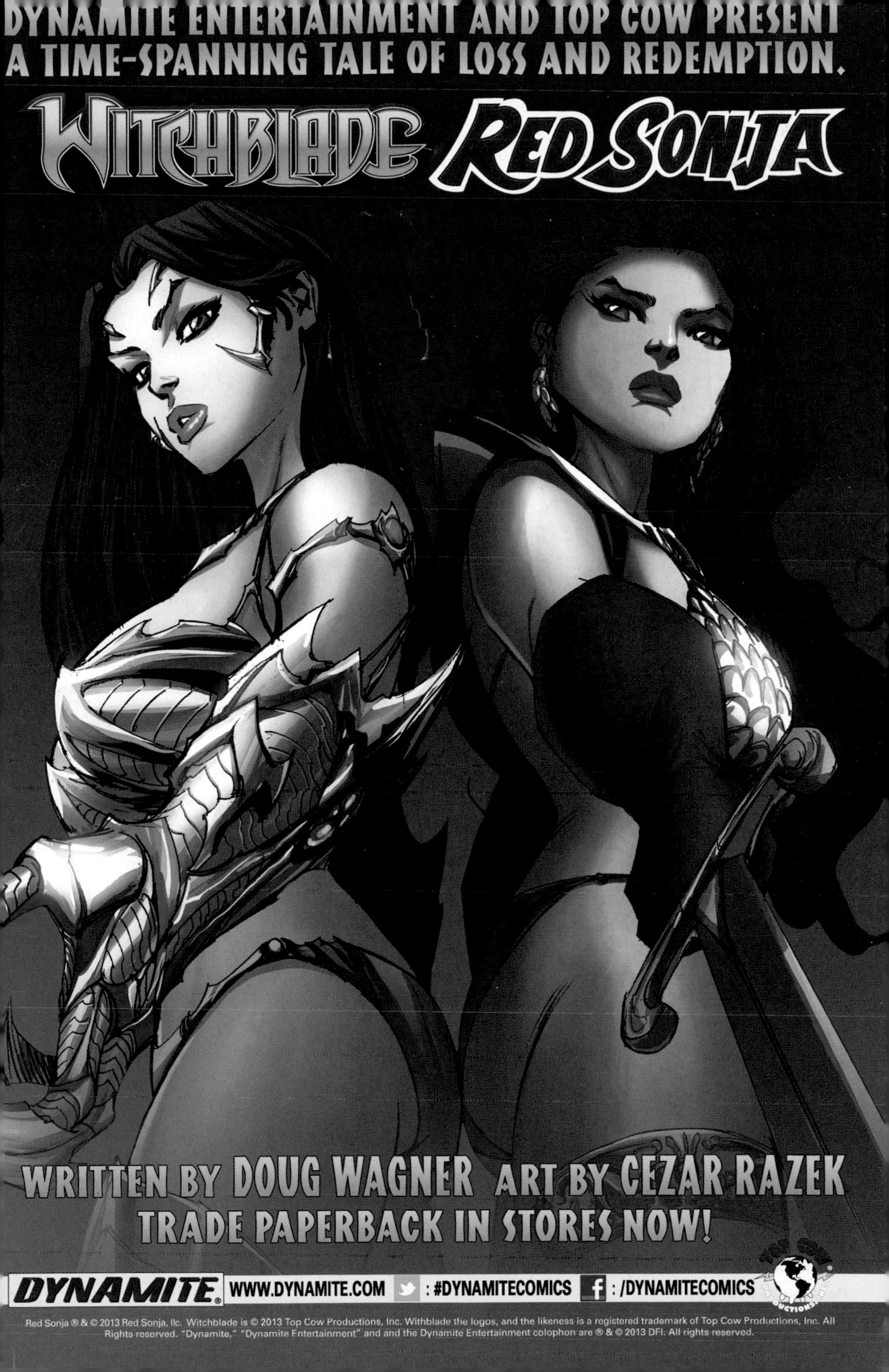

LOOK FOR THESE DYNAMITE GREATEST HITS!

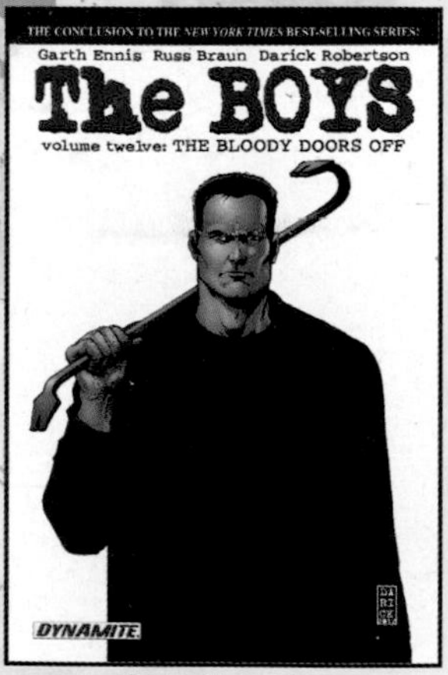
THE CONCLUSION TO THE NEW YORK TIMES BEST-SELLING SERIES!
Garth Ennis Russ Braun Darick Robertson
The BOYS
volume twelve: THE BLOODY DOORS OFF
DYNAMITE

**GARTH ENNIS
THE BOYS & MORE!**

(Garth Ennis') Battlefields V1: The Night Witches
Ennis, Braun

(Garth Ennis') Battlefields V2: Dear Billy
Ennis, Snejbjerg

(Garth Ennis') Battlefields V3: The Tankies
Ennis, Ezquerra

(Garth Ennis') The Complete Battlefields V1
Ennis, Braun, Ezquerra, more

(Garth Ennis') Battlefields V4: Happy Valley
Ennis, Holden

(Garth Ennis') Battlefields V5: The Firefiy and His Majesty
Ennis, Ezquerra

(Garth Ennis') Battlefields V6: Motherland
Ennis, Braun

(Garth Ennis') The Complete Battlefields V2
Ennis, Braun, Holden, more

The Boys V1 The Name of the Game
Ennis, Robertson

The Boys V2 Get Some
Ennis, Robertson, Snejbjerg

The Boys V3 Good For The Soul
Ennis, Robertson

The Boys V4 We Gotta Go Now
Ennis, Robertson

The Boys V5 Herogasm
Ennis, McCrea

The Boys V6 The Self-Preservation Society
Ennis, Robertson, Ezquerra

The Boys V7 The Innocents
Ennis, Robertson, Braun

The Boys V8 Highland Laddie
Ennis, McCrea

The Boys V9 The Big Ride
Ennis, Braun

The Boys V10: Butcher, Baker, Candlestickmaker
Ennis, Robertson

The Boys V11 Over the Hill With the Swords of a Thousand Men
Ennis, Braun

The Boys Definitive Edition V1
Ennis, Robertson

The Boys Definitive Edition V2
Ennis, Robertson

The Boys Definitive Edition V3
Ennis, Robertson, more

The Boys Definitive Edition V4
Ennis, Robertson, more

Dan Dare Omnibus
Ennis, Erskine

Jennifer Blood V1 A Woman's Work Is Never Done
Ennis, Batista, Baal, more

Jennifer Blood V2 Beautiful People
Ewing, Baal, more

Just A Pilgrim
Ennis, Ezquerra

The Ninjettes
Ewing, Casallos

Seven Brothers Omnibus
Ennis, Diggle, Kang, more

The Shadow V1 The Fire of Creation
Ennis, Campbell

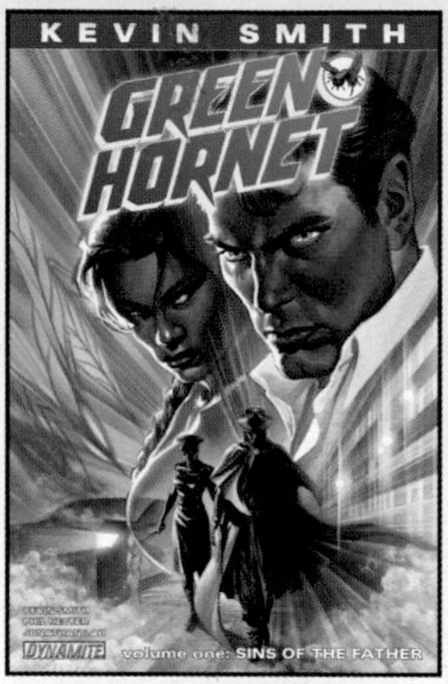
KEVIN SMITH
GREEN HORNET
DYNAMITE
volume one: SINS OF THE FATHER

**GREEN HORNET
KEVIN SMITH & MORE!**

(Kevin Smith's) Green Hornet V1 Sins of the Father
Smith, Hester, Lau

(Kevin Smith's) Green Hornet V2 Wearing 'o the Green
Smith, Hester, Lau

Green Hornet V3 Idols
Hester, Lau

Green Hornet V4 Red Hand
Hester, Smith, Vitorino, more

Green Hornet: Blood Ties
Parks, Desjardins

The Green Hornet: Year One V1 The Sting of Justice
Wagner, Campbell

The Green Hornet: Year One V2 The Biggest of All Game
Wagner, Campbell

The Green Hornet Parallel Lives
Nitz, Raynor

The Green Hornet Golden Age Re-Mastered
Various

Kato V1 Not My Father's Daughter
Parks, Garza, Bernard

Kato V2 Living in America
Parks, Bernard

Kato Origins V1 Way of the Ninja
Nitz, Worley

Kato Origins V2 The Hellfire Club
Nitz, Worley

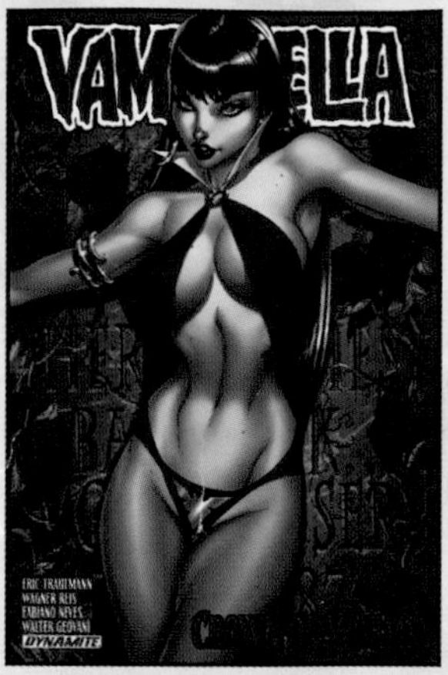
VAMPIRELLA
ERIC TRAUTMANN
WAGNER REIS
FABIANO NEVES
WALTER GEOVANI
DYNAMITE

VAMPIRELLA!

Vampirella Masters Series V1 Grant Morrison & Mark Millar
Morrison, Millar, more

Vampirella Masters Series V2 Warren Ellis
Ellis, Conner Palmiotti, more

Vampi Omnibus V1
Conway, Lau

Vampirella Masters Series V3 Mark Millar
Millar, Mayhew

Vampirella Masters Series V4 Visionaries
Moore, Busiek, Loeb, more

Vampirella Masters Series V5 Kurt Busiek
Busiek, Sniegoski, more

Vampirella Masters Series V6 James Robinson
Robinson, Jusko, more

Vampirella Archives V1
Various

Vampirella Archives V2
Various

Vampirella Archives V3
Various

Vampirella Archives V4
Various

Vampirella Archives V5
Various

Vampirella V1 Crown of Worms
Trautman, Reis, Geovani

Vampirella V2 A Murder of Crows
Trautman, Neves, more

Vampirella V3 Throne of Skulls
Trautman, Malaga, more

Vampirella And The Scarlet Legion
Harris, Malaga

Vampirella vs. Dracula
Harris, Rodriguez

RED SONJA!

Adventures of Red Sonja V1
Thomas, Thorne, More

Adventures of Red Sonja V2
Thomas, Thorne, More

Adventures of Red Sonja V3
Thomas, Thorne, More

Queen Sonja V1
Ortega, Rubi

Queen Sonja V2 The Red Queen
Nelson, Herbert

Queen Sonja V3 Coming of Age
Lieberman, Rubi

Queen Sonja V4 Son of Set
Nelson, Salazar

Red Sonja She-Devil With a Sword V1
Oeming, Carey, Rubi

Red Sonja She-Devil With a Sword V2: Arrowsmiths
Oeming, Rubi, more

Red Sonja She-Devil With a Sword V3: The Rise of Kulan Gath
Oeming, Rubi, more

Red Sonja She-Devil With a Sword V4: Animals & More
Oeming, Homs, more

Red Sonja She-Devil With a Sword V5: World On Fire
Oeming, Reed, Homs

Red Sonja She-Devil With a Sword V6: Death
Marz, Ortega, Reed, more

Red Sonja She-Devil With a Sword V7: Born Again
Reed, Geovani

Red Sonja She-Devil With a Sword V8: Blood Dynasty
Reed, Geovani

Red Sonja She-Devil With a Sword V9: War Season
Trautmann, Geovani, more

Red Sonja She-Devil With a Sword V10: Machines of Empire
Trautmann, Geovani, more

Red Sonja She-Devil With a Sword Omnibus V1
Oeming, Carey, Rubi, more

Red Sonja She-Devil With a Sword Omnibus V2
Oeming, Reed, Homs, more

Red Sonja She-Devil With a Sword Omnibus V3
Reed, Geovani

Red Sonja vs. Thulsa Doom V1
David, Lieberman, Conrad

Savage Red Sonja: Queen of the Frozen Wastes
Cho, Murray, Homs

Red Sonja: Travels
Marz, Ortega, Thomas, more

Sword of Red Sonja: Doom of the Gods (Red Sonja vs. Thulsa Doom 2)
Lieberman, Antonio

Red Sonja: Wrath of the Gods
Lieberman, Geovani

Red Sonja: Revenge of the Gods
Lieberman, Sampere

Savage Tales of Red Sonja
Marz, Gage, Ortega, more

ART BOOKS!

The Art of Howard Chaykin
The Art of Painted Comics
The Art of Ramona Fradon
The Art of Red Sonja
The Art of Vampirella
The Dynamite Art of Alex Ross
George Pérez: Storyteller
The Romita Legacy